꼭! 잡은 중학 영문법

Book 3

GRAMMAR
CATCH

Happy House

How to Use This Book

주요 문법 설명

내신 성적 향상을 위한 필수 영문법을 체계적으로 설명해 줍니다. 여러분이 보다 쉽게 이해할 수 있도록 학교 시험에 자주 출제되는 예문들을 담았습니다.

Grammar Check-Up

'내신 족집게 문제'를 풀기 위한 워밍업 단계로, 각 단원의 주요 문법에 관한 다양한 문제 풀이를 통해 기초 실력을 확인할 수 있습니다. 우리말 해석 및 영작 문제를 풀며 독해와 작문 실력을 향상시키며, Word Tip을 통해 문제 해결 능력을 키울 수 있습니다.

내신 족집게 문제

각 단원의 문법 사항 중에서 학교 시험에 자주 출제되는 주요 문법 문제들을 엄선하여 주관식과 객관식 문제로 구성했습니다. 문법 문제를 보다 쉽게 풀 수 있는 노하우를 알려드립니다.

수능 감각 기르기

사고력과 분석력을 키워 주는 문제들을 통해 중학교 영문법에 자신감을 갖게 됩니다. 앞서 학습한 단계의 문제들을 기반으로 수능 문제에 대한 감각을 키울 수 있도록 구성했습니다.

서술형 즐기기

그림이나 표를 이용한 서술형 문제를 다양하게 접할 수 있습니다. 앞서 학습한 Grammar Check-Up의 영작 문제에서 확장된 '한 단락 영작 학습'을 통해 Writing 실력을 향상시킬 수 있습니다.

Workbook

본책에서 학습한 내용을 복습하고 각 Unit 별로 더욱 다양한 유형의 문제들을 풀어 보면서 배운 문법을 완벽히 마스터할 수 있도록 도와줍니다.

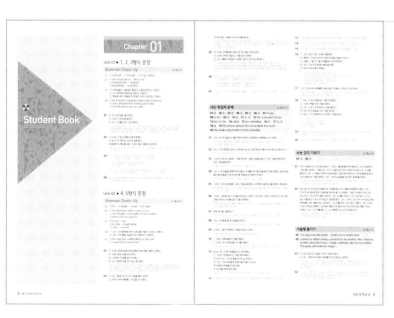

정답 및 해설

본책 및 워크북에서 여러분이 푼 문제들에 대한 정답과 저자의 명쾌한 설명이 담겨 있습니다. 문제를 풀면서 미처 생각하지 못하고 넘어간 부분을 확인하고, 틀린 문제는 다시 한 번 풀어 보세요.

Contents

Chapter 01

문장의 형식

Chapter 미리보기

1형식	주어 + 동사
2형식	주어 + 동사 + 주격 보어
3형식	주어 + 동사 + 목적어
4형식	주어 + 동사 + 간접목적어 + 직접목적어
5형식	주어 + 동사 + 목적어 + 목적격 보어

Still waters run deep.

▶ 고요한 물은 깊게 흐른다.

01 1, 2, 3형식 문장

A 1형식 문장

⟨주어 + 동사 + (수식어)⟩

ex • It doesn't matter.
• The train arrived at Seoul Station.
• There are a lot of animals in the Seoul Grand Park.

B 2형식 문장

⟨주어 + 동사 + 보어⟩

1 명사가 보어인 경우   ex • She became a famous singer.

2 형용사가 보어인 경우   ex • His voice is husky.

3 to부정사가 보어인 경우   ex • Her hope is to lose weight.

4 동명사가 보어인 경우   ex • His hobby is collecting stamps.

➊ 감각동사 (look, feel, sound, taste, smell 등) + 형용사

ex • You look happy.   • The flower smells good.

C 3형식 문장

⟨주어 + 동사 + 목적어⟩

1 명사가 목적어인 경우   ex • He owns a flower shop.

2 대명사가 목적어인 경우   ex • She took me to the museum.

3 to부정사가 목적어인 경우   ex • He decided to be a pianist.

4 동명사가 목적어인 경우   ex • She enjoyed collecting watches.

5 절이 목적어인 경우   ex • People say that seven is a lucky number.

➊ 목적어를 필요로 하는 타동사는 전치사와 함께 쓰지 않도록 조심한다.

marry (결혼하다), discuss (토론하다), attend (참석하다), enter (들어가다), resemble (닮다), reach (도착하다)

ex • They discussed their summer vacation. (○)
• They discussed about their summer vacation. (×)

Grammar Check-Up

01 다음 중 알맞은 것을 고르시오.

1) He   entered | went   the waiting room.

2) That sounds   strange | strangely .

3) He wants   to go | going   to ski | skiing .

02 다음 문장의 <u>틀린</u> 부분에 밑줄을 긋고 바르게 고쳐 쓰시오.

1) We discussed about the water pollution.   (→ _____)

2) My friend married with a Hungarian man.   (→ _____)

3) She looks very beautifully in a pink dress.   (→ _____)

1) pollution 오염

2) Hungarian
  헝가리의; 헝가리 사람

03 다음 문장을 우리말로 해석하고 문장의 형식을 쓰시오.

1) The leaves turn red and yellow in fall.

→ _____ (_____ 형식)

2) He hoped to win the lottery.

→ _____ (_____ 형식)

3) Once there lived an ugly princess in a village.

→ _____ (_____ 형식)

2) lottery 복권

3) once 옛날에, 한 때
  ugly 못생긴
  village 마을

04 다음 우리말을 영작하시오.

1) 그는 강남 고속버스 터미널에 도착했다.

→ _____

2) 그들은 어제 그 모임에 참석했다.

→ _____

3) 그녀는 다이어트를 하기로 결심했다.

→ _____

1) reach 도착하다
  Gangnam Express
  Bus Terminal
  강남 고속버스 터미널

2) attend 참석하다

3) go on a diet
  다이어트를 하다

Unit 02 4, 5형식 문장

A 4형식 문장

〈주어 + 동사 + 간접목적어 + 직접목적어〉

ex • They gave her a big hand.
  • She made me a pretty doll.

4형식 문장을 3형식 문장으로 바꾸기
4형식 주어 + 동사 + 간접목적어 + 직접목적어
3형식 주어 + 동사 + 직접목적어 + 전치사 + 간접목적어

ex • She sent her roommate a thank you card.
  → She sent a thank you card to her roommate.
  • He made his younger sister a paper boat.
  → He made a paper boat for his younger sister.

⊕ **4형식 문장을 3형식 문장으로 바꿀 때 사용되는 전치사**

• 전치사 to를 쓰는 동사 : give, send, write, tell, show, hand 등
• 전치사 for를 쓰는 동사 : buy, make, get, find, cook 등
• 전치사 of를 쓰는 동사 : ask 등

B 5형식 문장

〈주어 + 동사 + 목적어 + 목적격 보어〉

1 명사가 목적격 보어인 경우   **ex** • We named the cat Nari.

2 형용사가 목적격 보어인 경우   **ex** • The song made me happy.

3 to부정사가 목적격 보어인 경우   **ex** • He advised people not to drink too much.

4 동사원형이 목적격 보어인 경우   **ex** • Peeling onions makes me cry.

5 현재분사가 목적격 보어인 경우   **ex** • I saw a girl crying.

6 과거분사가 목적격 보어인 경우   **ex** • He had his sleeve shortened.

Tips
• 목적어와 목적격 보어와의 관계가 수동일 경우 과거분사를 쓴다.

⊕ **주의해야 할 5형식 동사들**

• 목적격 보어 자리에 to부정사가 오는 동사들(want, ask, advise, allow 등) → 〈동사 + 목적어 + to부정사〉
• 지각동사(see, watch, feel, hear 등) → 〈동사 + 목적어 + 동사원형/현재분사〉
• 사역동사(let, have, make) → 〈동사 + 목적어 + 동사원형〉

Grammar Check-Up

정답 및 해설 p.2

01 다음 중 알맞은 것을 고르시오.

1) She made carnations   for | to | of   her parents on Parents' Day.

2) She always makes me   laugh | laughing | to laugh .

3) The movie made us   sad | sadly | sadness .

4) He advised me   take | taking | to take   some medicine.

4) take some medicine
약을 먹다

02 다음 문장을 4형식은 3형식으로, 3형식은 4형식으로 바꾸어 쓰시오.

1) He asked me my sister's name.

→ _____

2) She bought her mother a red wallet.

→ _____

3) Jimin sent a parcel to me.

→ _____

2) wallet 지갑
3) parcel 소포

03 다음 문장의 <u>틀린</u> 부분에 밑줄을 긋고 바르게 고쳐 쓰시오.

1) She handed to me a notebook last night.   (→ _____)

2) She didn't hear the phone to ring.   (→ _____)

3) I had my suitcase carry by my brother.   (→ _____)

04 다음 문장을 우리말로 해석하고 문장의 형식을 쓰시오.

1) He made his daughter a white dress.

→ _____ (_____ 형식)

2) He made his daughter a diplomat.

→ _____ (_____ 형식)

05 다음 우리말을 영작하시오.

1) 그녀는 그가 빗속을 걸어가는 것을 보았다.

→ _____

2) 나는 그녀가 그와 결혼하길 원한다.

→ _____

1) in the rain 빗속에서

내신 족집게 문제

[01-06] 빈칸에 들어갈 수 <u>없는</u> 것을 고르시오.

01 He _____ to get a part-time job.

① wants   ② hopes
③ decided   ④ planned
⑤ gave up

02 The man who will marry my sister looks _____.

① generous   ② friendly
③ handsome   ④ politely
⑤ healthy

03 Her mother likes _____.

① to dance   ② reading books
③ them   ④ playing tennis
⑤ sleep in a tent

04 He made his son _____.

① happy   ② do homework
③ a kite   ④ to go to bed
⑤ a dentist

05 She _____ drawing a picture of you.

① loved   ② started
③ enjoyed   ④ liked
⑤ decided

06 She _____ me catch a butterfly.

① asked   ② made
③ helped   ④ watched
⑤ let

[07-08] 두 문장의 뜻이 같도록 빈칸에 알맞은 말을 쓰시오.

07 May I ask you a favor?

= May I ask a favor _____ _____?

08 He gave her a bunch of flowers.

= He gave a bunch of flowers _____

_____.

09 빈칸에 들어갈 알맞은 것을 고르시오.

She had him _____ a hole in the garden.

① to dig   ② dig
③ dug   ④ is digging
⑤ being dug

10 빈칸에 공통으로 들어갈 알맞은 것을 고르시오.

- She _____ to receive a scholarship.
- She _____ me to receive a scholarship.

① hoped   ② enjoyed
③ wanted   ④ planned
⑤ agreed

11 보기와 문장의 형식이 같은 것을 <u>두 개</u> 고르시오.

보기 He thought her to be beautiful.

① She forgot to return a book.
② My friend calls her daughter Yuri.
③ He made his wife a necklace.
④ Please pass me the pepper.
⑤ Please keep your room clean.

[12-15] 우리말과 일치하도록 빈칸에 알맞은 말을 쓰시오.

12 그는 그녀의 생일날 그녀에게 팔찌를 사 주었다.

→ He bought _____ a bracelet on her birthday.

→ He bought _____ _____

_____ _____ on her birthday.

13 나는 그녀에게 약간의 돈을 빌려주었다.

→ I _____ some money _____

_____.

14 나는 누군가 나의 이름을 부르는 것을 들었다.

→ I heard my name _____ by someone.

15 나는 어제 그녀가 말을 타는 것을 보았다.

→ I saw _____ _____ a horse yesterday.

16 다음 중 올바른 문장을 고르시오.

① He married with her ten years ago.
② Karen made dinner her boyfriend.
③ They discussed about their group work.
④ He wrote an email to his friend.
⑤ The train reached in Busan.

17 빈칸에 들어갈 알맞은 것을 <u>두 개</u> 고르시오.

He _____ a beautiful cabinet for his mother.

① gave　　　② showed
③ made　　　④ sent
⑤ bought

18 다음 중 올바른 문장을 고르시오.

① I let her to take a trip.
② She finished to write a book.
③ He found her diligently.
④ I saw a bird flying in the sky.
⑤ I heard he singing in the shower.

[19-20] 우리말과 일치하도록 주어진 단어를 알맞게 배열하시오.

19 그 의사는 팀에게 술을 너무 많이 먹지 말라고 충고했다.
(Tim, to, not, drink, advised, much, the doctor, too)

→ _____

20 그녀는 어제 그에게 열쇠고리를 만들어 주었다.
(she, for, made, yesterday, a key holder, him)

→ _____

정답 및 해설 p.3

01 다음 빈칸에 들어갈 말로 가장 적절한 것을 고르시오.

Last weekend I had the flu. It made me
Ⓐ_____. I didn't have enough energy to
get out of bed. At that time, I heard one of
my family members Ⓑ_____ the kitchen.
I hoped that was my mother. After a while,
she opened my room and found that I had
been sick. After I was taken good care of by
her, I felt better.

■ flu 유행성 감기

	Ⓐ		Ⓑ
①	to feel awful	–	enter
②	to feel awfully	–	enter
③	feel awful	–	enter
④	feel awful	–	enter into
⑤	feeing awful	–	enter into

02 다음 글의 밑줄 친 부분 중 어법상 틀린 것을 고르시오.

One day, while the old man ① was cutting
down a big tree near the river, his axe
② fell into the river. He sat down and began
③ to cry because that was the only old
axe he had. Then a god of the mountains
appeared and ④ asked him if a silver axe was
his. He shook his head. The god disappeared,
and then appeared again with a golden axe
and asked the same question. He answered
that that was not his. This time, the god
showed up with an iron axe. Seeing the iron
axe, he was very happy. He said that it was
his. The god of the mountains jumped into
the water and came up with the silver and
golden axes. He ⑤ gave both axes the old
man and went into the river.

■ axe 도끼   ■ appear 나타나다

01 다음 그림을 보고 보기의 단어들을 이용하여 문장을 완성하시오.

보기	smoke	to	a dog	the street
	him	cross	not	here

1)
I saw _____.

2)
I told _____.

02 다음 우리말을 읽고 바르게 영작하시오.

오늘은 어머니의 생신이다. 우리는 저녁에 깜짝 파티를 할
것이다. 나는 아버지께 어머니를 위한 선물을 사 오시라고
부탁했다. 또한 나는 남동생에게 집을 청소하라고 시켰다.
나는 어머니를 위해 생일케이크를 만들었다. 이 파티는
그녀를 행복하게 할 것이다.

Today is my mother's birthday. We will have a

surprise party in the evening.

_____

_____

_____

Chapter 02

시제

Chapter 미리보기

시제	시제의 형태	예문	시제	시제의 형태	예문
현재	동사원형(es)	He plays the piano every day.	현재완료	have/has + p.p	He has played the piano.
과거	동사원형 + -(e)d, 불규칙 동사	He played the piano.	과거완료	had + p.p	He had played the piano.
미래	will + 동사원형	He will play the piano.	미래완료	will have + p.p	He will have played the piano.
현재진행형	am/are/is + 동사원형-ing	He is playing the piano.	현재완료 진행형	have/has been + 동사원형-ing	He has been playing the piano.
과거진행형	was/were + 동사원형-ing	He was playing the piano.	과거완료 진행형	had been + 동사원형-ing	He had been playing the piano.
미래진행형	will be + 동사원형-ing	He will be playing the piano.	미래완료 진행형	will have been + 동사원형-ing	He will have been playing the piano.

Many hands make light work. 많은 손이 일을 가볍게 만든다.
▶ 백지장도 맞들면 낫다.

03 현재, 과거, 미래

현재시제	동사원형(es)	He plays the piano every day.
과거시제	동사원형 + -(e)d, 불규칙 동사	He played the piano.
미래시제	will + 동사원형	He will play the piano.

A 현재시제

현재의 반복적 동작이나 상태, 불변의 진리, 속담 등을 표현한다.

ex • I always drink coffee without sugar. (현재의 반복적 동작)
• Light travels faster than sound. (불변의 진리)
• Time is the great healer. (속담)

B 과거시제

과거의 동작이나 상태, 역사적 사실 등을 표현한다.
주로 과거를 나타내는 부사구(yesterday, ago, last 등)와 함께 쓴다.

ex • He got married five years ago. (과거의 동작)
• My father was sick yesterday. (과거의 상태)
• The French Revolution lasted from 1789 to 1799. (역사적 사실)

C 미래시제

미래에 일어날 동작이나 상태 등을 표현하며, 조동사 will이나 be going to, be about to를 사용한다.

ex • She will go abroad to study music.
• She is going to meet her grandparents soon.
• They are about to leave Seoul for France.

D 주의해야 할 시제

시간과 조건 부사절에서는 현재시제가 미래시제를 대신한다.

1 **시간 부사절을 이끄는 접속사 :** when, until, before, after, as soon as 등
2 **조건 부사절을 이끄는 접속사 :** if, unless 등

ex • I will wait for you until you come back home.
• If it is sunny tomorrow, we will go swimming.

—⊕ If it snows tomorrow, we will go skiing. (부사절 : ~한다면)
I don't know if it will snow tomorrow. (명사절 : ~인지 아닌지)

Grammar Check-Up

정답 및 해설 p.4

Note

O1 주어진 단어를 이용하여 문장을 완성하시오.

1) You should stay here until your mom _____ back. (come)

2) Japan _____ the American Navy in Hawaii in 1940. (attack)

3) If he _____ tomorrow, I will give this to him. (arrive)

4) I am sure that you _____ the exam next year. (pass)

2) attack 공격하다
   navy 해군

O2 주어진 말을 이용하여 다음 질문에 대한 대답을 쓰시오.

1) Ⓐ What does your sister do every morning?

   Ⓑ _____ (go swimming)

2) Ⓐ What did you do last weekend?

   Ⓑ _____ (wash my car)

3) Ⓐ What are you going to do this Saturday?

   Ⓑ _____ (take a trip to Jejudo)

O3 우리말과 일치하도록 빈칸에 알맞은 말을 쓰시오.

1) 영화가 막 시작되려고 한다.

   → The movie _____ _____ _____ start.

2) 아시안 게임이 자카르타에서 열릴 것이다.

   → The Asian Games _____ _____ held in Jakarta.

3) 그는 2년 전에 하버드 대학을 졸업했다.

   → He _____ from Harvard University two years ago.

2) hold 열다, 개최하다
3) graduate from
   ~을 졸업하다

O4 다음 우리말을 영작하시오.

1) 나는 하루에 세 번 이를 닦는다.

   → _____

2) 만약 내일 추우면, 나는 새 코트를 입을 것이다.

   → _____

3) 버스가 5분 전에 떠났다.

   → _____

Unit 04 진행형

현재진행형	am/are/is + 동사원형-ing	He is playing the piano.
과거진행형	was/were + 동사원형-ing	He was playing the piano.
미래진행형	will be + 동사원형-ing	He will be playing the piano.

A 현재진행형

현재 하고 있는 동작을 표현한다.

ex • A: What is your mom doing now?
  B: She is sleeping.
• Listen! She is playing the flute.

B 과거진행형

과거의 어느 한 순간 하고 있었던 동작을 표현한다.

ex • A: What were you doing at this time yesterday?
  B: I was making pizza.
• My mom was sleeping when I arrived.

C 미래진행형

미래의 어느 시점에 진행 중일 것으로 예상되는 일을 표현한다.

ex • My mom will be sleeping when I arrive.
• He will be swimming at this time tomorrow.

D 진행형에서 주의해야 할 사항

1 현재진행형은 가까운 미래에 일어날 확정된 일을 표현할 때 미래시제 대신 사용할 수 있으며, 이때 주로 미래 부사구(soon, tomorrow, next 등)와 함께 쓴다.

ex • The bus for New York is leaving soon.
• She is coming here this Saturday.

2 소유(have, belong to 등), 감정(like, love 등), 감각(see, hear, taste, smell 등), 인지(know 등)를 나타내는 동사들은 진행형으로 쓸 수 없다. 하지만 동작을 나타내는 동사로 쓰일 때는 진행형으로 쓸 수 있다.

ex • He has a lot of books. (○)
• He is having a lot of books. (×)
• He is having sandwiches for lunch. (○)
• These flowers smell good. (○)
• These flowers are smelling good. (×)
• He is smelling the flowers. (○)

Grammar Check-Up

정답 및 해설 p.4

01 다음 중 알맞은 것을 고르시오.

1) He   has | is having   many kinds of dictionaries.

2) She   is walking | was walking   along the street when she met her teacher.

3) Watch out! A truck   is coming | comes   here.

4) This electronic dictionary   belongs | is belonging   to me.

02 주어진 말을 이용하여 다음 질문에 대한 대답을 쓰시오.

1) **A** What is your father doing now?

B _____ (feed the cat)

2) **A** What was your sister doing at this time yesterday?

B _____ (lie on the grass)

03 밑줄 친 부분에 주의하여 다음 두 문장을 우리말로 비교 해석하시오.

1) The chef is tasting the soup. / It tastes too salty.

→ _____

2) He is coming to the party now. / He is coming to the party soon.

→ _____

04 다음 우리말을 영작하시오.

1) 할아버지께서는 지금 거실에서 낮잠을 주무시고 계신다.

→ _____

2) 어제 이맘때 나는 TV에서 영화를 보고 있었다.

→ _____

3) 내일 이맘때 나는 수영하고 있을 것이다.

→ _____

Note

1) dictionary 사전

4) electronic dictionary 전자사전

belong to ~에 속하다

1) feed 먹이를 주다

2) at this time yesterday 어제 이맘때

1) take a nap 낮잠을 자다

3) at this time tomorrow 내일 이맘때

A 현재완료의 용법

〈have/has + p.p(과거분사)〉의 형태이며, 과거의 어느 시점에서 현재까지의 경험, 계속, 완료, 결과를 나타낸다.

1 경험 : 과거에서부터 현재까지의 경험을 표현하며, '~한 적이 있다/없다'로 해석한다.
주로 ever, never, once, twice 등과 함께 쓰인다.

ex • I have never seen a movie star in person.

2 계속 : 과거부터 현재까지 계속하고 있는 일을 표현하며, '계속 ~해 오고 있다'로 해석한다.
주로 for, since 등과 함께 쓰인다.

ex • I have been in Germany for three years.

> **Tips**
> • 〈for + 기간〉 ~동안
> • 〈since + 특정한 시간〉
>   ~이래로

3 완료 : 과거부터 해 오던 일을 방금 끝냈다는 표현으로 '막 ~했다'로 해석한다.
주로 just, already, yet 등과 함께 쓰인다.

ex • They have just moved into this apartment.

> **Tips**
> • just 막, 금방
> • already
>   (긍정문) 이미, 벌써
> • yet
>   (부정문) 아직도
>   (의문문) 벌써

4 결과 : 과거에 일어난 일이 현재에 영향을 미치는 것을 표현하며, '~해서 그 결과 현재 …하다'로 해석한다.

ex • Her sister has lost her electronic dictionary.
= Her sister lost her electronic dictionary, so she doesn't have it.

B have gone to와 have been to

have gone to	~로 가 버렸다(그래서 지금 여기에 없다)	She has gone to China.
have been to	~에 가 본 적이 있다	She has been to China once.
	~에 갔다 왔다	I have been to the store.

C 현재완료와 함께 쓸 수 없는 것들

의문사 when, 과거 부사구(yesterday, ago, last 등)는 현재완료와 함께 사용할 수 없다.

ex • When have you finished it? (×) → When did you finish it? (○)
• The plane has landed an hour ago. (×) → The plane landed an hour ago. (○)

D 현재완료진행형

〈have/has been + 동사원형-ing〉 형태로 과거에 시작해서 현재까지 계속 진행 중인 동작을 강조할 때 사용한다.

ex • I have been studying English for two hours.

Grammar Check-Up

정답 및 해설 p.4

Note

01 다음 중 알맞은 것을 고르시오.

1) I have   been | gone   to Japan.

2) She has been in the hospital   for | since   three weeks.

3) He   has lost | lost   one of his teeth a week ago.

4) When   did | have   you read *Harry Potter*?

02 두 문장을 한 문장으로 바꿀 때 빈칸에 알맞은 말을 쓰시오.

1) She went to England. + She is there now.

   → She _____ _____ _____ England.

2) Sue came to Seoul ten years ago. + She still lives in Seoul.

   → Sue _____ _____ in Seoul for ten years.

3) It started to rain two days ago. + It is raining now.

   → It _____ _____ _____ for two days.

4) I lost my key. + I don't have it now.

   → I _____ _____ my key.

03 주어진 동사를 이용하여 문장을 완성하시오.

1) My father _____ ill in bed since last week. (be)

2) She _____ to a party last Saturday night. (go)

3) A year ago, I _____ the sea for the first time in my life. (see)

4) I _____ her since I _____ fifteen years old. (know, be)

04 주어진 말을 이용하여 다음 우리말을 영작하시오.

1) 나는 골프를 쳐 본 적이 없다. (never)

   → _____

2) 나는 여섯 시 이후로 계속 여기에 있었다. (since)

   → _____

3) 한국에 오신 지 얼마나 되었습니까? (how long)

   → _____

Unit 06 과거완료, 미래완료

A 과거완료

〈had + p.p〉의 형태이며, 과거의 한 시점을 기준으로 그 이전부터 그 기준 시점까지 동작의 완료, 결과, 경험, 계속을 나타낸다.

과거완료

기준 시점 과거　　　　현재

1 **완료** ex • Karen had already left by the time her mother got there.

2 **결과** ex • I found that I had lost my key.

3 **경험** ex • I had never seen any of Picasso's paintings before I visited the museum.

4 **계속** ex • She had been in Seoul for 2 years when I met her on the street.

B 과거완료진행형

〈had been + 동사원형-ing〉의 형태이며, 과거 이전부터 과거 기준 시점까지 계속 진행 중인 동작을 강조할 때 사용한다.

ex • She had been playing the cello for two hours when her mother came back home.

C 미래완료

〈will have + p.p〉의 형태이며, 예전부터 시작하여 미래 어느 시점에 완료, 결과, 경험, 계속을 나타낸다.

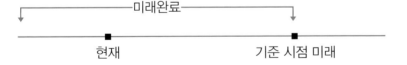

미래완료

현재　　　　기준 시점 미래

1 **완료** ex • She will have finished cleaning the house by two o'clock.

2 **결과** ex • He will have become a dentist by the time you get back to Korea.

3 **경험** ex • I will have been to America twice if I visit there next week.

4 **계속** ex • When he retires next month, he will have taught for 40 years.

Grammar Check-Up

01 다음 중 알맞은 것을 고르시오.

1) When I got up in the morning, he   had | has   already gone out.

2) If I go to Mt. Seorak again, I   will have climbed | have climbed   it three times.

02 우리말과 일치하도록 빈칸에 알맞은 말을 쓰시오.

1) 나는 숙제를 이미 다 했기 때문에 할 일이 거의 없었다.

→ I just had few things to do because I _____ my homework.

2) 만약에 그 영화를 한 번 더 본다면 나는 그것을 두 번 보게 되는 셈이다.

→ If I watch the movie once more, I _____ it twice.

3) 너는 9시에 집에 있었어. 그 전에는 어디 있었니?

→ You were at home at nine o'clock. Where _____ before that?

03 밑줄 친 부분에 주의하여 다음 문장을 우리말로 해석하시오.

1) By the time I see you, I will have graduated from high school.

→ _____

2) My sister told me that she had been busy for a week.

→ _____

1) graduate from ~을 졸업하다

04 우리말과 일치하도록 주어진 말을 바르게 배열하시오.

1) 그녀는 한국전쟁이 일어났을 때 10년 동안 서울에서 살았었다.

(in, Seoul, for, she, broke out, when, ten years, lived, the Korean War, had)

→ _____

2) 우리가 부산에 도착할 때 쯤이면 우리는 다섯 시간 운전을 하게 되는 셈이다.

(by the time, we, we, in, will, driven, arrive, for, Busan, five hours, have)

→ _____

내신 족집게 문제

[01-06] 빈칸에 들어갈 알맞은 것을 고르시오.

O1   Water _____ of oxygen and hydrogen.

① consists   ② is consisting
③ consisted   ④ will consist
⑤ has consisted

O2   The French Revolution _____ in 1789.

① starts   ② started
③ has started   ④ had started
⑤ is starting

O3   When my mom got home, we _____ in the yard.

① plays   ② is playing
③ will be playing   ④ has played
⑤ were playing

O4   Yesterday I saw my friend, Karen, on the street. At first, I didn't recognize her because she _____ a great deal of weight.

① has lost   ② had lost
③ have lost   ④ has been lost
⑤ had been lost

O5   I _____ afraid of dogs since I was a child.

① be   ② was
③ has been   ④ have been
⑤ had been

O6   I _____ here for four months by the time I leave this city.

① is   ② was
③ will have been   ④ have been
⑤ had been

O7   밑줄 친 부분이 어법상 틀린 것을 고르시오.

① He is about to start.
② One swallow doesn't make a summer.
③ Listen! The baby is crying.
④ She washes her hair every day.
⑤ He is cooking by the time I arrived.

[08-09] 두 문장의 뜻이 같도록 빈칸에 알맞은 말을 쓰시오.

O8   She went to Egypt. She is here now.

= She _____ _____ to Egypt.

O9   He started to play the piano an hour ago. He is playing it now.

= He _____ _____ _____ the piano for an hour.

10   보기의 밑줄 친 부분과 쓰임이 같은 것을 고르시오.

보기   She has never been there.

① I have known him for the past two years.
② I have had these shoes for three years.
③ The train for Busan has already left.
④ Have you ever been to China?
⑤ I haven't told him about the accident yet.

11   빈칸에 알맞은 시제를 바르게 연결한 것을 고르시오.

He _____ many beautiful pictures before he died. By next year, his pictures _____ kept in this museum for five years.

① has drawn – have been
② has drawn – will have been
③ has drawn – had been
④ had drawn – have been
⑤ had drawn – will have been

[12-14] 빈칸에 알맞은 단어를 순서대로 바르게 짝지은 것을 고르시오.

12
- It's been raining _____ I got up this morning.
- She has been on vacation _____ five days.
- I have lived here _____ 1999.

① for – since – since
② since – for – during
③ since – for – since
④ since – during – for
⑤ since – for – for

13
- If it _____ tomorrow, we will stay at home.
- I wonder if it _____ tomorrow.

① will rain – will rain   ② will rain – rains
③ rains – rains   ④ rains – will rain
⑤ rains – will rains

14
- It _____ sunny today.
- It _____ sunny yesterday.
- It _____ sunny since yesterday.

① is – was – has been
② is – was – was
③ is – has been – has been
④ was – was – was
⑤ was – has been – has been

15 다음 중 올바른 문장을 고르시오.
① As soon as he finishes dinner, he will take the children for a walk.
② When have you lost your bicycle?
③ He has bought this bicycle two years ago.
④ I have gone to Africa.
⑤ He will finish this work before he will leave.

16 다음 중 어법상 틀린 문장을 고르시오.
① Tim was driving a car at this time yesterday.
② The food is tasting spicy.
③ He is leaving at noon tomorrow.
④ Look! A girl is playing the violin on the street.
⑤ When I get up tomorrow morning, my mom will be reading a newspaper.

17 세 문장의 뜻이 같도록 빈칸에 알맞은 말을 쓰시오.

Two years have passed since he died.

= He _____ _____ dead for two years.

= He _____ two years ago.

[18-19] 우리말과 일치하도록 빈칸에 알맞은 말을 쓰시오.

18 그가 올 때까지 나는 바로 여기서 기다릴 것이다.
→ I will wait right here _____ _____

_____.

19 인류가 처음 나타났을 때 쯤 공룡은 이미 멸종되었다.
→ Dinosaurs _____ _____

_____ extinct by the time humankind first appeared.

20 우리말과 일치하도록 주어진 단어를 알맞게 배열하시오.

나는 이 나라에 온 이후로 이곳의 생활 방식을 많이 배워 왔다. (since, came, here, learned, to this country, a lot, the way of life, I, I, have, about)

→ _____

_____

01 다음 빈칸에 들어갈 말로 가장 적절한 것을 고르시오.

> When I **A**_____ spaghetti last weekend, I received a wedding invitation card. The card was from a friend with whom I **B**_____ in America before. Her wedding ceremony was on November 11th. I didn't know if I **C**_____ the ceremony because it was too far from here. Right then, I remembered promising her a few years ago that I would be at her wedding.

■ be sure to 반드시 ~하다   ■ attend 참석하다

	A	**B**	**C**
①	is making	– live	– will attend
②	is making	– had lived	– would attend
③	make	– have lived	– would attend
④	was making	– have lived	– will attend
⑤	was making	– had lived	– would attend

02 다음 글의 밑줄 친 부분 중 어법상 틀린 것을 고르시오.

> There ① have been a lot of reports of UFOs over the area of the Bermuda Triangle. Some people ② have suggested that the area is a UFO hunting ground, where humans ③ are kidnapped and taken to other worlds. They say, "In 1945, five navy airplanes of Flight 19 ④ have disappeared in this area." Another suggestion is that the Triangle is some kind of window connecting this world to another dimension. Under certain conditions, things might move from this life into another. Even the space shuttle ⑤ has lost compass directions and radio contact when flying over the Bermuda Triangle.

■ Bermuda Triangle 버뮤다 삼각지대   ■ kidnap 납치하다
■ dimension 차원   ■ compass 나침반

01 두 문장의 뜻이 같도록 주어진 동사를 알맞은 형태로 바꾸어 쓰시오.

1) Tim and Sue got married last year. Today is their first wedding anniversary.

→ They _____ married for a year. (be)

2) It started to snow yesterday. It is still snowing now.

→ It _____ since yesterday. (snow)

3) He arrived at Seoul Station at 5:10. The train left at 5 o'clock.

→ When he arrived at Seoul Station, the train _____. (already leave)

02 다음 우리말을 읽고 바르게 영작하시오.

1990년에 나는 속초에서 태어났다. 2000년 서울로 이사 왔을 때 나는 10년 동안 속초에서 살았었다. 2000년 이후로 나는 계속 서울에서 살고 있다.

_____

_____

_____

_____

Chapter

03

조동사

Chapter 미리보기

can	① 능력 (= be able to) ② 허락	① ~할 수 있다 ② ~해도 된다	had better	~하는 것이 좋다
may	① 허락 ② 추측	① ~해도 된다 ② ~일지도 모른다	would rather	차라리 ~하겠다
must	① 의무 (= have to) ② 추측	① ~해야 한다 ② ~임에 틀림없다	should have p.p	~했어야 했다
			shouldn't have p.p	~하지 말았어야 했다
should (= ought to)		~해야 한다	must have p.p	~했음에 틀림없다
would (과거의 습관)		~하곤 했다	may have p.p	~했을지도 모른다
used to (과거의 습관이나 상태)		~하곤 했다/~이었다	can't have p.p	~했을 리가 없다

Speak of the devil, and he will appear.
▶ 호랑이도 제 말하면 온다.

07 can, may, must, should

A can

1 능력 : '~할 수 있다'라는 의미이며, be able to로 바꾸어 쓸 수 있다.

> **ex** • Kate can (= is able to) play the flute.
> • The baby will be able to walk soon. (미래)

2 허락 : '~해도 된다'라는 의미이다.

> **ex** • You can use my cell phone.

3 약한 추측 : '~일 수 있다'라는 의미이다.

> **ex** • Jane can be a doctor.

B may

1 허락 : '~해도 된다'라는 의미이다.

> **ex** • May I come in?

2 약한 추측 : '~일지도 모른다'라는 의미이다.

> **ex** • Paul may come to the meeting.

C must

1 의무 : '~해야 한다'라는 의미이며, have to로 바꾸어 쓸 수 있다.

> **ex** • He must (= has to) go now.

2 강한 추측 : '~임에 틀림없다'라는 의미이다.

> **ex** • She must be a police officer.

의무	미래	will have to	Kate will have to apologize to him.
	과거	had to	Kevin had to finish it.
	부정문	don't have to = don't need to (~할 필요가 없다)	We don't have to go to school today.
		must not (~하면 절대로 안 된다)	You must not enter the room now.
추측	부정문	cannot (= can't) (~일 리 없다)	She cannot be a firefighter.

D should

'~해야 한다'라는 의미이며, ought to로 바꾸어 쓸 수 있다.

> **ex** • I think we should (= ought to) enter the tournament.
> • We should not (= ought not to) enter the tournament.

Grammar Check-Up

정답 및 해설 p.6

Note

O1 다음 문장을 지시대로 바꾸어 쓰시오.

1) Kevin can read and write English.

【미래】▶ _____

2) Kate must go to the hospital.

【과거】▶ _____

3) Paul ought to buy a new bike.

【부정문】▶ _____

O2 두 문장의 뜻이 같도록 빈칸에 알맞은 말을 쓰시오.

1) Kevin could remember phone numbers by heart.

= Kevin _____ _____ _____ remember

phone numbers by heart.

2) Jane doesn't have to carry the boxes.

= Jane doesn't _____ _____ carry the boxes.

1) by heart 외워서

O3 밑줄 친 부분에 주의하여 다음 문장을 우리말로 해석하시오.

1) We <u>must do</u> our best to make our dreams come true.

→ _____

2) Susan <u>must be</u> exhausted after climbing the mountain.

→ _____

3) Jane <u>may not</u> like the end of the story.

→ _____

1) come true 실현하다
2) exhausted 지친

O4 다음 우리말을 영작하시오.

1) 케이트(Kate)가 한국어 교사일 리 없다.

→ _____

2) 너는 여기서 길을 건너면 절대로 안 된다.

→ _____

3) 폴(Paul)은 돈을 빌릴 필요가 없었다.

→ _____

2) cross 건너다
3) borrow 빌리다

would, used to, had better, would rather

A would

1 will의 과거형

> **ex** • Ann said she would come home early.

2 과거의 습관 (~하곤 했다)

> **ex** • Paul would play football after school when he was younger.

3 요청, 권유, 부탁

> **ex** • Would you close the door for me, please?

4 would you like + 명사 / would you like to + 동사원형 (~하시겠습니까?)

> **ex** • Would you like some chocolate? / Would you like to join us?
>
> [비교] I would like to (= want to) meet the singer.

B used to

1 과거의 습관

> **ex** • We used to play table tennis on Saturday.

2 과거의 상태

> **ex** • There used to be a bakery next to the cafe.
>
> • I would be a student. (×)

Tips
• would는 과거의 습관으로 사용하지만 과거의 상태로는 사용하지 못한다.

⊕ • used to + 동사원형 (~하곤 했다)　　**ex** • I used to play the piano.
　• be used to + 동명사 (~하는 데 익숙하다)　　**ex** • I am used to getting up early.
　• be used to + 동사원형 (~하는 데 사용되다)　　**ex** • Wood is used to make desks.

C had better

'~하는 것이 좋다'라는 의미이며, 부정은 had better not이다.

> **ex** • You had better tell the truth. (= You'd better tell the truth.)
>
> • You'd better not watch TV all day.

D would rather

Tips
• would rather A than B
B하느니 차라리 A하는 것이 낫다

'차라리 ~하겠다'라는 의미이다.

> **ex** • It is cold outside. I would rather (= I'd rather) stay at home.
>
> • I am tired. I would rather not go out tonight.
>
> • I would rather (= I'd rather) watch TV than go to the movies with him.

Grammar Check-Up

01 다음 중 알맞은 것을 고르시오.

1) Kate   would like | would rather   to go to a classical concert.

2) You   would like | had better   go to the library tomorrow.

3) I   had better | would rather   go swimming than go climbing.

02 밑줄 친 부분을 바르게 고쳐 쓰시오.

1) You <u>would better finish</u> your homework first.

(→ _____)

2) He <u>would rather not to swim</u> in the sea.

(→ _____)

3) She <u>would be</u> an English teacher.   (→ _____)

4) <u>Would you like to</u> a sandwich?   (→ _____)

03 밑줄 친 부분에 주의하여 다음 문장을 우리말로 해석하시오.

1) I <u>would rather watch</u> TV at home than see the movie again.

→ _____

2) Kate <u>used to take</u> her puppy, Romeo, to the park.

→ _____

3) Kevin <u>is used to running</u> early in the morning.

→ _____

04 다음 우리말을 영작하시오.

1) 너는 내일 학교에 늦지 않는 것이 좋다.

→ _____

2) 나는 차라리 노래를 부르지 않는 것이 낫겠다.

→ _____

3) 그녀는 피아노를 치곤 했다.

→ _____

09 조동사 have p.p

A should have p.p

과거에 하지 않은 일에 대한 유감이나 후회를 나타내며, '~했어야 했다'라는 의미이다.

ex
- You should have come to the party. It was great!
- I should have finished my homework.

B shouldn't have p.p

과거에 한 일에 대한 유감이나 후회를 나타내며, '~하지 말았어야 했다'라는 의미이다.

ex
- I shouldn't have watched TV so long.
- Kate shouldn't have hidden her mistakes.

C must have p.p

과거의 일에 대한 강한 추측을 나타내며, '~했음에 틀림없다'라는 의미이다.

ex
- Kate must have left her textbook at home.
- I must have forgotten to bring my wallet.

D can't have p.p

과거의 일에 대한 강한 부정을 나타내며, '~했을 리가 없다'라는 의미이다.

ex
- You can't have seen him on the street. He went to Canada yesterday.
- Kate can't have played the piano. She doesn't know how to play it.

E may (= might) have p.p

과거의 일에 대한 약한 추측을 나타내며, '~했을지도 모른다'라는 의미이다.

ex
- Kate may have missed the bus.
- Kevin might have lost some weight.

Grammar Check-Up

O1 다음 중 알맞은 것을 고르시오.

1) Kate hasn't come home yet. Something 　must｜can't　 have happened to her.

2) Kevin was late for school. He 　may｜should　 have woken up late.

1) happen 일어나다

O2 빈칸에 알맞은 말을 보기에서 골라 쓰시오.

| 보기 | shouldn't have | should have | must have |

1) Ann lost her wallet. She _____ been more careful.

2) They passed the English test. They _____ studied hard.

3) Jane had a big lunch and got a stomachache. She _____ eaten so much.

O3 밑줄 친 부분에 주의하여 다음 문장을 우리말로 해석하시오.

1) Kevin shouldn't have made a mistake.

→ _____

2) Paul must have forgotten the appointment.

→ _____

3) Jane can't have won the English contest.

→ _____

1) make a mistake
　 실수를 하다
2) appointment 약속

O4 다음 우리말을 영작하시오.

1) 앤(Ann)은 숲에서 길을 잃어버렸는지도 모른다.

→ _____

2) 그는 약속을 지켰어야 했다.

→ _____

3) 케이트(Kate)가 그를 만났을 리가 없다.

→ _____

1) lose one's way
　 길을 잃다
2) keep one's promise
　 약속을 지키다

내신 족집게 문제

[01-04] 우리말과 일치하도록 빈칸에 알맞은 말을 쓰시오.

01 비가 올 것이다. 우리는 지금 집에 가는 것이 좋겠다.

→ It is going to rain. We _____

_____ go home now.

02 나는 그를 기다릴 필요가 없다.

→ I _____ _____ _____ wait

for him.

03 너는 시험 보는 동안에 부정행위를 해서는 절대로 안
된다.

→ You _____ _____ cheat during

the exam.

04 그녀는 레슬링 선수일 리 없다. 그녀는 너무 작다.

→ She _____ be a wrestler. She is so

small.

05 빈칸에 들어갈 수 <u>없는</u> 것을 고르시오.

The rumor about the singers _____ be true.

① can　　② have to　　③ must

④ may　　⑤ can't

06 빈칸에 알맞은 단어를 순서대로 바르게 짝지은 것을
고르시오.

• _____ you like to have lunch with me?

• He's got a headache. He _____ better
stay at home tonight.

① Have – have　　② Would – have

③ Would – had　　④ Would – would

⑤ Could – would

07 빈칸에 들어갈 알맞은 것을 고르시오.

Susan won an Olympic gold medal. She
_____ a lot of effort.

① must have made

② can't have made

③ should have made

④ shouldn't have made

⑤ must not have made

08 보기의 밑줄 친 부분과 의미가 <u>다른</u> 것을 고르시오.

보기　Kevin <u>may</u> know Kate.

① She <u>may</u> be a good teacher.

② He <u>may</u> be at home.

③ They <u>may</u> be sleeping now.

④ You <u>may</u> go now.

⑤ It <u>may</u> be true.

[09-11] 두 문장의 뜻이 같도록 빈칸에 알맞은 말을 쓰시오.

09 There was a bakery around the corner, but
there is a bookstore around the corner now.

= There _____ _____ _____ a
bakery around the corner.

10 I want to have some sandwiches.

= I _____ _____ _____ have
some sandwiches.

11 You should not play games for such a long
time.

= You _____ _____ _____ play
games for such a long time.

12 밑줄 친 조동사의 부정형이 잘못된 것을 고르시오.

① You had not better go there.

② I would rather not play with them.

③ Ann should not tell a lie.

④ We must not park here.

⑤ They don't have to pay for it.

[13-14] 밑줄 친 조동사의 의미가 나머지와 다른 것을 고르시오.

13 ① I could run a marathon.

② Kevin could play the violin.

③ Kate can speak English.

④ You can use my pen.

⑤ They could solve the puzzle.

14 ① Ann must give him the document today.

② Kevin must do his homework now.

③ You must be Jane's friend.

④ They must be careful with bombs.

⑤ I must use the password to log in.

15 두 문장의 뜻이 같지 않은 것을 고르시오.

① He could speak five languages.
= He was able to speak five languages.

② They must not play football here.
= They don't have to play football here.

③ I should listen to my parents.
= I ought to listen to my parents.

④ May I borrow your cell phone?
= Can I borrow your cell phone?

⑤ We have to turn off the computer after using it.
= We must turn off the computer after using it.

16 우리말과 일치하도록 주어진 단어를 알맞게 배열하시오.

나는 집에 있느니 차라리 도서관에 가겠다.
(rather, home, I, library, than, stay, go, the, at, would, to)

→ _____

[17-18] 빈칸에 알맞은 말을 보기에서 골라 알맞은 형태로 바꾸어 쓰시오.

보기 shouldn't   should   have   tell   save

17 I told her a lie. I regret it now. I _____
_____ _____ her a lie.

18 Ann spent all her money. She _____
_____ _____ some.

[19-20] 밑줄 친 부분의 쓰임이 어색한 문장을 고르시오.

19 ① I broke the vase. I shouldn't have touched it.

② They caught the thief last night. They can't have been brave.

③ Kevin lived in a big house. He may have been rich.

④ Paul had a car accident. He shouldn't have driven fast.

⑤ Karen's eyes were swollen. She must have cried last night.

20 ① Ann would go shopping on Sunday.

② Kevin used to be thin.

③ Jane used to be a guide.

④ Paul would be a music teacher.

⑤ Kate used to play table tennis with her family.

정답 및 해설 p.7

O1 다음 글의 밑줄 친 부분 중 어법상 **틀린** 것을 고르시오.

Poseidon was the god of the sea and the brother of Zeus. He was ① the second most powerful god. Poseidon protected all waters. Seamen worshiped him. His weapon was a trident. He ② could shake the earth with it. He loved Demeter but she ③ had rather have died than meet him. To avoid him Demeter asked him to make ④ the most beautiful animal in the world. So Poseidon ⑤ had to create the first horse to please her. At first he wasn't successful and created various other animals. Finally, he created the horse.

- seamen 선원들   - worship 숭배하다   - trident 삼지창

O2 다음 괄호 안에서 어법에 맞는 표현으로 가장 적절한 것을 고르시오.

According to a law to protect whales, ships Ⓐ(must / may) slow down in areas where whales are known to swim. Whales hear ships but Ⓑ(must / can't) easily get out of the way because they are much bigger than a bus. Adult whales can weigh 90,000 kilograms and be 12 to 15 meters long. Babies weigh about 900 kilograms and are about 4 meters long when they are born. Whales Ⓒ(may / must) look tough, but when a ship hits a whale, it can cause severe injuries.

- whale 고래   - weigh 무게가 나가다   - tough 강인한
- injury 부상

	Ⓐ		Ⓑ		Ⓒ
①	must	–	must	–	may
②	must	–	must	–	must
③	must	–	can't	–	may
④	may	–	can't	–	must
⑤	may	–	can't	–	may

O1 보기에서 알맞은 말을 골라 주어진 글을 완성하시오.

보기	had better	has to
	used to	doesn't have to

Kevin _____ be a firefighter. He wanted to establish his own small business. So he quit his job. He is good at making pizza. I think he _____ open a pizza restaurant. The shop _____ be big but the pizza _____ be delicious.

O2 다음 우리말을 읽고 바르게 영작하시오.

수잔 : 어제 나는 TV를 너무 많이 봤어. 나는 숙제를 했어야 했어.
케빈 : 나는 친구들과 하루 종일 놀지 말았어야 했어.
수잔 : 너도 숙제를 했을 리가 없구나.
케빈 : 하지만 앤은 숙제를 다한 게 틀림없어.

Susan : Yesterday I watched too much TV. _____

_____

Kevin : _____

_____

Susan : _____

_____

Kevin : _____

_____

Chapter

04

수동태
- ♣ **Unit 10** 수동태의 시제
- ♣ **Unit 11** 4, 5형식의 수동태
- ♣ **Unit 12** 여러 가지 수동태

Chapter 미리보기

	수동태 시제	예문
현재	am/are/is + p.p	A letter is written by me.
과거	was/were + p.p	A letter was written by me.
미래	will be + p.p	A letter will be written by me.
현재진행형	am/are/is + being + p.p	A letter is being written by me.
과거진행형	was/were + being + p.p	A letter was being written by me.
현재완료	have/has + been + p.p	A letter has been written by me.
과거완료	had been + p.p	A letter had been written by me.

What is done cannot be undone.
▶ 이미 한 것은 되돌릴 수 없다.

A 태

주어와 동사와의 관계를 말한다.

1 능동태 : 주어가 동사의 동작을 행하는 것을 말한다.

> **ex** • She helped the boy. (주어 she가 도움을 줌)

2 수동태 : 주어가 동사의 동작을 받거나 당하는 것을 의미하며, 형태는 〈be동사 + 과거분사(p.p)〉이다.

> **ex** • The boy was helped by her. (주어 the boy가 도움을 받음)

B 수동태 만드는 방법

> ⓐ 능동태의 목적어를 수동태의 주어 자리에 놓는다.
> ⓑ 동사를 〈be동사 + 과거분사(p.p)〉 형태로 바꾼다. 이때 be동사는 능동태 동사의 시제에 맞춘다.
> ⓒ 능동태의 주어를 〈by + 목적격〉으로 만든다.

> **ex** • Shakespeare   wrote   Hamlet. (능동태)
>
> → *Hamlet*   was written   by Shakespeare. (수동태)

C 수동태의 시제

1 현재시제 : am/are/is + 과거분사(p.p)

> **ex** • She opens the door. → The door is opened by her.

2 과거시제 : was/were + 과거분사(p.p)

> **ex** • His father built the house. → The house was built by his father.

3 미래시제 : will be + 과거분사(p.p)

> **ex** • We will paint the fence. → The fence will be painted by us.

4 진행형시제 : am/are/is/was/were + being + 과거분사(p.p)

> **ex** • I am writing a novel. → A novel is being written by me.

5 완료시제 : have/has/had + been + 과거분사(p.p)

> **ex** • He has opened the door. → The door has been opened by him.

Grammar Check-Up

정답 및 해설 p.7

O1 다음 중 알맞은 것을 고르시오.

1) My car   was parked | parked   in front of my house by my father.

2) Was the electric light bulb   inventing | invented   by Edison?

3) Karen   will be invited | will is invited   to the party.

4) Mr. Kim   taught | was taught   us math last semester.

2) electric light bulb 전구

4) semester 학기

O2 다음 문장을 수동태로 바꾸어 쓰시오.

1) The teacher will explain the lesson.

→ _____

2) A hurricane has destroyed the small village.

→ _____

3) She is taking children to the zoo.

→ _____

4) Waitresses and waiters serve customers.

→ _____

2) hurricane 허리케인
   destroy 파괴하다

4) serve 시중들다
   customer 손님, 고객

O3 다음 문장을 우리말로 해석하시오.

1) I was being interviewed by an employer at that time.

→ _____

2) Your exam reports will be sent to your parents next week.

→ _____

1) employer 고용주

2) exam report 성적표

O4 다음 우리말을 영작하시오.

1) 섬은 물로 둘러싸여 있다.

→ An island _____ .

2) 그는 학생들에 의해 존경을 받을 것이다.

→ He _____ .

1) surround 둘러싸다

2) respect 존경하다

Unit 11 4, 5 형식의 수동태

A 4형식 문장의 수동태

1 간접목적어와 직접목적어를 주어로 한두 가지 형태의 수동태가 가능하다.

> **ex** • He gave her a box of chocolate.
> → She was given a box of chocolate by him.
> → A box of chocolate was given to her by him.

2 단, write, buy, make, send 등은 직접목적어로만 수동태가 가능하다.

> **ex** • She bought her boyfriend a red tie.
> → A red tie was bought for her boyfriend by her. (○)
> → Her boyfriend was bought a red tie by her. (×)

Tips
- 4형식
  〈주어 + 동사 + 간접목적어 + 직접목적어〉
- 5형식
  〈주어 + 동사 + 목적어 + 목적격 보어〉

— ⊕ 직접목적어를 주어로 한 수동태를 만들 때 간접목적어 앞에 전치사를 쓴다.

- to를 쓰는 동사 : give, send, write, show 등
- for를 쓰는 동사 : buy, make 등
- of를 쓰는 동사 : ask 등

B 5형식 문장의 수동태

1 목적어만 수동태의 주어로 쓸 수 있다.

> **ex** • We named the street Elisabeth.
> → The street was named Elisabeth by us.

Tips
- 지각동사
  see, watch, feel, hear, touch 등
- 사역동사
  make, have 등

2 지각동사, 사역동사 등의 목적격 보어가 동사원형일 때 수동태에서는 to부정사로 바뀐다.

> **ex** • She made me set the table.
> → I was made to set the table by her.
> • He saw her play the flute.
> → She was seen to play the flute by him.

3 목적격 보어가 to부정사나 분사일 때 수동태에서는 그대로 온다.

> **ex** • He asked her to play the flute.
> → She was asked to play the flute by him.
> • He saw her playing the flute.
> → She was seen playing the flute by him.

Grammar Check-Up

Note

01 다음 중 알맞은 것을 고르시오.

1) The desk was   made | given   to the son by his father.

2) She   was allowed | allowed   to go on a trip by her parents.

3) They were seen   to buy | buy   flowers on the street by me.

4) This electronic dictionary was bought   for | to   my cousin by me.

4) electronic 전자의

02 다음 문장을 수동태로 바꾸어 쓰시오.

1) He told them to go straight.

→ _____

2) He made her 100 paper cranes.

→ _____

3) He made me keep meat in the refrigerator.

→ _____

4) My father gave me a pretty doll.

→ _____

2) paper crane 종이학
3) refrigerator 냉장고

03 다음 문장을 우리말로 해석하시오.

1) She was asked to wait for 30 minutes by Tim.

→ _____

2) Many questions are asked of mothers by children.

→ _____

04 우리말과 일치하도록 빈칸에 알맞은 말을 쓰시오.

1) 그가 샤워하면서 노래하는 것이 들렸다.

→ He _____ _____ _____ _____

in the shower by me.

2) 그녀는 부모님에 의해 지니(Jinny)라 불렸다.

→ She _____ _____ _____ by her parents.

여러 가지 수동태

A 조동사가 있는 문장의 수동태

〈조동사(can, will, must, should, may 등) + be + p.p〉의 형태이다.

ex
- You should send this letter.
  - → This letter should be sent by you.
- A repairman can repair our computer.
  - → Our computer can be repaired by a repairman.

B 동사구 수동태

동사를 수동태로 고치고 동사구 형태는 그대로 쓴다.

ex
- You should take care of your little sister.
  - → Your little sister should be taken care of by you.

C 〈by + 목적격〉의 생략

동작의 행위자가 불명확하거나 능동태의 주어가 일반적인 주어(we, they, people 등)일 때
〈by + 목적격〉은 생략이 가능하다.

ex
- This dictionary is designed for children. (행위자가 불명확)
- English and French are spoken in Canada. (일반적인 주어)

D by 이외의 다른 전치사를 쓰는 경우

be interested in	~에 흥미를 갖다	be pleased with/at/about	~에 기뻐하다
be surprised at/by	~에 놀라다	be covered with	~로 덮여있다
be known to	~에게 알려지다	be satisfied with	~에 만족하다
be filled with	~로 가득 차 있다	be made of	~로 만들어지다
be disappointed with	~에 실망하다	be made from	~로 만들어지다
be married to	~와 결혼하다	be worried about	~을 걱정하다

ex
- He is interested in collecting watches.
- The roof of my house is covered with snow.
- She was satisfied with her job.
- The department store was filled with toys for the holiday sale.
- Cheese is made from milk.

Grammar Check-Up

정답 및 해설 p.8

01 다음 중 알맞은 것을 고르시오.

1) All the flights   were canceled l canceled   because of fog.

2) The poor child was   looked after l looked after by   someone.

3) Her blouse is   made of l made by   cotton.

4) The Asian Games will   be held l hold   in this city.

1) cancel 취소하다
  fog 안개
4) hold (– held – held)
  열다, 개최하다

02 다음 문장을 수동태로 바꾸어 쓰시오.

1) We can solve the problem.

→ _____

2) Fallen leaves cover the bench.

→ _____

3) My sister threw the old letters away.

→ _____

2) fallen leaves 낙엽들

03 우리말과 일치하도록 빈칸에 알맞은 말을 쓰시오.

1) 이 교회는 1930년에 세워졌다.

→ This church _____ _____ in 1930.

2) 이 노래는 모든 사람들에게 알려져 있다.

→ This song is _____ _____ all the people.

3) 캐런은 한 부유한 남자와 결혼했다.

→ Karen _____ _____ _____ a rich man.

04 다음 우리말을 영작하시오.

1) 호수는 물고기로 가득 차 있다.

→ The lake _____.

2) 그녀는 그녀의 외모에 만족했다.

→ She _____.

2) appearance 외모

내신 족집게 문제

[01-03] 다음 문장을 수동태로 바꿀 때 빈칸에 들어갈 알맞은 것을 고르시오.

01 I kept meat in the refrigerator.

→ Meat _____ in the refrigerator by me.

① keeps   ② is kept   ③ is keeping
④ was kept   ⑤ has kept

02 They have changed the date of the meeting.

→ The date of the meeting _____ by them.

① is changed
② was been changed
③ has been changed
④ have been changed
⑤ is being changed

03 He told her to see a doctor.

→ She _____ a doctor by him.

① was told to see   ② was told see
③ was told seeing   ④ was telling to see
⑤ was telling see

04 보기의 문장을 수동태로 바르게 바꾼 것을 고르시오.

보기 He bought his girlfriend a necklace.

① His girlfriend was bought a necklace by him.
② His girlfriend was bought for a necklace by him.
③ A necklace was bought for his girlfriend by him.
④ A necklace was bought to him by his girlfriend.
⑤ A necklace was bought for him by his girlfriend.

[05-08] 다음 문장을 수동태로 바꿀 때 빈칸에 들어갈 알맞은 말을 쓰시오.

05 She should take care of the baby.

→ The baby _____ _____

_____ _____ _____ by her.

06 She made me this key holder.

→ This key holder _____ _____

_____ _____ _____

_____.

07 My father made me study English.

→ I _____ _____ _____

_____ _____ by my father.

08 They are painting the wall of my house.

→ The wall of my house _____

_____ _____ by them.

09 다음 문장을 능동태로 바꿀 때 빈칸에 들어갈 알맞은 말을 쓰시오.

She will be invited to his birthday party by Intae.

→ Intae _____ _____ her to his birthday party.

10 빈칸에 들어갈 알맞은 것을 <u>두 개</u> 고르시오.

A thief was seen _____ her purse by her.

① steal   ② to steal   ③ stealing
④ stole   ⑤ stolen

11 빈칸에 들어갈 수 <u>없는</u> 것을 고르시오.

The new bag was _____ to her by her father.

① made ② given ③ shown
④ sent ⑤ handed

12 빈칸에 공통으로 들어갈 알맞은 전치사를 쓰시오.

• He was disappointed _____ her.
• He is satisfied _____ his success.

13 빈칸에 알맞은 단어를 순서대로 바르게 짝지은 것을 고르시오.

They _____ his behavior.

→ His behavior _____ them.

① laughed – was laughed by
② laughed at – was laughed at by
③ laughed – was laughed at
④ laughed at – was laughed at
⑤ laughed by – was laughed by

[14-15] 빈칸에 들어갈 알맞은 것을 고르시오.

14 The thief _____ by the police yesterday.

① arrests ② arrested
③ is arrested ④ was arrested
⑤ has been arrested

15 He may _____ to Germany by his company in December.

① send ② is sent ③ have sent
④ is sending ⑤ be sent

16 밑줄 친 부분이 어법상 <u>틀린</u> 것을 고르시오.

① He <u>was born</u> in Seoul in 1992.
② The speech <u>was found</u> boring by me.
③ A new hospital <u>will be built</u> next year.
④ He <u>sent</u> his parents a thank-you card.
⑤ The police <u>were caught</u> a bank robber.

17 다음 중 올바른 문장을 고르시오.

① The cat was ran over by the car.
② She was not interesting in playing the guitar.
③ She was heard take a shower.
④ The tree is planted by my father when I was young.
⑤ The car has been washed by my sister.

18 두 문장의 뜻이 같도록 빈칸에 주어진 단어의 알맞은 형태를 쓰시오.

They _____ gold in California in 1848. (discover)

→ Gold _____ in California in 1848.

[19-20] 우리말과 일치하도록 주어진 단어를 알맞은 형태로 바꾸어 문장을 완성하시오.

19 그녀는 부모님으로부터 해외 유학 가는 것을 허락받았다. (allow, study abroad)

→ She _____ by her parents.

20 내일 축구 경기가 열릴 것이다. (hold)

→ The soccer game _____ tomorrow.

O1 다음 괄호 안에서 어법에 맞는 표현으로 가장 적절한 것을 고르시오.

> Sweet potatoes are native to Central America. In 1492, Christopher Columbus **A** (brought / were brought) them to Europe. By the 16th century, they were brought to the Philippines by Spanish explorers and to Africa, India, and southern Asia by Portuguese. In the mid-20th century, they **B** (introduced / were introduced) to the United States. Sweet potatoes are common food in many Asian and Latin American cultures. Today, most sweet potatoes **C** (produce / are produced) in Korea, China, Japan, Indonesia and Vietnam.

- native 본산지　　■ century 세기　　■ explorer 탐험가
- Portuguese 포르투갈 사람들

	A	**B**	**C**
①	brought	– introduced	– produce
②	brought	– were introduced	– are produced
③	brought	– introduced	– are produced
④	were brought	– were introduced	– produce
⑤	were brought	– were introduced	– are produced

O2 다음 글의 밑줄 친 부분 중 어법상 틀린 것을 고르시오.

> The Taj Mahal in Agra, India ① has often described as the most beautiful building in the world since it ② was built three centuries ago. It ③ was designed by a Turkish architect, and it ④ took 20,000 workers 200 years to complete it. The Taj Mahal ⑤ was built by a Muslim, Emperor Shah Jahan, in memory of his dear wife and queen at Agra, India.

- describe 묘사하다　　■ architect 건축가
- complete 완성하다　　■ dear 사랑하는

O1 주어진 단어를 알맞은 형태로 바꾸어 능동태 문장과 수동태 문장을 완성하시오.

1) invent, the telephone

Alexander Graham Bell _____

_____ in 1876.

→ The telephone _____

_____.

2) elect, president

We _____

_____ in 2002.

→ Roh Moonhyun _____

_____.

O2 다음 우리말을 읽고 바르게 영작하시오.

어제 한 자동차 사고가 보도되었다. 아무도 죽지 않았지만 100명이 부상을 당했다. 그들은 병원으로 옮겨졌다. 모든 사람들이 그들을 걱정했다.

_____

_____

_____

_____

_____

- report 보도하다　　■ injure 다치게 하다　　■ carry 옮기다

Chapter

05

to부정사

Chapter 미리보기

want, ask tell, allow expect + 목적어 + to부정사	I asked him to help me. My mom told me to study hard. My dad allows me to watch TV.
see, hear, feel listen to + 목적어 + 동사원형/현재분사	I saw her laugh/laughing. She heard him cry/crying.
let make have + 목적어 + 동사원형	She will let you know your grade. Ann made me do it for her. Paul had us wash the dishes.
help + 목적어 + 동사원형/to부정사 get + 목적어 + to부정사	I helped her (to) make the kite. She got him to clean the room.

It is never too late to mend.
▶ 잘못을 고치는 데 늦는 법은 없다.

Unit **13** 명사적 용법, 의문사 + to부정사

A 명사적 용법

1 주어 역할 : to부정사가 문장에서 주어 역할을 하며, '~하는 것은/이'이라고 해석한다.
주어 역할을 하는 to부정사구를 문장 뒤에 보내어 진주어(진짜 주어)라고 하고, 빈 주어 자리에는
아무 뜻이 없는 it을 써서 가주어(가짜 주어)라고 한다.

ex • To solve the problem of pollution is not easy.
→ It is not easy to solve the problem of pollution.
(가주어)　　　　　　　　　(진주어)

2 목적어 역할 : to부정사가 문장에서 목적어 역할을 하며, '~하는 것을, ~하기를'이라고 해석한다.
want, decide, expect, plan, promise, wish 등은 to부정사를 목적어로 취한다.

ex • Ann wanted to go to the swimming pool after school.
• John planned to do volunteer work during the summer vacation.

3 보어 역할 : to부정사가 문장에서 보어 역할을 하며, '~하는 것(이다)'이라고 해석한다.

ex • His hope is to become a fashion designer.
• My dream is to travel around the world.

⊕ to부정사의 부정 → not/never + to부정사

ex • Paul expected not to fail the exam.

B 의문사 + to부정사

문장에서 주어, 목적어, 보어 역할을 한다.

• what + to부정사 : 무엇을 ~할지
• when + to부정사 : 언제 ~할지
• where + to부정사 : 어디서 ~할지
• how + to부정사 : 어떻게 ~할지

ex • We don't know what to say.
• She doesn't know when to meet us.
• I don't know where to have lunch.
• He doesn't know how to do it.

⊕ 〈의문사 + to부정사〉 = 〈의문사 + 주어 + should + 동사원형〉

ex • Ann doesn't know what to buy for Paul.
= Ann doesn't know what she should buy for Paul.

Note

01 다음 중 알맞은 것을 고르시오.

1) It was not easy   for finding | to find | find   her in the crowd.

2) We didn't know where   going | to go | go .

3) Kate expected   meeting | to meet | meet   John in the auditorium.

🖉
1) crowd 군중
3) auditorium 강당

02 다음 문장의 <u>틀린</u> 부분에 밑줄을 긋고 바르게 고쳐 쓰시오.

1) Ann asked me to not tell it to Paul.   (→ ＿＿＿＿＿)

2) Kevin knew how finding the way to the highway. (→ ＿＿＿＿＿)

3) John decided taking an English language course in Canada.

(→ ＿＿＿＿＿)

🖉
2) highway 고속도로

03 두 문장의 뜻이 같도록 문장을 완성하시오.

1) To see a shooting star in the city is difficult.

= It ＿＿＿＿＿＿＿＿＿＿＿＿＿ .

2) Paul didn't know where to get off the bus.

= Paul didn't know where ＿＿＿＿＿＿＿＿＿ .

🖉
1) shooting star 별똥별
2) get off (버스에서) 내리다

04 밑줄 친 부분에 주의하여 다음 문장을 우리말로 해석하시오.

1) Kate <u>decided not to be</u> late for school.

→ ＿＿＿＿＿＿＿＿＿＿＿＿＿＿＿

2) My uncle doesn't know <u>what to do</u> next.

→ ＿＿＿＿＿＿＿＿＿＿＿＿＿＿＿

05 다음 우리말을 영작하시오.

1) 어머니는 나에게 게임을 하지 말라고 말씀하셨다.

→ ＿＿＿＿＿＿＿＿＿＿＿＿＿＿＿

2) 내 취미는 모형 자동차를 만드는 것이다.

→ ＿＿＿＿＿＿＿＿＿＿＿＿＿＿＿

3) 외국어를 배우는 것은 흥미롭다.

→ ＿＿＿＿＿＿＿＿＿＿＿＿＿＿＿

🖉
2) model car 모형 자동차
3) foreign language 외국어

Unit 14 형용사적 용법과 부사적 용법

A 형용사적 용법

to부정사가 문장에서 앞의 명사나 대명사를 수식하여, '〜하는', '〜할'로 해석한다.

1 명사 수식

> **ex** • Paul has a book to read.
>
> • Ann has a pen to write with. (→ write with a pen)
>
> • Ann has a pen to write. (×)

2 be + to부정사

> ① 예정 **ex** • Ann was to leave for London.
> ② 의무 **ex** • I am to finish my homework by tomorrow.
> ③ 가능 **ex** • No one was to be found in this building.
> ④ 의도 **ex** • If you are to buy a new MP3 player, you should save some money.
> ⑤ 운명 **ex** • We are to meet each other.

B 부사적 용법

to부정사가 동사나 형용사를 수식하여 목적, 감정의 원인, 결과, 판단 등의 의미를 나타낸다.

1 목적 (〜하기 위하여)

> **ex** • We went to the shop to buy hats.
> = We went to the shop in order to buy hats.

2 감정의 원인 (〜해서, 〜하니)

감정을 나타내는 형용사(happy, glad, pleased, excited, surprised, sad 등) + to부정사

> **ex** • Ann was pleased to meet Paul again.
> • John was surprised to find an old English book in this bookstore.

3 결과 (〜해서 …하다)

> **ex** • Her grandmother lived to be one hundred years old.

4 형용사 수식 (〜하기에)

> **ex** • This question is difficult to answer.

5 판단 (〜하다니, 〜하는 것을 보니)

> **ex** • You must be foolish to say such a thing.

Grammar Check-Up

01 다음 문장의 틀린 부분에 밑줄을 긋고 바르게 고쳐 쓰시오.

1) He was to marrying her.　　　　　　　　　(→ _____)

2) They were excited hear the news.　　　　　(→ _____)

3) I need a house to live.　　　　　　　　　　(→ _____)

4) If you are take an English exam, you should study harder.

　　　　　　　　　　　　　　　　　　　　　　(→ _____)

02 문장이 완성되도록 서로 연결하시오.

1) Ramyeon is easy　•　　　　　　　•　ⓐ to be seen.

2) Kate studied hard　•　　　　　　•　ⓑ to cook.

3) No one was　•　　　　　　　　•　ⓒ to improve her English.

improve 향상시키다

03 두 문장의 뜻이 같도록 빈칸에 알맞은 말을 쓰시오.

1) John is going to move to Suwon.

　= John _____ _____ move to Suwon.

2) Kevin left home early in order to take the first train.

　= Kevin left home early _____ take the first train.

04 밑줄 친 부분에 주의하여 다음 문장을 우리말로 해석하시오.

1) Ann baked a chocolate cake to celebrate Paul's birthday.

　→ _____

2) My sister grew up to be a veterinarian.

　→ _____

1) celebrate 축하하다
2) veterinarian 수의사

05 다음 우리말을 영작하시오.

1) 그녀는 유럽에 가기 위해 돈을 모으고 있다.

　→ _____

2) 케이트(Kate)가 그렇게 하는 것을 보니 현명함에 틀림없다.

　→ _____

1) save 모으다
2) wise 현명한

지각동사, 사역동사

A 동사 + 목적어 + to부정사

want, ask, tell, allow, expect 등과 같은 동사는 목적격 보어로 to부정사를 취한다.

want, ask tell, allow + 목적어 + to부정사 expect	I asked him <u>to help</u> me. My mom told me <u>to study</u> hard. My dad allows me <u>to watch</u> TV.

B 지각동사

see, hear, feel, smell 등과 같은 지각동사는 목적격 보어로 동사원형이나 현재분사를 취한다.

see hear, feel + 목적어 + 동사원형/현재분사 listen to smell	I saw her <u>laugh/laughing</u>. She heard him <u>cry/crying</u>. He felt someone <u>look/looking</u> at him.

➊ see, hear, listen to, feel, smell 등과 같은 지각동사는 목적격 보어로 to부정사를 사용하지 않는다.

ex ▸ • I saw him to run away. (×)

C 사역동사

let, make, have와 같은 사역동사는 목적격 보어로 동사원형을 취한다.

let make + 목적어 + 동사원형 have	She will let you <u>know</u> your grade. Ann made me <u>do</u> it for her. Paul had us <u>wash</u> the dishes.
help + 목적어 + 동사원형/to부정사 get + 목적어 + to부정사	I helped her <u>(to) make</u> the kite. She got him <u>to clean</u> the room.

➊ let, make, have 같은 사역동사도 지각동사처럼 목적격 보어로 to부정사를 사용하지 않는다. 하지만, 사역동사는 지각동사와는 달리 목적격 보어로 현재분사를 사용할 수 없다.

ex ▸ • They made me to feel happy. (×)
• He made her waiting for an hour. (×)

Grammar Check-Up

정답 및 해설 p.10

Note

01 다음 중 알맞은 것을 고르시오.

1) I asked her   come | to come | coming .

2) Let me   help | to help | helping   you.

3) Ann heard him   snore | to snore | snored   terribly.

4) Paul had her   look after | to look after   his parrot.

3) snore 코를 골다
   terribly 심하게
4) look after 돌보다
   parrot 앵무새

02 다음 문장의 틀린 부분에 밑줄을 긋고 바르게 고쳐 쓰시오.

1) My dad told me do my best.　　　　　　(→ _____)

2) Kate got him take her dog to the vet.　　(→ _____)

3) Kevin helped me finding a part time job.　(→ _____)

1) do one's best
   최선을 다하다
2) vet 수의사
3) a part time job
   시간제 일자리

03 밑줄 친 부분에 주의하여 다음 문장을 우리말로 해석하시오.

1) Ann saw me waiting for Paul.

→ _____

2) Henry had her fetch his glasses.

→ _____

3) John expected them to bring some sandwiches.

→ _____

2) fetch 가지고 오다

04 다음 우리말을 영작하시오.

1) 앤(Ann)은 누군가 그녀를 지켜보고 있는 것을 느꼈다.

→ _____

2) 제인(Jane)은 그에게 빨래를 하라고 시켰다.

→ _____

3) 케이트(Kate)는 무언가 타는 냄새를 맡았다.

→ _____

2) do the laundry
   빨래를 하다
3) burn 타다

16 to부정사 구문

A too + 형용사/부사 + to부정사 = so + 형용사/부사 + that + 주어 + can't

'너무 ~해서 …할 수 없다'라는 의미이다.

1 문장의 주어 = to부정사의 의미상 주어

ex
- Kate is too small to wear those jeans.
  → Kate is so small that she can't wear those jeans.
- Jane was too stubborn to listen to others.
  → Jane was so stubborn that she didn't listen to others.

2 문장의 주어 ≠ to부정사의 의미상 주어

ex
- It was too cold for us to swim in the sea.
  → It was so cold that we couldn't swim in the sea.
- The bike is too big for him to ride.
  → The bike is so big that he can't ride it.

B 형용사/부사 + enough + to부정사 = so + 형용사/부사 + that + 주어 + can

'~하기에 충분히 …하다'라는 의미이다.

1 문장의 주어 = to부정사의 의미상 주어

ex
- She is clever enough to answer the question.
  → She is so clever that she can answer the question.
- He was kind enough to help the disabled.
  → He was so kind that he could help the disabled.

2 문장의 주어 ≠ to부정사의 의미상 주어

ex
- The water is fresh enough for us to use.
  → The water is so fresh that we can use it.

C seem + to부정사

'~인/하는 것 같다'라는 의미이다.
〈주어 + seem + to부정사〉 = 〈It seems/seemed that + 주어 + 동사〉

ex
- Kevin seems to be sad.
  → It seems that Kevin is sad.
- Susan seemed to like him.
  → It seemed that Susan liked him.

Grammar Check-Up

정답 및 해설 p.10

01 다음 중 알맞은 것을 고르시오.

1) The Internet seems   be | to be | being   slow to use.

2) This milk is   enough fresh | fresh enough   to drink.

3) This road is   enough | too   narrow for cars to pass.

3) narrow 좁은

02 두 문장의 뜻이 같도록 빈칸에 알맞은 말을 쓰시오.

1) Kevin is too big to wear this.

= Kevin is _____ _____ _____ _____

_____ wear this.

2) Paul ran fast enough to win the race.

= Paul ran _____ _____ _____ _____

_____ win the race.

3) Ann seems to have some problems.

= It seems that _____ _____ _____

_____.

03 밑줄 친 부분에 주의하여 다음 문장을 우리말로 해석하시오.

1) They are <u>so small that they can't</u> be basketball players.

→ _____

2) Susan woke up <u>so early that she could</u> see the sunrise.

→ _____

3) He <u>seemed to know</u> the answer.

→ _____

2) wake up 깨다, 일어나다
sunrise 해돋이

04 to부정사를 이용하여 다음 우리말을 영작하시오.

1) 그 물은 너무 뜨거워서 마실 수가 없다.

→ _____

2) 앤(Ann)은 정직한 것 같다.

→ _____

17 to부정사의 의미상 주어와 시제

A to부정사의 의미상 주어

1 **for + 목적격** : to부정사의 의미상 주어와 문장의 주어가 다르면 to부정사 앞에 〈for + 목적격〉을 to부정사의 의미상 주어로 사용한다.

2 **of + 목적격** : 사람의 성질을 나타내는 형용사가 앞에 오는 경우에는 〈of + 목적격〉을 to부정사의 의미상 주어로 사용한다.

가주어 + be동사	형용사	의미상 주어	진주어
It is	difficult, impossible, easy 등	for her	to write a poem.
It is	kind, nice, wise, foolish, silly 등	of you	to say that.

⊕ 관용적 표현

- It is time for me to do my homework. (~할 시간이다)
- It took an hour for us to get there. (~하는 데 …의 시간이 걸리다)

B to부정사의 시제

1 **단순형**(to + 동사원형) : 본동사의 시제와 같거나 이후의 시제를 나타낸다.

> ex · She seemed to be nice. = It seemed that she was nice.
>   (과거)   (과거)
> · I expect to meet the singer. = I expect that I will meet the singer.
>   (현재)   (미래)

2 **완료형**(to have p.p) : 본동사의 시제보다 이전의 시제를 나타낸다.

> ex · Kate seems to have trusted him. = It seems that Kate trusted him.
>   (현재)   (과거)
> · Ann seemed to have been tired. = It seemed that Ann had been tired.
>   (과거)   (과거완료)

C 대부정사

to부정사의 반복을 피하기 위하여 to만을 사용하는데, 이것을 대부정사라고 한다.

> ex · A: Would you like to go to the movies?
>   B: Yes, I'd like to (go to the movies).

Note

O1 다음 중 알맞은 것을 고르시오.

1) It was kind   for | of | to   him to help the handicapped.

2) It is difficult   for | of | to   them to keep the secret.

3) **A** Do you want to play football with us?   **B** Yes, I want   for | of | to .

✎
1) the handicapped
장애인들

O2 두 문장의 뜻이 같도록 빈칸에 알맞은 말을 쓰시오.

1) Ann seems to be happy.

= It seems that _____.

2) Ann seems to have been happy.

= It seems that _____.

3) **A** We are going to the movies. Would you like to join us?

B I would love to.

(= I would love _____.)

O3 밑줄 친 부분에 주의하여 다음 문장을 우리말로 해석하시오.

1) It is <u>wise of them to plan</u> ahead.

→ _____

2) Paul <u>seemed to have known</u> the answer.

→ _____

3) Jane <u>hopes to get</u> free concert tickets.

→ _____

✎
1) ahead 미리

O4 주어진 말로 시작하여 다음 우리말을 영작하시오.

1) 앤(Ann)은 제인(Jane)과 잘 지내는 것 같다.

→ Ann _____.

2) 그가 그 영어책을 해석하는 것은 쉽다.

→ It _____.

3) 천천히 운전하는 것을 보니 그녀는 신중하구나.

→ It _____.

✎
1) get along with
～와 잘 지내다
2) translate 해석하다
3) careful 신중한

내신 족집게 문제

O1 빈칸에 들어갈 수 <u>없는</u> 것을 고르시오.

It is _____ of you to do it.

① kind　　② wise　　③ easy
④ careful　　⑤ silly

[02-05] 우리말과 일치하도록 빈칸에 알맞은 말을 쓰시오.

O2 존은 그 기계를 어떻게 사용하는지 몰랐다.

→ John didn't know _____ _____

_____ the machine.

O3 그는 이야기할 친구가 없다.

→ He doesn't have a _____ _____

_____ _____.

O4 할아버지에게 자리를 양보하다니 그는 친절했다.

→ It was nice _____ _____ to give
up his seat to the old man.

O5 제인은 그를 반 친구들 앞에서 울게 만들었다.

→ Jane made him _____ in front of her
classmates.

O6 빈칸에 공통으로 들어갈 study의 알맞은 형태를 쓰시오.

• Ann is planning _____ abroad. (study)

• Henry bought an English dictionary
_____. (study)

O7 보기의 밑줄 친 부분과 용법이 같은 것을 고르시오.

보기 Ann <u>is to leave</u> for London tomorrow.

① They were to meet again.
② He is to finish the work by next week.
③ If you are to be a doctor, you should study
harder.
④ No one was to be found on the street.
⑤ He is to run a marathon next month.

[08-09] 빈칸에 들어갈 알맞은 것을 <u>두 개</u> 고르시오.

O8 Henry saw her _____ on the phone.

① to talk　　② talked　　③ talking
④ talk　　⑤ to talking

O9 Paul helped me _____ my keys.

① to find　　② finding　　③ find
④ found　　⑤ to finding

10 밑줄 친 to부정사의 용법이 나머지와 <u>다른</u> 것을 고르시오.

① She doesn't know where <u>to go</u>.
② He decided <u>to go</u> to medical school.
③ It is difficult <u>to believe</u> a liar.
④ My dream is <u>to become</u> a professional golfer.
⑤ I bought some flowers <u>to give</u> them to my
mom.

[11-12] 두 문장의 뜻이 같도록 빈칸에 알맞은 말을 쓰시오.

11
I was so tired that I could sleep all day.

= I was _____ _____ _____

_____ all day.

12
The question is so difficult that he can't answer it.

→ The question is _____ _____

_____ _____ _____

_____.

13 대화의 밑줄 친 부분 중 생략할 수 있는 것을 괄호 안에 넣으시오.

A: Do you want to go swimming with us?

B: Yes, I want to go swimming with you.

[14-15] 두 문장의 뜻이 같도록 문장을 완성하시오.

14
Ann seemed to be angry with me.

= It _____.

15
Paul seemed to have had a bad dream.

= It _____.

[16-17] 다음 중 어법상 틀린 문장을 고르시오.

16
① He told me to study English every day.
② She heard him complaining about the bathroom.
③ I got him to pick them up from the airport.
④ She had him fixing it.
⑤ He helped her to cross the bridge.

17
① She is too young to go to a university.
② It isn't wise of you to say that.
③ She is strong enough to lift the box.
④ He didn't know when to leaving.
⑤ Please give me a chair to sit on.

18 밑줄 친 부분을 부정하는 문장으로 바꾸어 쓰시오.

Ann asked him to leave her alone.

→ _____

19 보기의 밑줄 친 to부정사와 용법이 같은 것을 고르시오.

보기 Kate met Susan to go to the second-hand bookstore.

① It is foolish of him to do that.
② I am really glad to find this old toy.
③ He lived to be eighty years old.
④ We went to the bakery to buy some bread.
⑤ She has some friends to play with.

20 두 문장의 뜻이 같지 않은 것을 고르시오.

① She seems to be kind.
= It seems that she is kind.
② He seemed to be stubborn.
= It seemed that he was stubborn.
③ She seems to have enjoyed the party.
= It seems that she enjoyed the party.
④ He seemed to have been ill.
= It seemed that he was ill.
⑤ It seemed that he was a magician.
= He seemed to be a magician.

정답 및 해설 p.11

O1 다음 글의 밑줄 친 부분 중 어법상 틀린 것을 고르시오.

Cupid was the son of Venus. He was a beautiful boy. He carried arrows. Some arrows made people ① love each other. Others made people ② to hate each other. Venus was jealous of Psyche. Venus asked Cupid ③ to make Psyche love the ugliest man in the world. But Cupid fell in love with Psyche. He visited her every night. He told her ④ not to look at him, but she was curious and saw him. Then he left her. Psyche searched the world for him. The sky god Zeus allowed her ⑤ to live forever so that she could be with Cupid.

■ arrow 화살   ■ jealous 질투하는

O2 다음 괄호 안에서 어법에 맞는 표현으로 가장 적절한 것을 고르시오.

Giant pandas are one of the rarest mammals in the world. About 2,000 giant pandas live in the mountains of China. Another 200 giant pandas live in zoos mostly in China. More and more people destroy the panda's natural habitat to build their houses. It is hard **A**(of / for) them to keep a lot of their habitat and their food — wild bamboo plants. **B**(To keep / Keeping) the giant panda from becoming extinct, conservationists are planning **C**(to create / creating) a place where pandas can comfortably live.

■ rare 희귀한   ■ mammal 포유류   ■ habitat 서식지
■ extinct 멸종된   ■ conservationist 자연보호론자

	A	**B**	**C**
①	of	To keep	to create
②	of	To keep	creating
③	for	To keep	to create
④	for	Keeping	creating
⑤	for	Keeping	to create

O1 주어진 단어를 이용하여 대화를 완성하시오.

1) **Susan** : Kate lost her puppy. I met her yesterday and she seemed _____ _____. (sad)

2) **Jerry** : I saw Susan yesterday. She looked slimmer. Susan seems _____ _____. (lose, weight)

3) **Harry** : Look! Ann is having lunch with a boy. It seems that _____. (have, boyfriend)

O2 다음 우리말을 읽고 바르게 영작하시오.

오늘날 우주여행은 단지 꿈만은 아니다. 달에 가는 것은 가능하다. 우리는 모든 훈련을 통과할 만큼 충분히 강해야 한다. 지금 우리는 너무 비싸서 달에 갈 수 없지만 나는 언젠가는 달에 가기를 희망한다.

Space traveling is not just a dream today.

_____

_____

_____

_____

■ training 훈련   ■ someday 언젠가는

Chapter 06

동명사

- ♠ Unit 18 동명사의 기본 개념
- ♠ Unit 19 to부정사와 동명사
- ♠ Unit 20 동명사의 의미상 주어와 시제

Chapter 미리보기

동명사만을 목적어로 하는 동사		enjoy, finish, give up, mind, avoid + 동명사	
to부정사만을 목적어로 하는 동사		want, wish, hope, decide, plan, expect, promise + to부정사	
동명사와 to부정사를 모두 목적어로 하는 동사	의미가 같은 경우	begin, start, like, love, hate + to부정사/동명사	
	의미가 다른 경우	remember + to부정사 (~할 것을 기억하다)	remember + 동명사 (~했던 것을 기억하다)
		forget + to부정사 (~할 것을 잊다)	forget + 동명사 (~했던 것을 잊다)
		regret + to부정사 (~해서 유감이다)	regret + 동명사 (~했던 것을 후회하다)
		stop + to부정사 (~하기 위하여 멈추다)	stop + 동명사 (~하는 것을 멈추다)
		try + to부정사 (~하려고 노력하다)	try + 동명사 (시험 삼아 ~해보다)

Casting pearls before swine. 돼지 앞에 진주를 던져주기.

▶ 돼지 목에 진주 : 값어치를 모르는 사람에게는 보물도 아무 소용 없다.

Unit 18 동명사의 기본 개념

A 동명사의 역할

동명사는 문장에서 주어, 목적어, 보어 역할을 한다.

1 주어 역할 : '~하는 것은/것이'로 해석한다.

> ex ● Doing exercise is good for your health.
>   ● Speaking English is not easy.

— ⊕ 동명사가 주어일 경우 단수 취급하므로 항상 단수 동사와 같이 사용한다.

> ex ● Playing with friends is fun. (O)
>   ● Playing with friends are fun. (×)

2 목적어 역할 : '~하는 것을'로 해석한다.

① 동사의 목적어

> ex ● Ann enjoys riding a bike.
>   ● John finished painting his room.

② 전치사의 목적어

> ex ● Jane left without saying anything.

3 보어 역할 : '~하는 것(이다)'으로 해석한다.

> ex ● His hobby is collecting toy figures.
>   ● Her job is cleaning the house.

B 동명사의 부정

동명사의 부정은 동명사 앞에 not 또는 never를 사용한다.

> ex ● Kevin is sorry for not calling you back.
>   ● Kate is proud of never being absent from school.

C 동명사 구문

```
• can't help + 동명사 : ~하지 않을 수 없다
• have a hard time + 동명사 : ~하는 데 힘든 시간을 보내다
• stop/keep A from + 동명사 : A가 ~하는 것을 막다
• look forward to + 동명사 : ~하기를 고대하다
• feel like + 동명사 : ~하고 싶다
```

> ex ● Ann can't help laughing.   ● John had a hard time cleaning the attic.
>   ● Ann stopped Paul from going.   ● I am looking forward to seeing you again.
>   ● I feel like going to the movies.

Grammar Check-Up

정답 및 해설 p.12

O1 다음 중 알맞은 것을 고르시오.

1) Jane is interested in   go | going   to the moon.

2)   Help | Helping   others is a good thing to do.

3) Ann is proud of   telling not | not telling   a lie.

4) Kate finished   to write | writing   an essay about pollution.

5) They looked forward   to meet | to meeting   friends.

🖉
3) be proud of
   ~을 자랑스러워 하다
4) essay 작문
   pollution 공해

O2 다음 문장의 <u>틀린</u> 부분에 밑줄을 긋고 바르게 고쳐 쓰시오.

1) Talking to friends are fun.   (→ _____)

2) Her job is write novels.   (→ _____)

O3 밑줄 친 부분에 주의하여 다음 문장을 우리말로 해석하시오.

1) The police officer couldn't <u>keep the thief from running away</u>.

→ _____

2) Paul was sorry <u>for not telling the truth</u>.

→ _____

3) <u>Having good friends</u> is very important in your life.

→ _____

🖉
1) run away 도망가다

O4 다음 우리말을 영작하시오.

1) 그녀의 직업은 관광객을 안내하는 것이다.

→ _____

2) 케이트(Kate)는 외국인과 이야기하는 것을 즐긴다.

→ _____

3) 앤(Ann)은 울지 않을 수가 없었다.

→ _____

🖉
1) guide 안내하다
   tourist 관광객

19 to부정사와 동명사

A 동명사만을 목적어로 하는 동사

enjoy, finish give up mind, avoid } + 동명사	Paul enjoys playing football. Ann gave up playing games. Do you mind opening the window?

B to부정사만을 목적어로 하는 동사

want, wish, hope decide, plan expect, promise } + to부정사	Jane wants to invite Ann for dinner. Harry decided to climb Mt. Everest. Paul promised to come to my birthday party.

C 동명사와 to부정사를 모두 목적어로 하는 동사

1 의미의 차이가 없는 경우

begin, start like, love hate } + to부정사/동명사	Ann began to learn/learning Spanish. John likes to play/playing chess. We hate to eat/eating spinach.

2 의미가 달라지는 경우

remember + to부정사 remember + 동명사	I remembered to call Kate. (~할 것을 기억하다) I remember calling Ann. (~한 것을 기억하다)
forget + to부정사 forget + 동명사	Harry won't forget to meet Jane. (~할 것을 잊다) Harry won't forget meeting Jane. (~한 것을 잊다)
regret + to부정사 regret + 동명사	I regret to say that you didn't pass the exam. (~해서 유감이다) Jane regrets yelling at Paul. (~한 것을 후회하다)
stop + to부정사 stop + 동명사	Jane stopped to send him a letter. (~하기 위하여 멈추다) Jane stopped sending him a letter. (~하는 것을 그만두다)
try + to부정사 try + 동명사	John tried to open the bottle. (~하려고 노력하다) John tried opening the bottle. (시험 삼아 ~해보다)

Grammar Check-Up

정답 및 해설 p.12

01 다음 중 알맞은 것을 고르시오.

1) My dad promised   to buy | buying   me a new school bag.

2) Ann finished   to make | making   lunch.

3) Kate avoided   meeting | to meet   Paul.

4) I regret   to inform | informing   you that you didn't gain admission to Harvard University.

🖉

4) admission 입학 허가

02 다음 문장의 **틀린** 부분에 밑줄을 긋고 바르게 고쳐 쓰시오.

1) Do you mind close the door?   (→ _____)

2) Harry wants meeting Jane on Saturday.   (→ _____)

3) I haven't brought my textbook. I remember to leave it on the bed.

(→ _____)

03 밑줄 친 부분에 주의하여 다음 문장을 우리말로 해석하시오.

1) Harry won't <u>forget to meet</u> Jane.

→ _____

2) Harry won't <u>forget meeting</u> Jane.

→ _____

3) John <u>stopped to buy</u> her flowers.

→ _____

4) John <u>stopped buying</u> her flowers.

→ _____

04 다음 우리말을 영작하시오.

1) 존(John)은 폴(Paul)에게 전화했던 것을 후회한다.

→ _____

2) 그는 영어 소설을 쓰려고 노력했다.

→ _____

3) 나는 약을 먹어야 하는 것을 기억했다.

→ _____

🖉

3) take some medicine
약을 먹다

Unit 19 ✤ **65**

20 동명사의 의미상 주어와 시제

A 동명사의 의미상 주어

1 **동명사의 의미상 주어를 사용하지 않는 경우**

① 문장의 주어 = 동명사의 의미상 주어

> **ex** • We enjoy playing the violin.

② 동명사의 의미상 주어가 일반인일 경우

> **ex** • Seeing is believing.

2 **동명사의 의미상 주어를 사용하는 경우** : 문장의 주어 ≠ 동명사의 의미상 주어

동명사의 의미상 주어는 동명사 앞에 위치하며 소유격이나 목적격을 사용한다.

문장의 주어	동사	동명사의 의미상 주어	동명사
She	likes	his/him	coming to my birthday party.
They	don't mind	her	staying with them.

B 동명사의 시제

1 **단순형(동사원형-ing)** : 동명사의 시제가 본동사의 시제와 같거나 이후의 시제를 나타낸다.

> **ex** • She was afraid of walking alone at night.
>
> = She <u>was</u> afraid that she <u>walked</u> alone at night.
>   (과거)   (과거)
>
> • He is afraid of failing the exam.
>
> = He <u>is</u> afraid that he <u>will</u> fail the exam.
>   (현재)   (미래)

2 **완료형(having p.p)** : 동명사의 시제가 본동사의 시제보다 이전의 시제를 나타낸다.

> **ex** • He is proud of having finished the work.
>
> = He <u>is</u> proud that he <u>finished</u> the work.
>   (현재)   (과거)
>
> • I was proud of having won first prize.
>
> = I <u>was</u> proud that I <u>had won</u> first prize.
>   (과거)   (과거완료)

Grammar Check-Up

Note

01 다음 중 알맞은 것을 고르시오.

1) He doesn't like   she | her   being late.

2) Ann was proud of   have | having kept   her promise.

3) She hates   he | his   smoking.

2) keep one's promise
∼의 약속을 지키다

02 두 문장의 뜻이 같도록 문장을 완성하시오.

1) Kevin is surprised that she is a famous singer.

   = Kevin is surprised at _____.

2) Kate is ashamed that he told a lie.

   = Kate is ashamed of _____.

2) ashamed 부끄러운

03 밑줄 친 부분에 주의하여 다음 문장을 우리말로 해석하시오.

1) Do you <u>mind his sitting</u> next to you?

   → _____

2) Kate is <u>excited about making</u> new friends.

   → _____

3) Ann <u>remembers having paid</u> for the jeans.

   → _____

04 우리말과 일치하도록 주어진 말을 바르게 배열하시오.

1) 앤은 그가 집으로 돌아와서 놀랐다.

   (home, was, his, at, Ann, coming, surprised)

   → _____

2) 해리는 그녀가 비웃어서 화가 났다.

   (him, at, Harry, was, about, laughing, her, angry)

   → _____

3) 존은 일등상을 받았던 것을 자랑스러워 한다.

   (first, of, John, proud, having, is, prize, won)

   → _____

2) laugh at 비웃다

내신 족집게 문제

01 대화의 빈칸에 들어갈 알맞은 말을 쓰시오.

A: Was it hard for her to make friends?
B: Yes, she had a hard _____ _____ friends.

02 빈칸에 공통으로 들어갈 do의 알맞은 형태를 쓰시오.

• Kate didn't do her homework. She forgot _____ her homework. (do)
• Kevin started _____ his homework. (do)

03 빈칸에 들어갈 알맞은 것을 <u>두 개</u> 고르시오.

_____ for the final exam is stressful.

① Prepare ② Prepared ③ Preparing
④ To prepare ⑤ To preparing

04 빈칸에 들어갈 수 <u>없는</u> 것을 고르시오.

Tom _____ going rock climbing.

① enjoys ② began ③ gave up
④ avoided ⑤ planned

05 빈칸에 공통으로 들어갈 수 <u>없는</u> 것을 고르시오.

• She _____ to eat breakfast.
• He _____ playing table tennis.

① started ② hates ③ likes
④ decided ⑤ loves

[06 - 08] 우리말과 일치하도록 주어진 동사를 이용하여 빈칸을 채우시오.

06 앤은 실수했던 것을 후회한다.
→ Ann regrets _____ a mistake. (make)

07 헨리는 친구들에게 인사하기 위해 멈췄다.
→ Henry stopped _____ hello to his friends. (say)

08 폴은 나무에 물을 주어야 하는 것을 기억했다.
→ Paul remembered _____ the plants. (water)

09 두 문장의 뜻이 같도록 빈칸에 들어갈 알맞은 것을 고르시오.

Yesterday I called her several times but she didn't answer the phone.
= I tried _____ her yesterday.

① call ② called ③ be calling
④ to call ⑤ to being called

10 보기의 밑줄 친 부분과 쓰임이 같지 <u>않은</u> 것을 고르시오.

보기 Paul finished <u>playing</u> a game.

① Her job is <u>traveling</u> around the world.
② Ann remembered <u>meeting</u> him at the party.
③ <u>Writing</u> a novel is not that easy.
④ The child is afraid of <u>sleeping</u> alone.
⑤ Jane is <u>singing</u> in the bathroom.

[11-12] 두 문장의 뜻이 같도록 빈칸에 알맞은 말을 쓰시오.

11
Tom is proud that she graduated from a university.

= Tom is proud of _____ _____

_____ from a university.

12
Henry was ashamed that he didn't help the handicapped.

= Henry was ashamed of _____

_____ the handicapped.

[13-14] 주어진 동사를 빈칸에 알맞은 형태로 바꾸어 쓰시오.

13
I am looking forward to _____ to school again. (go)

14
We feel like _____ today. (sing)

15 밑줄 친 부분을 부정하는 문장으로 바꾸어 쓰시오.

Thank you for <u>asking</u> me a question.

→ Thank you _____.

16 다음 중 어법상 틀린 문장을 고르시오.

① I expect to study abroad.

② Kate avoided to eat at night.

③ Kevin promised to buy us lunch.

④ We gave up going to Jejudo.

⑤ I hope to become a car designer.

17 다음 중 올바른 문장을 고르시오.

① He stopped her from fall.

② She had a hard time to find a house to live.

③ I looked forward to talk to her again.

④ They couldn't help eating chocolate.

⑤ Snow kept me from drive a car.

18 우리말과 일치하도록 빈칸에 알맞은 말을 쓰시오.

제인은 그가 게임을 하는 것을 싫어한다.

→ Jane hates _____ _____ games.

19 빈칸에 들어갈 알맞은 것을 고르시오.

Her job is _____ robots.

① make   ② making   ③ made
④ to be made ⑤ being made

20 두 문장의 뜻이 같지 <u>않은</u> 것을 고르시오.

① Henry seemed to be intelligent.
   = It seemed that Henny was intelligent.

② Terry remembers to meet Kate.
   = Terry met Kate and he remembers it.

③ Paul forgot boiling the water.
   = Paul boiled the water and then he forgot about it.

④ Ann is afraid of dying young.
   = Ann is afraid that she will die young.

⑤ Jane likes swimming in the sea.
   = Jane likes to swim in the sea.

정답 및 해설 p.13

O1 다음 글의 밑줄 친 부분 중 어법상 틀린 것을 고르시오.

Apollo was the son of Zeus. He was the god of music, and he ① played a golden lyre. He was also the god of truth, and ② could not tell a lie. He was the archer who used a silver bow. He was interested in ③ heal. He was ④ famous for his oracle at Delphi. People traveled to it from all over the Greek world ⑤ to know their future.

- lyre 수금(악기)　■ archer 사수　■ heal 치료하다
- oracle 신탁

O2 다음 괄호 안에서 어법에 맞는 표현으로 가장 적절한 것을 고르시오.

Cancer researchers try **A**(to discover / discovering) why some people get cancer and others do not. The main reasons are genetic problems and certain environmental or behavioral problems. Cancer occurs when cells begin **B**(to grow / grow) in an unusual way. Normal body cells grow over a period of time until they die. But cancer cells continue to grow until they **C**(to form / form) tumors.

- cancer 암　■ genetic 유전자의　■ environmental 환경적인
- behavioral 행동의　■ cell 세포　■ tumor 종양

	A	**B**	**C**
①	to discover	– to grow	– to form
②	to discover	– grow	– to form
③	to discover	– to grow	– form
④	discovering	– grow	– form
⑤	discovering	– to grow	– form

O1 다음 표를 참고하여 문장을 완성하시오.

Tue.	I took an English exam.
Wed.	I didn't bring the English textbook.
Fri.	I am going to go to the dentist.
Sat.	I am going to meet Kate.

Today is Thursday.

1) I remember _____
　 on Tuesday.

2) I forgot _____
　 on Wednesday.

3) I won't forget _____
　 on Friday.

4) I will remember _____
　 on Saturday.

O2 다음 우리말을 읽고 바르게 영작하시오.

케이트(Kate)는 코미디를 보는 것을 즐긴다. 그녀의 꿈은 코미디언이 되는 것이다. 그녀는 우리를 웃게 만든다. 우리는 웃지 않을 수 없다. 언젠가 우리는 그녀를 TV쇼에서 보기를 기대한다.

_____

_____

_____

_____

- comedies 코미디, 희극　■ comedian 코미디언, 희극배우
- someday 언젠가

Chapter 07

분사
- ☢ **Unit 21** 분사의 용법
- ☢ **Unit 22** 분사구문
- ☢ **Unit 23** 주의해야 할 분사구문 ①
- ☢ **Unit 24** 주의해야 할 분사구문 ②

Chapter 미리보기

		현재분사	과거분사
형태		동사원형 + -ing	동사원형 + -ed 또는 불규칙 변화
명사수식	의미	~하고 있는(진행, 능동 의미)	~된, ~당한(완료, 수동 의미)
	예문	a dancing girl a girl dancing on the stage	a broken vase a vase broken by Mary
주격 보어		주어와 보어가 능동관계 The game was exciting.	주어와 보어가 수동관계 We were excited.
목적격 보어		목적어와 목적격 보어가 능동관계 I saw her crying.	목적어와 목적격 보어가 수동관계 I heard my name called.
분사구문		Seeing her, he ran away. (Seeing은 주절의 주어 he와 능동관계)	Seen from the hill, the rock looks like a turtle. (Seen은 주절의 주어 the rock과 수동관계)

Let sleeping dogs lie. 잠자는 개는 누워있게 놔둬라.
▶ 긁어 부스럼 만들지 말아라.

21 분사의 용법

A 현재분사와 과거분사의 비교

현재분사는 〈동사원형 + -ing〉이며 진행형에서 사용된다.
과거분사는 〈동사원형 + -ed〉이며 완료시제와 수동태에서 사용된다.

ex
- They were playing computer games then.
- She has just arrived at Seoul Station.
- Your car was parked near the post office.

B 현재분사와 과거분사의 역할

분사는 형용사처럼 명사를 수식하거나 보어 자리에 올 수 있다.

1 명사 수식

	현재분사(동사원형 + -ing)	과거분사(동사원형 + -ed)
해석	~하고 있는, ~하는	~된, ~당한
의미	진행, 능동	수동, 완료

ex
- a barking dog (짖고 있는 개)
- a stolen watch (도난당한 시계)

⊕ 분사가 목적어, 보어, 수식어와 함께 올 경우 명사 뒤에서 수식한다.

ex
- The man wearing a red hat is my brother.
- The email sent to me last night was shocking.

2 주격 보어 : 〈주어 + 동사 + 분사〉의 형태로 현재분사는 주어와 보어가 능동관계이고, 과거분사는 주어와 보어가 수동관계이다.

ex
- The children sat surrounding their father. (주어 The children이 둘러싸는 것)
- The man sat surrounded by his children. (주어 The man이 둘러싸인 것)
- The movie bored me.
  → The movie was boring. (주어 The movie가 지루하게 하는 것)
  → I felt bored. (주어 I가 지루해지는 것)

Tips
목적어와 목적격 보어가
능동관계일 때

- 〈have + 목적어 +
  동사원형〉
- 〈get + 목적어 + to
  + 동사원형〉

3 목적격 보어 : 〈주어 + 동사 + 목적어 + 분사〉의 형태로 현재분사는 목적어와 목적격 보어가 능동관계이고, 과거분사는 목적어와 목적격 보어가 수동관계이다.

ex
- I saw my sister keeping a diary in English. (목적어 my sister가 일기를 씀)
- I had/got the computer fixed. (목적어 the computer가 수리됨)

Grammar Check-Up

정답 및 해설 p.13

O1 다음 중 빈칸에 알맞은 것을 고르시오.

1) Ⓐ How was the movie last night?
   Ⓑ It was   disappointing | disappointed   .

2) The class bored the students. It was a   boring | bored   class.
   The students were   boring | bored   .

3) I heard the rain   falling | fallen   all night.

4) She got her shoes   to polish | polished | polishing   .

O2 우리말과 일치하도록 주어진 말을 빈칸에 알맞은 형태로 쓰시오.

1) 파티에 초대받은 사람들은 가면을 써야 한다.

   → The people _____ to the party should wear a mask. (invite)

2) 나는 길에서 옆집 사는 사람을 만났다.

   → I met a man _____ next door on the street. (live)

3) 나는 길에서 귀여운 소녀가 울고 있는 것을 보았다.

   → I watched a cute girl _____ on the street. (weep)

4) 나는 호텔에서 손목시계를 도난당했다.

   → I had my watch _____ at the hotel. (steal)

O3 밑줄 친 부분에 주의하여 다음 문장을 우리말로 해석하시오.

1) The people waiting for the bus in the rain wore yellow raincoats.

   → _____

2) He read *The Old Man and the Sea*, a novel written by Ernest Hemingway.

   → _____

O4 분사를 이용하여 다음 우리말을 영작하시오.

1) 나는 경찰 한 명이 그 도둑을 추격하는 것을 보았다.

   → _____

2) 그는 어제 그 지붕을 수리하도록 시켰다.

   → _____

Note

1) disappoint 실망시키다
4) polish 닦다, 광내다

3) weep 울다

1) chase 추격하다
2) repair 수리하다

Unit 21 ⚘ **73**

22 분사구문

A 분사구문의 개념

분사구문이란 부사절을 분사가 있는 문장으로 바꾼 것을 말한다. 즉, 〈접속사 + 주어 + 동사〉를
〈동사원형 + -ing〉의 형태로 바꾸는 것이다.

B 분사구문을 만드는 방법

> ⓐ 접속사를 생략한다.
> ⓑ (주절과 종속절의 주어가 같을 때) 주어를 없앤다.
> ⓒ 동사원형에 -ing를 붙인다.

ex • While he played with the ball, he became hungry.
  → Playing with the ball, he became hungry.

━⊕ 부정문의 분사구문은 〈not + 분사〉의 형태로 쓴다.

ex • If you don't go to bed now, you will get up late.
  → Not going to bed now, you will get up late.

C 분사구문의 의미

1 때 : when, as (～할 때), while (～동안에), after (～한 후에), as soon as (～하자마자) 등

ex • Walking into my office, I found Karen using my phone.
  = When I walked into my office, I found Karen using my phone.

2 이유 : because, as, since (～ 때문에) 등

ex • Not knowing his telephone number, I couldn't call him.
  = Because I didn't know his telephone number, I couldn't call him.

3 조건 : if (만약 ～라면) 등

ex • Turning to the right, you can see my house.
  = If you turn to the right, you can see my house.

4 양보 : though, although (비록 ～이지만) 등

ex • Admitting he is right, I cannot agree with him.
  = Though I admit he is right, I cannot agree with him.

5 부대상황 : 동시 동작 → as (～하면서), 연속 동작 → and (그리고 나서)

ex • Waving his hand, he got on the train.
  = As he waved his hand, he got on the train.

Grammar Check-Up

01 밑줄 친 부분을 분사구문으로 바꾸어 쓰시오.

1) <u>As I thought they might be thirsty</u>, I gave them something to drink.

→ _____, I gave them something to drink.

2) <u>While she was crossing the street</u>. she was run over by a car.

→ _____, she was run over by a car.

1) thirsty
　갈증이 난, 목마른

2) run over
　(차 등이 사람·동물을) 치다

02 두 문장의 뜻이 같도록 빈칸에 알맞은 말을 쓰시오.

1) Not eating lunch, we were very hungry.

= _____ _____ _____ eat lunch, we were

very hungry.

2) Getting a good grade, he wasn't satisfied with it.

= _____ _____ _____ a good grade, he

wasn't satisfied with it.

2) be satisfied with
　~에 만족하다

03 밑줄 친 부분에 주의하여 다음 문장을 우리말로 해석하시오.

1) <u>Not being able to speak Spanish</u>, he couldn't understand what she said.

→ _____

2) <u>Arriving at the party</u>, I saw my friend Tim standing alone.

→ _____

04 우리말과 일치하도록 빈칸을 채우시오. 그리고 두 번째 문장은 분사구문으로 만드시오.

1) 그는 버스에서 내릴 때 미끄러졌다.

→ When _____, he slipped.

→ _____, he slipped.

2) 비록 그녀는 독일에서 1년 동안 살았지만 독일어를 배우지 않았다.

→ Although _____ for a year, she didn't learn German.

→ _____ for a year, she didn't learn German.

1) get off (버스에서) 내리다
　slip 미끄러지다

2) Germany 독일

주의해야 할 분사구문 ①

A 분사구문의 시제

분사구문의 시제는 단순형(동사원형 + -ing)과 완료형(having p.p)이 있다.

1 단순형(동사원형 + -ing) : 주절과 종속절의 시제가 같거나 이후의 시제일 때 사용한다.

> ex • Because I felt tired, I went to bed early.
> (과거)   (과거)
>   → Feeling tired, I went to bed early.
>
> • If you go straight, you will see Seoul Station.
> (현재)   (미래)
>   → Going straight, you will see Seoul Station.

2 완료형(having p.p) : 종속절의 시제가 주절보다 이전의 시제일 때 사용한다.

> ex • Because she lived in France for a year, she speaks French well.
> (과거)   (현재)
>   → Having lived in France for a year, she speaks French well.
>
> • After we had bought our tickets, we went into the theater.
> (과거완료)   (과거)
>   → Having bought our tickets, we went into the theater.

B 능동태와 수동태 문장에서의 분사구문 비교

	단순형	완료형
능동태 문장	동사원형 + -ing	having p.p
수동태 문장	(being) p.p	(having been) p.p
	→ being, having been은 생략 가능	

> ex • As he was given all the information, he could get the right answer.
>   → (Being) Given all the information, he could get the right answer.
>
> • As he had been praised by the teacher, he worked hard.
>   → (Having been) Praised by the teacher, he worked hard.

Grammar Check-Up

Note

01 다음 중 알맞은 것을 고르시오.

1) Talking | Talked   on the phone to her friend, she bought some carnations.

2) Writing | Written   in Spanish, the letter was hard for me to read.

3) Losing | Having lost   my cell phone yesterday, I can't call you.

02 다음 문장을 분사구문으로 바꾸어 쓰시오.

1) As it had been painted in a dark color, it needed some bright lights.

→ _____

2) As the car was imported from Germany, it was very expensive.

→ _____

3) As I slept well last night, I feel very good today.

→ _____

2) import 수입하다

03 다음 문장을 우리말로 해석하시오.

1) Compared with European people, Asian people are not so good at expressing their feelings.

→ _____

2) Having seen the movie twice before, I don't want to see it again.

→ _____

1) compare 비교하다

04 우리말과 일치하도록 주어진 말을 바르게 배열하시오. (단, 동사를 알맞은 형태로 바꿀 것)

1) 나는 시험에 연필을 가지고 오지 않았기 때문에 하나 빌려야 했다.

(a pencil, to the exam, not, have, have to, bring, I, one, borrow)

→ _____

2) 그는 기말고사로 지쳤기 때문에 일찍 잠자리에 들었다.

(final exams, by, he, go, exhaust, bed, early, to)

→ _____

Unit 24 주의해야 할 분사구문 ②

A 접속사 + 분사구문

분사구문을 만들 때 접속사를 생략하는 것이 원칙이나 뜻을 명확히 하기 위해서 접속사를 분사구문 앞에 붙이는 경우가 있다.

ex
- While I was staying in America, I was helped by some Koreans.
  = Staying in America, I was helped by some Koreans.
  = While staying in America, I was helped by some Koreans.

B 독립 분사구문

분사구문을 만들 때 주절과 종속절의 주어가 다르면 분사구문에 주어를 그대로 쓴다.

ex
- When school was over, they played soccer on the playground.
  = School being over, they played soccer on the playground.
- Because it was so hot, we went swimming.
  = It being so hot, we went swimming.

C 무인칭 독립 분사구문

독립 분사구문에서 주어가 막연한 일반인일 때 관용적으로 사용한다.

• generally speaking	→ 일반적으로 말하면
• frankly speaking	→ 솔직하게 말하면
• strictly speaking	→ 엄격하게 말하면
• considering ~	→ ~을 고려해 본다면
• judging from ~	→ ~으로 판단해 보건데

ex
- Frankly speaking, he failed the exam.
- Considering her age, she looks young.
- Judging from his appearance, he must be a rich man.

D with + 목적어 + 분사

동시동작을 의미하며, '~을 …하면서'로 해석한다.

1 〈with + 목적어 + 현재분사〉: 목적어가 행동을 하는 능동의 의미

　　ex • The man was smoking with his wife knitting beside him.

2 〈with + 목적어 + 과거분사〉: 목적어가 행동을 받는 수동의 의미

　　ex • He sat under a tree with his eyes closed.

Grammar Check-Up

정답 및 해설 p.14

O1 밑줄 친 부분을 분사구문으로 바꾸어 쓰시오.

1) As it is a fine day, we will go out for a walk.

→ _____, we will go out for a walk.

2) If we judge from his accent, he must be from China.

→ _____, he must be from China.

3) As soon as the train arrived at Seoul Station, it began to rain.

→ _____, it began to rain.

2) judge 판단하다

O2 다음 중 알맞은 것을 고르시오.

1) Speaking frankly | Frankly speaking , he is not handsome.
2) After taking | take | taken   off his shoes, he went into the house.
3) Considered | Considering   everything, he must have been sick yesterday.
4) He sat in the armchair with his eyes closed | closing .

2) take off ~을 벗다
3) must have p.p
 ~했음에 틀림없다
4) armchair 안락의자

O3 밑줄 친 부분에 주의하여 다음 문장을 우리말로 해석하시오.

1) The wind blowing very hard, we went out to buy something to eat.

→ _____

2) Before asking a librarian for help, you should try to find the book.

→ _____

1) blow (바람 등이) 불다
2) librarian 도서관 사서

O4 우리말과 일치하도록 빈칸에 알맞은 말을 쓰시오.

1) 캐런(Karen)은 선생님이 질문하지 않으면 수업 시간에 말을 하지 않는다.

→ If the teacher _____ _____ _____
_____, Karen doesn't talk in class.

→ _____ _____ _____ _____
_____ _____, Karen doesn't talk in class.

2) 일반적으로 말하면 한국 사람들은 근면하다.

→ _____ _____, Koreans are diligent.

2) diligent
 부지런한, 근면한

내신 족집게 문제

01 빈칸에 들어갈 알맞은 것을 <u>두 개</u> 고르시오.

There was a big car _____ in front of my house.

① parking ② parked ③ was parking
④ was parked ⑤ which was parked

02 빈칸에 알맞은 단어를 순서대로 바르게 짝지은 것을 고르시오.

Sumi is going to Europe next week. She has never been there before. It will be an _____ experience for her. Taking a trip is _____. She is really _____ about going to Europe.

① excited – exciting – excited
② excited – exciting – exciting
③ excited – excited – excited
④ exciting – exciting – excited
⑤ exciting – exciting – exciting

03 밑줄 친 분사의 쓰임이 틀린 것을 고르시오.

① There are a lot of <u>fallen</u> leaves on the street.
② <u>Barking</u> dogs never bite.
③ The women <u>attending</u> the meeting are my teachers.
④ I felt somebody <u>touching</u> my back.
⑤ Don't sit with your leg <u>crossing</u>.

[04-05] 주어진 말을 빈칸에 알맞은 형태로 바꾸어 쓰시오.

04 The email _____ to me last night was shocking. (send)

05 She had her blood pressure _____. (check)

06 빈칸에 들어갈 수 <u>없는</u> 것을 고르시오.

I _____ my mother playing the guitar.

① watched ② found ③ made
④ saw ⑤ heard

[07-08] 다음 문장을 분사구문으로 바꿀 때 빈칸에 알맞은 말을 쓰시오.

07 As I didn't want to wake the baby, I closed the door quietly.

→ _____ _____ to wake up the baby, I closed the door quietly.

08 As we had spent nearly all our money, we couldn't stay at a hotel.

→ _____ _____ nearly all our money, we couldn't stay at a hotel.

[09-12] 빈칸에 알맞은 단어를 순서대로 바르게 짝지은 것을 고르시오.

09
• _____ his friends to his party, he was busy preparing for it.
• _____ to her birthday party, he couldn't go there because of his illness.

① Invited – To invite ② Invited – Inviting
③ Inviting – Invited ④ Inviting – To invite
⑤ Invite – inviting

10
• He got his friend _____ a letter.
• We finally got our clothes _____.

① reading – to clean ② reading – cleaned
③ read – to clean ④ to read – clean
⑤ to read – cleaned

11
- The pianist _____ to us is my brother.
- The boy _____ on the floor is Tom.

① knowing – lying   ② knew – lying
③ known – lying   ④ known – lay
⑤ known – lain

12
- The concert was _____.
- We were _____ by the concert.

① boring – bored   ② boring – boring
③ to bore – bored   ④ bored – bored
⑤ bored – boring

13 다음 중 올바른 문장을 고르시오.

① Pleased with my grade, she took me to Everland.
② Writing in easy English, the book is fit for beginners.
③ Judge from his big car, he cannot be poor.
④ Comparing with his house, my house is small.
⑤ Sitting up late last night, I am very tired.

14 두 문장의 뜻이 같지 않은 것을 고르시오.

① As I've finished my homework, I am free now.
= Having finished my homework, I am free now.
② When she was asked to sing a song, she refused to.
= Asking to sing a song, she refused to.
③ While he was cleaning the room, he found some coins.
= Cleaning the room, he found some coins.
④ Though I like listening to music, I don't sing well.
= Liking listening to music, I don't sing well.
⑤ If it is hot tomorrow, we will go swimming.
= It being hot tomorrow, we will go swimming.

15 두 문장의 뜻이 같도록 빈칸에 알맞은 말을 쓰시오.

Studying English, she always uses an English-English dictionary.
= _____ studying English, she always uses an English-English dictionary.

16 밑줄 친 부분이 어법상 틀린 것을 고르시오.

① He heard his name called.
② I had my students write a letter to their parents.
③ I watched something crawling on my arm.
④ The language spoken in Mexico is Spanish.
⑤ The story made me shocking.

[17-18] 우리말과 일치하도록 빈칸에 알맞은 말을 쓰시오.

17 일반적으로 말하면 여자가 남자보다 더 오래 산다.
→ _____ _____, women live longer than men.

18 앨리스는 그녀의 집을 파랗게 칠하라고 시켰다.
→ Alice _____ her house _____ in blue.

[19-20] 우리말과 일치하도록 주어진 단어를 알맞게 배열하시오.

19 기차를 기다리고 있던 한 소년이 나에게 몇 시인지 물었다. (what time, a train, waiting, was, for, asked, a boy, it, me)
→ _____
_____

20 나는 답장을 받지 못했기 때문에 다시 그에게 편지를 썼다. (I, again, having, to him, an answer, a letter, received, not, wrote)
→ _____
_____

정답 및 해설 p.15

O1 다음 글의 밑줄 친 부분 중 어법상 **틀린** 것을 고르시오.

> Bill Gates is a computer programmer and businessman. In 1955, he was born in Seattle, Washington. In 1973, he attended Harvard, majoring in law. ① After dropping out of Harvard at the age of 18, he ② founded the Microsoft Corp. with Paul Allen. In 1980, IBM asked him ③ to develop the operating system ④ used in its first personal computer. In 1995, he produced the Windows 95 operating system. This system made Microsoft the world's largest producer of software, ⑤ given him a lot of wealth. However, he has been sharing his fortune. He created the largest charitable foundation in the USA.

- drop out of ~을 중퇴하다   - operating system 운영 체계
- charitable foundation 자선재단

O2 다음 밑줄 친 동사의 형태가 바르게 짝지어진 것을 고르시오.

> **A** Establish in 1872, Yellowstone National Park is America's first national park. **B** Locate in Wyoming, Montana, and Idaho, it is home to a large variety of wildlife **C** include bears, wolves, bison, and elk. Old Faithful, a collection of the world's most extraordinary geysers and hot springs, and the Grand Canyon of the Yellowstone are preserved within Yellowstone National Park.

- establish 설립하다   - extraordinary 대단한
- geyser 간헐천   - preserve 보존하다

	A		B		C
①	Establishing	–	Located	–	including
②	Establishing	–	Locating	–	including
③	Established	–	Located	–	including
④	Established	–	Located	–	included
⑤	Established	–	Locating	–	included

O1 다음 문장을 보기와 같이 분사구문으로 만드시오.

> 보기 Though she is old, she still feels young.
> → Being old, she still feels young.

1) While I was talking to my mom on the phone, I heard the doorbell ring.

→ _____

_____

2) As he didn't want to cook dinner, he ate out.

→ _____

_____

3) Because she lost her dog yesterday, she still feels sad.

→ _____

_____

O2 다음 우리말을 읽고 바르게 영작하시오.

나는 축구에 관심이 있다. 어제 나는 매우 흥미진진한 축구 경기를 보았다. 경기장에 있던 사람들 모두가 흥분했다. 선수들은 지쳤지만 최선을 다했다.

_____

_____

_____

_____

_____

- stadium 경기장

Chapter 08

비교구문

Chapter 미리보기

as + 형용사/부사 원급 + as	~만큼 …한
비교급 + than	~보다 더 …한

최상급 = 비교급 + than any other + 단수 명사
      = No (other) + 단수 명사 ~ 비교급 + than
      = No (other) + 단수 명사 ~ as + 형용사/부사 원급 + as
	가장 ~한

as + 원급 + as possible	가능한 한 ~하게
배수사 + as + 원급 + as	~배로 더 …한
비교급 + and + 비교급	점점 더 ~한
the + 비교급, the + 비교급	~할수록 더 …한
one of the + 최상급 + 복수 명사	가장 ~한 것 중의 하나
the + 최상급 + (that) + 주어 + have + ever p.p	지금까지 ~한 것 중에 가장 …한

The grass is always greener on the other side of the fence.
언제나 울타리 저 편의 잔디가 더 푸르다.

▶ 남의 떡이 항상 더 커 보인다.

25 원급, 비교급, 최상급

A as + 형용사/부사 원급 + as

'~만큼 …한'이란 뜻이며, 두 개 또는 그 이상을 비교하여 양쪽이 동등한 것을 나타내는 것으로 원급비교라고 한다.

ex
- Ann is as old as Jane.
- David speaks as slowly as Ann.

- This book is not as expensive as that one.
  = This book is not so expensive as that one.
  = This book is less expensive than that one.
  = That book is more expensive than this one.
  = This book is cheaper than that one.

B 비교급 + than

'~보다 …한'이란 뜻이며, 비교하는 대상 중 어느 한쪽이 더 잘하거나 못하는 것을 나타낸다.

ex
- My room is larger than Jane's.
- Kate is healthier than Susan.

C the + 최상급 + in/of

'~중에 가장 …한'이란 뜻이며, 비교의 대상이 되는 것 가운데 가장 최고이거나 좋음 등을 나타낸다.

ex
- This is the oldest building in Korea.
- Kate is the smartest of all.

D 비교급과 최상급 만들기

ⓐ 1음절 단어 : -er, -est	tall	taller	tallest
ⓑ -y로 끝난 경우 : -y를 i로 고치고 -er, -est를 붙인다.	easy	easier	easiest
ⓒ 〈단모음 + 단자음〉으로 끝난 경우 : 마지막 자음을 한 번 더 쓰고 -er, -est를 붙인다.	hot	hotter	hottest
ⓓ 2음절이나 3음절 이상의 단어 : 앞에 more, most를 붙인다.	interesting	more interesting	most interesting
ⓔ 불규칙 변화	good/well	better	best
	bad/ill	worse	worst
	many/much	more	most
	little	less	least

Grammar Check-Up

정답 및 해설 p.15

Note

O1 주어진 단어의 원급, 비교급, 최상급을 이용하여 문장을 완성하시오.

1) Ann is _____ as Paul. (creative)

2) John is _____ than Tom. (foolish)

3) Kate is _____ student in her school. (stubborn)

4) Winter is _____ of all seasons. (cold)

1) creative 창의적인
3) stubborn 고집이 센

O2 다음 문장의 <u>틀린</u> 부분에 밑줄을 긋고 바르게 고쳐 쓰시오.

1) This is the hotter place in the world.　　(→ _____)

2) I can run as faster as Jane can.　　(→ _____)

3) Kevin is more taller than Kate.　　(→ _____)

4) Kate studies English most than I do.　　(→ _____)

O3 두 문장의 뜻이 같도록 빈칸에 알맞은 말을 쓰시오.

1) Jane is not as attractive as Kate.

= Kate is _____ _____ than Jane.

2) The chair is less comfortable than the sofa.

= The chair is _____ _____ _____ as the sofa.

1) attractive 매력적인
2) comfortable 편한

O4 다음 우리말을 영작하시오.

1) 버스는 평상시만큼 붐볐다.

→ _____

2) 폴(Paul)은 우리 반에서 가장 호기심이 강한 학생이다.

→ _____

3) 샘(Sam)은 내가 생각했던 것보다 더 이기적이다.

→ _____

1) crowded 붐비는
   usual 평소의
2) curious 호기심 있는
3) selfish 이기적인

원급과 비교급의 여러 가지 용법

A as + 원급 + as possible

'가능한 한 ~하게'라는 의미로 〈as + 원급 + as + 주어 + can/could〉로 바꾸어 쓸 수 있다.

ex • I will be back as soon as possible.
  = I will be back as soon as I can.
 • They ran as fast as possible.
  = They ran as fast as they could.

B 배수사(twice, three times 등) + as + 원급 + as ~

'~보다 …배 더 −한/하게'라는 의미로 〈배수사 + 비교급 + than〉으로 바꾸어 쓸 수 있다.

ex • This house is four times as big as that one.
  = This house is four times bigger than that one.
 • The man is twice as heavy as the boy.
  = The man is twice heavier than the boy.

C 비교급 강조

much, far, even, a lot, still + 비교급 : '훨씬 더 ~한'

ex • Kate is much happier than before.
 • Paul is far more famous than Harry.

D 비교급 + and + 비교급

'점점 더 ~한'이라는 의미이다.

ex • It is getting hotter and hotter.
 • Susan is becoming more and more popular in her school.

E the + 비교급, the + 비교급

'~할수록 더 …하다'라는 의미이다.

ex • The bigger, the better.
 • The more you know, the more you want to know.

Grammar Check-Up

정답 및 해설 p.15

Note

01 다음 중 알맞은 것을 고르시오.

1) This bell is   very | much   louder than that one.

2) Her eyes are getting   big and big | bigger and bigger .

3) The story is becoming   more interesting and more interesting |
   more and more interesting .

4)   The most | The more   you have,   the most | the more   you want to
   have.

🖉 _____
1) loud 소리가 큰

02 두 문장의 뜻이 같도록 빈칸에 알맞은 말을 쓰시오.

1) Kate will finish it as soon as possible.

   = Kate will finish it as soon as _____ _____.

2) This road is four times as wide as that one.

   = This road is four times _____ _____ that one.

03 밑줄 친 부분에 주의하여 다음 문장을 우리말로 해석하시오.

1) Her book is three times as thick as his book.

   → _____

2) Writing Arabic is much more difficult than writing English.

   → _____

3) The hotter it is, the more we want to eat ice cream.

   → _____

🖉 _____
2) Arabic 아랍어

04 다음 우리말을 영작하시오.

1) 폴(Paul)은 가능한 한 빨리 그것을 너에게 보내줄 것이다.

   → _____

2) 이 타워는 저것보다 두 배가 높다.

   → _____

3) 나는 공부를 할수록 더 많이 알고 싶다.

   → _____

Unit 27 최상급의 여러 가지 용법

A 원급과 비교급을 이용한 최상급 표현

> the + 최상급 + in/of
> = 비교급 + than any other + 단수 명사 (비교급)
> = No (other) + 단수 명사 ~ 비교급 + than (비교급)
> = No (other) + 단수 명사 ~ as + 형용사/부사 원급 + as (원급)

ex
- Kate is the kindest girl in my class.
  = Kate is kinder than any other girl in my class. (비교급)
  = No (other) girl in my class is kinder than Kate. (비교급)
  = No (other) girl in my class is as kind as Kate. (원급)
- Rain is the most famous singer in Korea.
  = Rain is more famous than any other singer in Korea. (비교급)
  = No (other) singer in Korea is more famous than Rain. (비교급)
  = No (other) singer in Korea is as famous as Rain. (원급)
- Sarah is the worst singer in the club.
  = Sarah is worse than any other singer in the club. (비교급)
  = No (other) singer in the club is worse than Sarah. (비교급)
  = No (other) singer in the club is as bad as Sarah. (원급)

B one of the + 최상급 + 복수 명사

'가장 ~한 것/사람들 중의 하나'라는 의미이다.

ex
- David is one of the best doctors in the United States.
- Venice is one of the most beautiful cities in the world.
- Today is one of the happiest days of my life.

C the + 최상급 + (that) + 주어 + have ever p.p

'지금까지 ~한 것 중에 가장 …한'이라는 의미이다.

ex
- This is the saddest movie that I have ever seen.
- This is the most delicious pizza that I have ever eaten.
- This is the funniest book that Sally has ever read.

Note

01 다음 중 알맞은 것을 고르시오.

1) Paul is one of the best   student | students   in my school.

2) Kate is   the cutest | cuter   than any other girl in my class.

3) Susan is   happier | the happiest   person that I have ever met.

02 보기의 문장과 뜻이 같도록 빈칸을 채우시오.

> 보기 Kevin is the smartest student in my school.

1) Kevin is _____ _____ any other student in my school.

2) No other student in my school is _____ _____ Kevin.

3) No _____.

03 밑줄 친 부분에 주의하여 다음 문장을 우리말로 해석하시오.

1) This is one of the oldest wooden houses in the world.

→ _____

2) Tom was the most handsome boy that I have ever met.

→ _____

3) No singer is as good as Kevin.

→ _____

🖉 _____

1) wooden house
목조 가옥

04 우리말과 일치하도록 주어진 말을 바르게 배열하시오.

1) 이것은 내가 읽은 책 중에서 가장 재미있는 책이다.

(read, have, book, ever, I, is, most, the, this, interesting, that)

→ _____

2) 케이트는 세계에서 가장 유명한 화가이다.

(any, more, world, the, Kate, than, in, is, painter, famous, other)

→ _____

3) 어떤 배우도 케빈보다 인기가 많지는 않다.

(Kevin, more, is, no, famous, actor, than)

→ _____

내신 족집게 문제

[01-04] 두 문장의 뜻이 같도록 빈칸에 알맞은 말을 쓰시오.

01 The magazine is 5,000 won and the book is 10,000 won.

= The book is _____ _____

_____ as the magazine.

02 Tom ate lunch as quickly as possible.

= Tom ate lunch as quickly as _____

_____ .

03 Friendship is the most important thing in my life.

= Nothing is _____ _____ as friendship in my life.

04 Kate is the smartest student in my class.

= Kate is _____ than _____

_____ _____ in my class.

[05-06] 보기의 문장과 같은 뜻이 되도록 빈칸에 알맞은 말을 쓰시오.

보기 Kevin is not as strong as Paul.

05 = Paul is _____ than _____ .

06 = Kevin is _____ _____ than Paul.

[07-08] 빈칸에 들어갈 알맞은 것을 고르시오.

07 Kate has _____ English books than I have.

① many　　② good　　③ much
④ most　　⑤ more

08 Susan is _____ than any other player in our team.

① much　　② good　　③ the best
④ better　　⑤ more

09 다음 중 어법상 틀린 문장을 고르시오.

① My uncle is much busier than my aunt.
② *Harry Potter* is the most interesting book I have ever read.
③ The rose is one of the most popular flower in the world.
④ It is becoming more and more crowded.
⑤ Kate is the kindest girl in my class.

10 빈칸에 들어갈 수 <u>없는</u> 것을 고르시오.

Kate is _____ happier than before.

① a lot　　② much　　③ very
④ far　　　⑤ even

11 우리말과 일치하도록 주어진 단어를 이용하여 빈칸을 채우시오.

그 영화는 점점 더 인기가 좋아졌다.

→ The movie was getting _____

_____ . (popular)

[12-14] 우리말과 일치하도록 빈칸에 알맞은 말을 쓰시오.

12 수잔은 우리학교에서 가장 웃긴 학생 중의 한 명이다.

→ Susan is _____ of _____

_____ _____ in my school.

13 이것은 내가 본 것 중에 최고의 영화이다.

→ This is _____ _____ _____

that I _____ _____ _____.

14 우리가 더 높이 올라갈수록 날씨는 더 추워질 것이다.

→ _____ _____ we go up,

_____ _____ it is.

[15-16] 문장의 의미가 나머지와 다른 것을 고르시오.

15 ① Susan is the most attractive girl in the room.
② Susan is more attractive than any other girl in the room.
③ Susan is as attractive as other girls in the room.
④ No other girl in the room is as attractive as Susan.
⑤ No other girl in the room is more attractive than Susan.

16 ① This cloth is not as long as that one.
② This cloth is longer than that one.
③ This cloth is less long than that one.
④ This cloth is shorter than that one.
⑤ This cloth is not so long as that one.

[17-18] 주어진 단어를 알맞은 형태로 바꾸어 빈칸에 쓰시오.

17 This is the _____ restaurant in our town.
(bad)

18 Susan plays the piano _____ than I do.
(well)

19 대화의 빈칸에 들어갈 알맞은 것을 고르시오.

A: I haven't decided which internet service provider to use.

B: _____

① The fast, the best.
② The faster, the best.
③ The faster, the better.
④ The fastest, better.
⑤ Fast, good.

20 두 문장의 뜻이 같지 않은 것을 고르시오.

① His hair is not as long as her hair.
= Her hair is longer than his hair.
② Kate is the most adventurous student in my school.
= No other student in my school is as adventurous as Kate.
③ Kevin spoke as slowly as possible.
= Kevin spoke as slowly as he could.
④ These shoes are twice cheaper than those ones.
= Those shoes are twice as cheap as these ones.
⑤ Susan is more generous than any other member in the club.
= No other member in the club is more generous than Susan.

수능 감각 기르기

01 다음 글의 밑줄 친 부분 중 어법상 틀린 것을 고르시오.

> Hermes was the son ① of Zeus. He was ② the cleverest of the Greek gods, and he delivered messages from Zeus to all the other gods. He was ③ fastest than any other god. He wore winged sandals, a winged hat, and carried a magic wand. He was ④ also the god of travelers who crossed boundaries. He guided ⑤ dead people on their way to the underworld.

- winged 날개 달린
- magic wand 마법의 지팡이
- boundary 경계선
- underworld 저승

02 다음 괄호 안에서 어법에 맞는 표현으로 가장 적절한 것을 고르시오.

> Caffeine is naturally produced in the leaves and seeds of many plants. It is also produced artificially and added to certain foods. Caffeine is in tea leaves, coffee beans, chocolate, many soft drinks, and pain killers. Some people are **A** (very / much) more sensitive to caffeine because they have not taken it **B** (as many as / as much as) others. **C** (The more / The most) sensitive to caffeine people are, the more they will feel changes in mood.

- seed 씨앗
- artificially 인공적으로
- pain killer 진통제
- sensitive 민감한
- mood 기분

A	**B**	**C**
① very	– as many as	– The more
② very	– as much as	– The most
③ very	– as many as	– The more
④ much	– as many as	– The most
⑤ much	– as much as	– The more

서술형 즐기기

정답 및 해설 p.17

01 보기와 같은 의미가 되도록 다음 문장을 완성하시오.

> **보기** The Nile is the longest river in the world.

1) The Nile is _____ in the world.

2) No _____ the Nile.

3) No _____ the Nile.

02 다음 우리말을 읽고 바르게 영작하시오.

런던은 세계에서 가장 아름다운 도시들 중 하나이다. 나는 작년 여름에 런던에 갔다. 런던은 방문할수록 더 많이 다시 방문하고 싶어진다. 나는 영국 박물관에 갔다. 그것은 내가 가 본 중에서 최고의 박물관이다. 나는 거기에서 미이라를 보았다. 그것은 놀라운 경험이었다.

_____

_____

_____

_____

It was an amazing experience.

- British Museum 영국 박물관
- mummy 미이라

Chapter 09

접속사

Chapter 미리보기

명령문 + and/or	명령문 + and + 주어 + 동사 (~해라, 그러면 …할 것이다) 명령문 + or + 주어 + 동사 (~해라, 그렇지 않으면 …할 것이다)
상관접속사	both A and B → 복수 동사 either A or B, neither A nor B → 동사는 B의 수에 일치 not only A but also B = B as well as A → 동사는 B의 수에 일치
명사절을 이끄는 접속사	that (목적절인 경우 that 생략 가능), if/whether (~인지 아닌지)
부사절을 이끄는 접속사	• when, as, while, until, before, after • if (만약 ~한다면), unless (만약 ~하지 않는다면) • as, since, because, now that (~때문에) • so ~ that + 주어 + can = enough to + 동사원형 (너무 ~해서 …하다) • so ~ that + 주어 + can't = too ~ to + 동사원형 (너무 ~해서 …할 수 없다) • though, although, even though, even if (비록 ~이지만)

Where there is a will, there is a way.

▶ 뜻이 있는 곳에 길이 있다.

A 명령문 + and

'~해라, 그러면 …할 것이다'라는 의미이다.

ex • Try your best, and you will pass the exam.
= If you try your best, you will pass the exam.

B 명령문 + or

'~해라, 그렇지 않으면 …할 것이다'라는 의미이다.

ex • Hurry up, or you will miss the train.
= If you do not hurry up, you will miss the train.
= Unless you hurry up, you will miss the train.

C 상관접속사

상관접속사란 2개 이상의 단어가 상관관계를 가지는 접속사를 말한다.

⊕ 상관접속사를 쓸 때 동사의 수의 일치

both A and B + 복수동사
either A or B, neither A nor B, not A but B
not only A but also B, B as well as A → 동사는 B의 수에 일치

1 both A and B : 'A와 B 둘 다' (복수 동사)

ex • Both Kate and I are going to London tomorrow.
• Paul likes both apples and pears.

2 either A or B : 'A이거나 B' (동사는 B의 수에 일치)

ex • Either Kevin or I am afraid of spiders.
• She will buy either the book or the magazine.

3 neither A nor B : 'A도 B도 아닌' (동사는 B의 수에 일치)

ex • Neither Kate nor I like mathematics.
• He has neither a pen nor a pencil.

4 not only A but also B = B as well as A : 'A뿐만 아니라 B도' (동사는 B의 수에 일치)

ex • Not only Kevin but also I enjoy swimming.
= I as well as Kevin enjoy swimming.

5 not A but B : 'A가 아니고 B' (동사는 B의 수에 일치)

ex • Not Kate but I am the class president.
• Sally is not a singer but a dancer.

Grammar Check-Up

Note

O1 다음 중 알맞은 것을 고르시오.

1) Neither Kate   or｜nor｜and   Kevin knew you.

2) Either Paul   or｜nor｜and   John became a vet.

3) Both Jane and I   is｜are｜am   students.

4) Not only Kevin but also I   likes｜like   swimming.

2) vet 수의사

O2 두 문장의 뜻이 같도록 빈칸에 알맞은 말을 쓰시오.

1) Study hard, and you will get a good grade.

= _____ _____ _____ _____, you will get a good grade.

2) Wake up now, or you will be late for school.

= _____ _____ _____ _____ up now, you will be late for school.

3) Not only Kate but also I wanted to read the book.

= _____ as _____ _____ _____ wanted to read the book.

1) grade 성적

O3 밑줄 친 부분에 주의하여 다음 문장을 우리말로 해석하시오.

1) <u>Go to bed early, and</u> you won't be tired.

→ _____

2) <u>Speak slowly, or</u> I can't understand you.

→ _____

3) <u>Neither Kate nor Kevin</u> made any mistakes.

→ _____

O4 다음 우리말을 영작하시오.

1) 그녀가 아니라 그가 영어를 유창하게 말할 수 있다.

→ _____

2) 케빈(Kevin)뿐만 아니라 나도 점심을 먹는다.

→ _____

1) fluently 유창하게

명사절을 이끄는 접속사, 간접의문문

A 명사절을 이끄는 접속사

1 **that** : that이 목적어 역할을 할 경우에는 생략할 수 있다.

> ex
> • That Bell invented the telephone is true.
> • I know (that) John won the contest.
> • The fact is that Sally can't swim.

2 **whether/if** : '~인지 아닌지'로 해석한다.

> ex
> • I asked her whether she would go to the classical concert (or not).
> • We don't know if she will come.
> • Paul wants to know if Kate likes roses.

B 간접의문문

간접의문문은 의문문이 문장의 일부로 되어 있는 것을 말한다.

1 **의문사가 있는 간접의문문** : 의문사가 있는 간접의문문의 어순은 〈의문사 + (주어) + 동사〉이다.

> ex
> • I don't know who made it.
> • Do you know where they went for dinner?
> • Do you know where did they go for dinner? (×)

2 **의문사가 없는 간접의문문** : 의문사가 없는 간접의문문의 어순은 〈if/whether + 주어 + 동사〉이다.

> ex
> • Harry asked if I knew Jane.
> • I wonder whether he answered the question.
> • I wonder whether did he answer the question. (×)

3 **동사 think, believe의 간접의문문** : 주절에 think, believe, guess 등의 동사가 올 때는 의문사가 문장 맨 앞으로 나온다.

> ex
> • What do you think the problem is? (○)
> • Do you think what the problem is? (×)
>
> • When do you think he left? (○)
> • Do you think when he left? (×)
>
> • Who do you believe the thief is? (○)
> • Do you believe who the thief is? (×)

Note

O1 다음 중 알맞은 것을 고르시오.

1) Ann thinks   that | what   John made a lot of effort.

2) Paul wonders   that | whether   Sarah had a boyfriend.

3) Do you know   that | what   she wants to buy for him?

1) make an effort
   노력하다

2) wonder 궁금해하다

O2 다음 문장의 <u>틀린</u> 부분에 밑줄을 긋고 바르게 고쳐 쓰시오.

1) Do you think who she talked to?   (→ _____)

2) What do you know he wants to do?   (→ _____)

3) Do you know what did they eat for lunch? (→ _____)

O3 다음 질문에 알맞은 대답을 완성하시오.

1) Ⓐ Will she take English lessons?

   Ⓑ I don't know _____ .

2) Ⓐ What did he do last night?

   Ⓑ I don't know _____ .

O4 우리말과 일치하도록 주어진 말을 바르게 배열하시오.

1) 나는 그녀가 우리 클럽에 가입할 것인지 궁금하다.
   (join, will, whether, wonder, our, she, I, club)

   → _____

2) 당신은 그가 신뢰하는 사람이 누구라고 생각합니까?
   (trusts, think, who, he, you, do)

   → _____

3) 당신은 누가 그 빌딩을 설계했는지 아십니까?
   (building, do, who, know, the, designed, you)

   → _____

2) trust 신뢰하다, 믿다

Unit 30 부사절을 이끄는 접속사

A 시간의 부사절을 이끄는 접속사

when, as, while, after, before, until 등이 있다.

ex
- After she went home, he arrived. = Before he arrived, she went home.
- I found my old diary while I was cleaning my room.
  [비교] While Kate likes English, Jason likes mathematics. (~하는 반면에)

B 조건의 부사절을 이끄는 접속사

if, unless (= if ~ not) 등이 있다.

ex
- If it is sunny tomorrow, I will go fishing.
- If I do not visit my grandparents, I will see you tomorrow.
  = Unless I visit my grandparents, I will see you tomorrow.

➖⊕ 시간과 조건의 부사절에서는 미래시제 대신 현재시제를 사용한다.

ex
- When I finish my homework, I will go out. (○)
- When I will finish my homework, I will go out. (×)

C 이유의 부사절을 이끄는 접속사

as, since, because, now that 등이 있다.

ex
- As Kate was absent from school, she couldn't take the final exam.
  [비교] As she entered the shop, they were shouting at each other. (~할 때)
- Kevin was late for school since he overslept.
  [비교] Kevin has lived here since 2000. (~이래로)
- Kevin was crying because he dropped his ice cream.
  [비교] Kate couldn't watch TV last night because of a power outage. (because of + 명사)
- Now that you finished your homework, you can watch TV.

D 결과의 부사절을 이끄는 접속사

so ~ that + 주어 + can/can't

ex
- Paul was so shy that he couldn't look at the girl he likes.
  [비교] Ann is studying hard so that she can pass the test. (~하도록, ~하기 위하여)

E 양보의 부사절을 이끄는 접속사

although, though, even though, even if 등이 있다.

ex
- Although my grandfather is 100 years old, he is healthy.

Grammar Check-Up

정답 및 해설 p.17

O1 다음 중 알맞은 것을 고르시오.

1) Kate became a professional golfer   when | because   she was 16.

2)   Now that | Though   he saved some money, he can buy a new MP3 player.

3) Jane is   so hungry that | hungry so that   she can eat anything.

2) save 모으다

O2 다음 문장의 <u>틀린</u> 부분에 밑줄을 긋고 바르게 고쳐 쓰시오.

1) They will go shopping if they will have time.   (→ _____)

2) Kate gave Paul her favorite book because of she likes him.

(→ _____)

3) Unless you don't like the book, I want to have it.   (→ _____)

O3 밑줄 친 부분에 주의하여 다음 문장을 우리말로 해석하시오.

1) <u>As</u> Kate was adventurous, she went on an expedition to the Amazon.

→ _____

2) Ann stayed up late last night <u>since</u> she had to prepare for the exam.

→ _____

3) Kevin has been playing the piano <u>since</u> he was six.

→ _____

1) expedtion 탐험

2) stay up late
늦게까지 깨어 있다

O4 우리말과 일치하도록 주어진 말을 바르게 배열하시오.

1) 폴이 기말고사에서 실패하지 않는다면 대학을 졸업할 것이다.
(the final exam, his university, Paul, graduate, he, unless, will, from, fails)

→ _____

2) 케빈은 키가 크지 않지만 농구를 잘한다.
(basketball, not, he, although, at, Kevin, tall, good, is, is)

→ _____

1) graduate from
~을 졸업하다

내신 족집게 문제

[01-05] 두 문장의 뜻이 같도록 빈칸에 알맞은 말을 쓰시오.

01 If you don't take a taxi, you will be late for the meeting.

= _____ you take a taxi, you will be late for the meeting.

02 Kate likes apples and I like apples, too.

= _____ Kate _____ I like apples.

03 Kate doesn't like the movie. Kevin doesn't like the movie, either.

= _____ Kate _____ Kevin likes the movie.

04 Jane as well as I is a baseball player.

= Not _____ _____ _____
_____ _____ _____ a
baseball player.

05 Before Ann went to school, she had breakfast.

= After Ann _____ _____, _____
_____ _____ _____.

06 빈칸에 알맞은 단어를 순서대로 바르게 짝지은 것을 고르시오.

• I don't know _____ she will come.
• I think _____ he gets along with us.

① that – that
② that – if
③ if – that
④ if – if
⑤ that – whether

07 주어진 단어를 알맞은 형태로 바꾸어 빈칸에 쓰시오.

Not Paul but I _____ to pay for the tickets.
(have)

08 빈칸에 들어갈 알맞은 것을 고르시오.

She wondered _____ they heard the rumor.

① that
② whether
③ what
④ which
⑤ who

[09-12] 우리말과 일치하도록 빈칸에 알맞은 말을 쓰시오.

09 열심히 일해라, 그러면 너는 그것을 일찍 끝낼 수 있을 것이다.

→ Work hard, _____ you will finish it earlier.

10 코트를 가져가라, 그렇지 않으면 감기에 걸릴 것이다.

→ Take your coat, _____ you will catch a cold.

11 당신은 그녀가 누구라고 생각합니까?

→ _____ _____ _____
_____ she is?

12 당신은 누가 그 질문에 대답했는지 아십니까?

→ _____ _____ _____
_____ _____ the question?

13 밑줄 친 부분의 쓰임이 나머지와 <u>다른</u> 것을 고르시오.

① I think <u>that</u> he is honest.

② Ann knows <u>that</u> Paul is coming to the party.

③ We thought <u>that</u> was a great idea.

④ It is important <u>that</u> you do some exercise.

⑤ Jane knew <u>that</u> he lost the important match.

[14-15] 빈칸에 들어갈 수 <u>없는</u> 것을 고르시오.

14

We rode bikes _____ it was rainy.

① though   ② although   ③ even though

④ if   ⑤ even if

15

_____ Kate is ill, she couldn't go to school.

① Since   ② Because   ③ As

④ Now that   ⑤ Though

[16-17] 밑줄 친 부분이 어법상 <u>틀린</u> 것을 고르시오.

16 ① <u>Where do you think</u> he lives?

② <u>Do you know who</u> likes Ann?

③ <u>I wonder if</u> he has a girlfriend.

④ <u>I don't know whether</u> he passed the English exam.

⑤ <u>Do you think what</u> Edison invented?

17 ① I wonder <u>if she will go</u> to the movies.

② Do you know <u>when we will arrive</u> there?

③ I will do my homework <u>after I will watch</u> TV.

④ We won't go out <u>if it is windy</u>.

⑤ They will go shopping <u>when they finish their work</u>.

[18-19] 밑줄 친 접속사의 쓰임이 <u>어색한</u> 것을 고르시오.

18 ① My mom couldn't sleep <u>until</u> I came home.

② Sue was sad <u>as</u> her pet died last night.

③ Ann went to Canada <u>so</u> she wanted to improve her English.

④ The phone rang <u>while</u> I was sleeping.

⑤ Paul couldn't play football <u>since</u> he broke his leg.

19 ① He has lived here <u>since</u> he was ten.

② Take your umbrella, <u>or</u> you will get wet.

③ Neither Kate <u>or</u> Kevin want to go out with their friends.

④ She will be in trouble <u>unless</u> she finds the key.

⑤ Stay here, <u>and</u> you will be safe.

20 두 문장의 뜻이 같지 <u>않은</u> 것을 고르시오.

① Ann is so nervous that she can't do that.
= Ann is too nervous to do that.

② Now that he failed the English test, he has to take another English test.
= Though he failed the English test, he has to take another English test.

③ John was so hungry that he could eat anything.
= John was hungry enough to eat anything.

④ If I don't go out, I will watch the game on TV.
= Unless I go out, I will watch the game on TV.

⑤ I lost the game because I made a mistake.
= I lost the game because of a mistake I made.

정답 및 해설 p.18

01 다음 글의 밑줄 친 부분 중 어법상 <u>틀린</u> 것을 고르시오.

> Zeus was the god of the sky ① and ruler of the gods. Zeus defeated his father Cronus. ② After that he became the greatest ruler of the gods. He is ③ not only the god of justice but also the god of mercy. He protected weak people and punished wicked people. His weapon was a thunderbolt. He threw the thunderbolt ④ when someone made him angry. He punished people ⑤ unless they lied or broke their promises.

- justice 정의
- mercy 자비
- wicked 사악한
- thunderbolt 번개

01 두 문장의 뜻이 같도록 문장을 완성하시오.

1) Jerry lost his wallet. He bought a new one.

= Because _____

_____ .

2) Jennifer had a sandwich for lunch. Then she went shopping with Kate.

= Before _____

_____ .

3) David has to study hard, otherwise he will fail the math test.

= Unless _____

_____ .

02 다음 괄호 안에서 어법에 맞는 표현으로 가장 적절한 것을 고르시오.

> Ozone is a gas and is produced naturally in the stratosphere. This ozone layer protects us **A** (because / because of) it absorbs a lot of the sun's harmful ultraviolet(UV) rays. But there are some holes in the ozone layer **B** (because / because of) man-made chemicals. These destroy the ozone. The holes in the layer are getting bigger. **C** (Even though / As) a lot of countries try not to use those chemicals, there are still a lot of them in the stratosphere.

- stratosphere (지구 대기의) 성층권
- ozone layer 오존층
- ultraviolet rays 자외선

A	**B**	**C**
① because of	– because	– Even though
② because of	– because	– As
③ because of	– because of	– Even though
④ because	– because of	– As
⑤ because	– because of	– Even though

02 다음 우리말을 읽고 바르게 영작하시오.

케이트 : 너는 이것이 무엇이라고 생각하니?
수잔 : 나는 그것이 앤을 위한 선물이라고 생각해.
케이트 : 너는 누가 이것을 앤에게 주었는지 아니?
수잔 : 응, 폴이 주었어. 해리 또한 그녀에게 선물을 주었어.
케이트 : 그러면 너는 앤이 누구를 좋아한다고 생각하니?
수잔 : 나는 앤이 그들 중 한 명을 좋아하는지 모르겠어.

Kate : _____

Susan : I think it is a present for Ann. _____

Kate : _____

Susan : Yes, Paul did. Harry also gave her a present.

Kate : _____

Susan : _____

Chapter 10

관계사

Chapter 미리보기

관계사	관계대명사		관계부사	
역할	접속사 + (대)명사		접속사 + 부사 = 전치사 + 관계대명사	
선행사	사람	who	장소(the place)	where = in/at/on/to which
	사물, 동물	which	시간(the time)	when = in/at/on which
	사람, 사물, 동물	that	이유(the reason)	why = for which
	선행사 포함	what	방법(the way)	how = in which

However humble it may be, there is no place like home.
▶ 아무리 보잘것없다 할지라도 집 같은 곳은 없다.

관계대명사 who, which, that

A 관계대명사의 개념

관계대명사는 접속사와 (대)명사 역할을 하며, who, which, that이 대표적이다.

Tips
• 관계대명사절은 선행사를 수식한다.

선행사	주격	소유격	목적격
사람	who/that	whose	whom/that
시물, 동물	which/that	whose/of which	which/that

ex • I don't know the girl who is standing there. (나는 저기에 서 있는 소녀를 모른다.)
(선행사) (관계대명사절)

• This is the house which he built last year. (이것은 그가 작년에 지은 집이다.)
(선행사) (관계대명사절)

B 주격 관계대명사

Tips
• 주격 관계대명사가 이끄는 관계사절 안에 있는 동사는 선행사의 수에 일치시킨다.

주격 관계대명사(who, which, that)는 관계대명사절에서 주어 역할을 한다.

ex • I saw the boy. + He broke the window.
  → I saw the boy who/that broke the window.
• The car is broken. + It is in front of my house.
  → The car which/that is in front of my house is broken.

C 소유격 관계대명사

소유격 관계대명사(whose)는 관계대명사절에서 소유격 역할을 한다.

ex • I know the boy. + His bicycle is broken.
  → I know the boy whose bicycle is broken.
• I live in the house. Its roof is blue.
  → I live in the house whose roof is blue.

D 목적격 관계대명사

목적격 관계대명사(who(m), which, that)는 관계대명사절에서 목적어 역할을 한다. whom 대신 that이 많이 쓰인다.

ex • I liked the boy. + I met him yesterday.
  → I liked the boy who(m)/that I met yesterday.
• I liked the book. + I read it last week.
  → I liked the book which/that I read last week.

01 다음 중 알맞은 것을 고르시오.

1) The woman   whose | which | that   I was dancing with stepped on my toe.

2) I couldn't find the man   whose | who | that   car was blocking the driveway.

3) I know the girls that   is | are   good at playing computer games.

02 빈칸에 들어갈 알맞은 관계대명사를 쓰시오.

1) I am reading a book _____ was written by Ernest Hemingway.

2) I apologized to the woman _____ coffee I spilled.

3) The waitress _____ served us was very impolite.

03 관계대명사를 이용하여 다음 두 문장을 한 문장으로 쓰시오.

1) Look at the house. + Its windows were broken.

→ _____

2) The taxi driver was friendly. + He took me to the airport.

→ _____

04 다음 문장을 우리말로 해석하시오.

1) Have you heard about the earthquake that occurred in Japan?

→ _____

2) The person who showed me the way to the bank spoke too fast.

→ _____

05 다음 우리말을 영작하시오.

1) 나는 남편이 교수인 여자를 알고 있다.

→ _____

2) 내가 어제 읽었던 책은 '오만과 편견(Pride and Prejudice)'이다.

→ _____

32 주의해야 할 관계대명사

A 관계대명사 that만 사용하는 경우

1 사람과 동물, 사람과 사물이 선행사일 때

Tips
• the very + 명사
바로 그 ~

2 선행사 앞에 서수, 최상급, the only, the very, the same 등이 올 때

3 something, anything, nothing, everything이 선행사일 때

> **ex** • Look at the boy and his dog that are coming here.
> • I found the very man that I wanted to marry.

B 관계대명사 what

what은 선행사를 포함하고 있으며, '~것'으로 해석한다. 따라서 what 앞에는 선행사가 없고, the thing which로 바꾸어 쓸 수 있다.

> **ex** • This is the thing. + I wanted it.
> → This is the thing which I wanted.
> → This is what I wanted.
> • Did you hear what he said?
> • What I have to do is to protect animals.

C 관계대명사의 생략

1 목적격 관계대명사 which, who(m), that은 생략이 가능하다.

Tips
• 목적격 관계대명사 뒤에는 〈주어 + 동사〉가 온다.

> **ex** • I am looking for a ring (which) I lost here.

2 〈주격 관계대명사 + be동사〉에서 주격 관계대명사와 be동사는 함께 생략이 가능하다.

> **ex** • The woman (who is) singing on the street looks like my friend.
> • I am reading a book (which was) written by Jane Austin.

D 전치사 + 관계대명사

전치사의 목적어로 쓰인 관계대명사는 〈전치사 + 관계대명사〉의 형태로 쓸 수 있으며, 목적격 관계대명사를 생략할 때 전치사는 반드시 뒤로 보낸다. that은 〈전치사 + 관계대명사〉로 쓰지 않는다.

> **ex** • Do you know the man whom Jenny got married to?
> = Do you know the man to whom Jenny got married? (○)
> = Do you know the man Jenny got married to? (○)
> = Do you know the man to that Jenny got married? (×)

Note

O1 다음 중 알맞은 것을 고르시오.

1) That | What | Which   I saw yesterday in the street was terrible.

2) This is the building in   that | which | what   my friend lives.

3) The son of   which | whom | that   she was proud won the race.

O2 빈칸에 들어갈 알맞은 관계대명사를 쓰시오.

1) I know _____ you did last summer.

2) There are children of _____ you should take care.

3) This is the worst movie _____ I have ever seen.

O3 다음 문장 중 생략할 수 있는 부분을 괄호 안에 넣으시오.

1) The girl who is talking to Minyeong is from China.

2) I come from a city which is located on the east coast.

3) The butterfly that I caught yesterday is yellow and black.

4) The teacher whom I met last weekend gave me good advice.

🖉
2) coast 해안
4) advice 조언, 충고

O4 두 문장의 뜻이 같도록 빈칸에 알맞은 말을 쓰시오.

1) This is the thing which I want to have.

= This is _____ I want to have.

2) He is the actor that we talked about.

= He is the actor _____ _____ we talked.

3) Our solar system is in a galaxy called the Milky Way.

= Our solar system is in a galaxy _____ _____ called

the Milky Way.

🖉
3) solar system 태양계
   galaxy 은하

O5 주어진 말을 이용하여 다음 우리말을 영작하시오.

1) 나무로 만들어진 울타리가 우리 집을 둘러싸고 있다. (surround, be made of)

→ The fence _____ .

2) 그녀의 가방 속에 있는 것은 잡지책 한 권이다. (what, magazine)

→ _____

33 관계부사

A 관계부사의 정의

관계부사는 접속사와 부사 역할을 하며, 전치사와 관계대명사로 바꾸어 쓸 수 있다. 관계부사는 장소, 시간, 이유, 방법 등 선행사에 따라 where, when, why, how를 쓴다.

선행사	관계부사	전치사 + 관계대명사
장소(the place, the town, the country)	where	in/on/at which
시간(the time, the year, the season)	when	in/on/at which
이유(the reason)	why	for which
방법(the way)	how	in which

B where

장소가 선행사일 때

ex ・ This is the house. + I lived in the house.
= This is the house which I lived in.
= This is the house in which I lived.
= This is the house where I lived.

C when

시간이 선행사일 때

ex ・ I can't remember the day when I first met you.
= I can't remember the day on which I first met you.

D why

이유가 선행사일 때

ex ・ I don't know the reason why she missed the first train.
= I don't know the reason for which she missed the first train.

E how

방법이 선행사일 때 the way나 how 둘 중 하나만 쓴다.

ex ・ I want to know how he folds paper cranes.
= I want to know the way he folds paper cranes.
= I want to know the way in which he folds paper cranes.
= I want to know the way how he folds paper cranes. (×)

01 빈칸에 들어갈 알맞은 관계부사를 쓰시오.

1) Monday is the day _____ I don't like to go to school.

2) Please tell me the shop _____ we can buy water and bread.

3) I don't know the reason _____ she has gone to China.

3) have gone to
~로 가 버렸다

02 다음 문장들의 뜻이 같도록 빈칸에 알맞은 말을 쓰시오.

1) The town which I live in is very small.

= The town _____ _____ I live is very small.

= The town _____ I live is very small.

2) Tell me the reason why you have a long face.

= Tell me the reason _____ _____ you have a long face.

2) have a long face
우울한 얼굴을 하고 있다

3) This is how he fixed the computer.

= This is _____ _____ he fixed the computer.

4) Four o'clock is the time at which my train arrives.

= Four o'clock is the time _____ my train arrives.

03 다음 문장을 우리말로 해석하시오.

1) The house where I was born was destroyed by a hurricane.

→ _____

2) I will never forget the first day when I arrived in Europe.

→ _____

04 우리말과 일치하도록 주어진 말을 바르게 배열하시오. (단, 관계부사를 넣을 것)

1) 네가 학교에 지각한 이유를 내게 말해라.

(the reason, you, me, tell, are, for, late, school)

→ _____

2) 우리가 여름방학을 보냈던 그 마을은 아름다웠다.

(beautiful, the village, spent, we, was, our summer vacation)

→ _____

Unit 34 관계사의 용법

A 관계사의 제한적 용법과 계속적 용법

제한적 용법	계속적 용법
관계사 앞에 콤마가 없다.	관계사 앞에 콤마가 있다.
• 관계대명사 : who, which, that, what • 관계부사 : when, where, how, why	• 관계대명사 : who, which • 관계부사 : when, where
목적격 관계대명사 생략 가능	관계대명사 생략 불가능

1 제한적 용법

ex • I have two friends who are dentists.
  (나는 치과의사인 친구들이 두 명 있다. → 친구가 둘 이상)

2 계속적 용법

ex • I have two friends, who are dentists.
  (나는 두 명의 친구가 있고, 그 친구들은 치과의사이다. → 친구가 둘 뿐)

⊕ 관계대명사 that은 계속적 용법에서 사용할 수 없다.

ex • I have two friends, who are dentists. (○)
  • I have two friends, that are dentists. (×)

B 관계사의 전환

계속적 용법에 사용된 관계대명사는 〈접속사(and, but, for, though 등) + 대명사〉, 관계부사는 〈접속사 + 부사〉로 바꾸어 쓸 수 있다.

ex • He threw away the apples, which (= for they) were rotten.
  • He didn't employ the woman, who (= though she) spoke English well.
  • She pointed at the map, which (= and it) was on the wall.
  • I visited Hungary last month, when (= and then) I met Jane's boyfriend.
  • I went to Sokcho, where (= and there) I stayed for a week.

C 관계대명사 which

관계대명사 which는 선행사로 구나 절이 올 수 있다.

ex • Karen was late, which surprised me. (which의 선행사는 Karen was late이다.)

01 다음 중 알맞은 것을 고르시오.

1) She opened the present,   which | that | who   came from her father.

2) Miss Kim,   whom | that | which   we met yesterday, teaches math.

3) I met Tim yesterday,   which | when   he told me the news.

4) Her boss fired her,   which | that | who   made her angry.

4) fire 해고하다

02 두 문장의 뜻이 같도록 빈칸에 알맞은 말을 쓰시오.

1) I don't like the pants, for they are too tight.

= I don't like the pants, _____ are too tight.

2) She had three daughters, and they got married.

= She had three daughters, _____ got married.

3) We went to Busan, and there we spent our vacation.

= We went to Busan, _____ we spent our vacation.

03 다음 문장을 우리말로 해석하시오.

1) She told me her phone number, which I wrote down on the paper.

→ _____

2) Yesterday I met Peter, who told me he would get married.

→ _____

3) Next week I'm going to Canada, where my sister lives.

→ _____

04 우리말과 일치하도록 주어진 말을 바르게 배열하시오.

1) 나는 그 학생에게 벌을 주었는데, 왜냐하면 숙제를 안 했기 때문이다.

(the student, who, do, punished, didn't, his homework, I)

→ _____

1) punish 벌주다

2) 그는 나에게 책을 한 권 주었는데, 나는 그것을 두 번 읽었다.

(which, he, a book, read, twice, me, gave, I)

→ _____

Unit 35 복합관계사

복합관계사는 관계사에 -ever를 붙인 것으로, 복합관계대명사는 명사절이나 양보 부사절을 이끌고, 복합관계부사는 양보 부사절이나 시간·장소 부사절을 이끈다.

A 명사절

복합관계대명사절이 전체 문장에서 주어나 목적어 역할을 한다.

복합관계대명사	명사절(선행사 + 관계대명사)	해석
whoever	anyone who	누구나, 누구든지
whichever	any(thing) which	어느 것이든지
whatever	anything that	무엇이든지, 무엇이나

ex • Whoever (= Anyone who) will meet me may come home.
   • Choose whichever (= any(thing) which) you want to buy.
   • I will give her whatever (= anything that) she wants.

B 부사절

1 **양보 부사절** : 관계사 + -ever = no matter + 관계사

복합관계대명사	양보 부사절	복합관계부사	양보 부사절
whoever	no matter who (누구일지라도)	whenever	no matter when (언제 ~일지라도)
whichever	no matter which (어느 것일지라도)	wherever	no matter where (어디 ~일지라도)
whatever	no matter what (무엇일지라도)	however	no matter how (아무리 ~해도)

ex • Whoever (= No matter who) may break this vase, he will be scolded.
   • Whatever (= No matter what) you may do for me, I can't trust you.
   • However (= No matter how) rich you may be, you can't buy it.

2 **시간이나 장소를 나타내는 부사절** : 관계부사 + -ever = 선행사 + 관계부사

복합관계대명사	시간·장소 부사절	해석
whenever	at any time when	~할 때마다, 언제든지
wherever	at any place where	~은 어디에나, 어디든지

ex • You can come whenever you want.
   • I have a car. I can take you wherever you want to go.

Grammar Check-Up

O1 다음 중 알맞은 것을 고르시오.

1) He will talk to   whoever | whatever   will listen to him.

2) You may say   whatever | whenever   is on your mind.

3)   Whenever | However   much she may eat, she never gets fat.

4) You may leave   whenever | however   you want.

O2 두 문장의 뜻이 같도록 빈칸에 알맞은 말을 쓰시오.

1) No matter what you may say, I will not believe you.

= _____ you may say, I will not believe you.

2) No matter how late you may be, you have to phone me.

= _____ late you may be, you have to phone me.

3) Anyone who wants to succeed should work hard.

= _____ wants to succeed should work hard.

4) No matter where you may go, I will follow you.

= _____ you may go, I will follow you.

O3 다음 문장을 우리말로 해석하시오.

1) However carefully I write a letter, I always make mistakes.

→ _____

2) I won't change my mind whatever you may do for me.

→ _____

3) You may watch whichever movie you like.

→ _____

O4 우리말과 일치하도록 문장을 완성하시오.

1) 너는 아무리 피곤해도 네 숙제를 끝내야 한다.

→ _____, you should do your homework.

2) 네가 하고 싶은 것은 무엇이든지 해도 좋다.

→ You may do _____.

내신 족집게 문제

[01-05] 빈칸에 들어갈 알맞은 관계대명사를 보기에서 골라 쓰시오.

보기   whom   that   what   which   whose

01 My brother, _____ you once met, is visiting us next week.

02 Do you know the name of the girl _____ bag was stolen?

03 The song to _____ I listened last night was very good.

04 Budapest is the most beautiful city _____ I have ever visited.

05 I can't agree with _____ you have just said.

06 두 문장에 공통으로 들어갈 관계대명사를 쓰시오.

- The machine _____ broke down has just been fixed.
- He is the very man _____ I want to marry.

07 밑줄 친 what의 용법이 나머지와 다른 것을 고르시오.

① I am happy to do what I love best.
② He asked me what her name was.
③ What we have to do is to save money.
④ What is beautiful is not always good.
⑤ This is what I want to have.

08 밑줄 친 부분 중 생략할 수 없는 것을 고르시오.

① I live in a house which was built 100 years ago.
② The dress which she bought yesterday was too small.
③ Please show me the pictures that you took in Europe.
④ The man who is parking a car there is my dad.
⑤ She is the woman about whom I told you.

[09-11] 두 문장의 뜻이 같도록 빈칸에 알맞은 말을 쓰시오.

09 Tell me the hotel at which you want to stay in Seoul.

= Tell me the hotel _____ you want to stay in Seoul.

10 Do you know the way she made the cheesecake?

= Do you know _____ she made the cheesecake?

11 Anyone who will meet me should call me first.

= _____ will meet me should call me first.

12 다음 중 어법상 틀린 문장을 고르시오.

① Do you remember the place that you parked your car in?
② Do you remember the place you parked your car in?
③ Do you remember the place in which you parked your car?
④ Do you remember the place in that you parked your car?
⑤ Do you remember the place where you parked your car?

[13-15] 빈칸에 들어갈 관계사를 순서대로 바르게 짝지은
것을 고르시오.

13
- Winter is the season _____ it snows a lot.
- Tell me the reason _____ your mother scolded you.

① why – why
② why – when
③ when – why
④ when – when
⑤ which – why

14
- I went to Busan, _____ is famous for its beautiful beach.
- I went to Busan, _____ I stayed for a week.

① that – that
② that – where
③ where – where
④ which – where
⑤ where – which

15
- Look at the man and his car _____ are over there.
- The man for _____ you are waiting is very handsome.
- My friend has a car _____ color is red.

① which – that – whom
② which – whom – whose
③ that – that – whom
④ that – whom – whose
⑤ that – whom – which

16 다음 중 올바른 문장을 고르시오.
① Tell me the way how you got out of danger.
② He threw away the apples, that were rotten.
③ This is the house where he lives in.
④ The building whose wall is pink is my house.
⑤ The people whom I met in America was very kind.

17 보기의 밑줄 친 when과 쓰임이 같은 것을 고르시오.

보기 I can't forget the day <u>when</u> he left for New Zealand.

① It was raining when I went out.
② Don't drive a car when you are sleepy.
③ She asked me when my mother had come home.
④ Do you know when he will leave for New Zealand?
⑤ I was born in the year when the Olympic Games were held in Seoul.

18 우리말과 일치하도록 빈칸에 공통으로 들어갈 알맞은 말을 쓰시오.

- 너는 아무리 배가 고파도 천천히 먹어야 한다.
  → _____ hungry you may be, you should eat slowly.
- 아무리 보잘것없어도 집 같은 장소는 없다.
  → _____ humble it may be, there is no place like home.

[19-20] 우리말과 일치하도록 주어진 단어를 알맞게 배열하시오.

19 그녀가 파티에 데리고 온 그 남자가 저기에 서 있다.
(over there, she, the man, whom, to, is standing, brought, the party)

→ _____

_____

20 너는 우리가 작년에 머물렀던 호텔 이름을 아니?
(the hotel, know, where, do, stayed, you, of, we, last year, the name)

→ _____

_____

정답 및 해설 p.21

O1 다음 괄호 안에서 어법에 맞는 표현으로 가장 적절한 것을 고르시오.

> J. K. Rowling first thought of *Harry Potter* while she was riding a train in 1990. She wrote the book in a cafe with her baby next to her. It took several years to finish the first book. In 1996, she tried to publish the book. However, 12 publishers rejected her book. At last, a woman **A** (who / which) was working for a publisher had an interest in her book. *Harry Potter and the Sorcerer's Stone*, **B** (who / which) was published in 1998, was popular. Both kids and their parents wanted to read the book. The second and third books were published, too. The *Harry Potter* series have appeared on bestseller's lists all over the world. In an interview, J. K. Rowling said, "I am a very lucky person because I can do **C** (that / what) I love best in the world."

	A		**B**		**C**
①	who	–	which	–	that
②	who	–	which	–	what
③	who	–	who	–	what
④	which	–	who	–	what
⑤	which	–	who	–	that

O2 다음 글의 밑줄 친 부분 중 어법상 **틀린** 것을 고르시오.

> Kate and her husband went on a drive to the desert ① where they had never been before. The road ② that they traveled on went up into the mountains and then down the mountains into a flat area ③ which were very dry. The wind was blowing very hard and her husband, ④ whose car was very small, was worried about ⑤ keeping his car on the road.

O1 관계부사를 사용하여 주어진 문장을 보기처럼 다시 쓰시오.

> **보기** I was born on that day.
> → My birthday is the day when I was born.

1) Jesus was born on the day.

→ Christmas is the day _____

_____.

2) Many books are kept for reading in the place.

→ A library is the place _____

_____.

3) The Korean War broke out in that year.

→ 1950 was the year _____

_____.

O2 다음 우리말을 읽고 바르게 영작하시오.

나는 친구가 한 명 있다. 그는 내가 원하는 것은 무엇이든지 준다. 그는 내가 그를 필요로 할 때는 언제든지 나와 함께 한다. 그는 아무리 피곤할지라도, 나를 도와준다.

_____

_____

_____

_____

Chapter 11

일치와 화법

Chapter 미리보기

	평서문	의문문	명령문
전달 동사	say → say say to → tell	ask	tell ask advise order
형태	• say + (that) + 주어 + 동사 • tell + 목적어 + (that) + 주어 + 동사	• ask + (목적어) + 의문사 + (주어) + 동사 • ask + (목적어) + if + 주어 + 동사	• tell/ask/advise + 목적어 + to + 동사원형
예문	• He said, "I am happy." → He said that he was happy. • He said to me, "You look sad." → He told me that I looked sad.	• He said to me, "What is it?" → He asked me what it was. • He said to me, "Can you swim?" → He asked me if I could swim.	• He said to me,"Open it." → He told me to open it.

No news is good news.
▶ 무소식이 희소식이다.

36 수의 일치

A 주어와 동사의 수의 일치

주어가 단수일 때는 단수 동사, 주어가 복수일 때는 복수 동사로 일치시킨다.

> **ex** • He and I are the same age.
> • That book that I got from my parents was very interesting.

Tips
- 단수 동사
  is, was, has, had,
  일반동사 + -(e)s
- 복수 동사
  are, were, have, had,
  일반동사의 원형

B 주의해야 할 수의 일치

1 '-s'로 끝나는 나라 이름이나 과목명은 단수 취급한다.

나라 이름	Unites States, Philippines, Netherlands 등
과목명	mathematics, physics, economics, politics 등

> **ex** • The United States is very big.
> • Mathematics is easy for her.

2 each, every 다음에는 단수 동사가 온다.

> **ex** • Each of my friends is coming here.
> • Every child needs parent's love.

3 〈some/all/half/most/분수 + of + 단수 명사〉 → 단수 동사
〈some/all/half/most/분수 + of + 복수 명사〉 → 복수 동사

> **ex** • Most of the students have a cell phone.
> • Most of the cheese is rotten.

4 a number of와 the number of의 차이

a number of + 복수 명사	복수 동사	많은 ~
the number of + 복수 명사	단수 동사	~의 수

> **ex** • A number of students were late.
> • The number of students is thirty.

5 **the + 형용사** : '~하는 사람들'이란 의미로 복수 동사가 온다.

> **ex** • The poor have a lot of problems.

Tips
- the poor
  = poor people
  가난한 사람들

6 시간, 거리, 중량, 가격 등이 하나의 단위로 취급될 때 단수 동사가 온다.

> **ex** • Ten miles is too far to walk.

Grammar Check-Up

01 다음 중 알맞은 것을 고르시오.

1) Physics   is | are   my favorite subject.

2) Each of the students   have | has   an MP3 player.

3) The book about insects   was | were   interesting.

4) Three quarters of the earth   is | are   covered with water.

1) physics 물리학

3) insect 곤충

4) three quarters 3/4

02 다음 문장의 틀린 부분에 밑줄을 긋고 바르게 고쳐 쓰시오.

1) The apples that I bought at the shop was very expensive.

(→ _____)

2) Half of the students in the class comes from Korea. (→ _____)

3) Every teachers need a laptop computer.   (→ _____)

4) Eight hours are enough for me to sleep.   (→ _____)

03 빈칸에 주어진 단어의 알맞은 형태를 쓰시오.

1) No news _____ good news. (be)

2) Everybody in my family _____ singing and dancing. (enjoy)

3) The Philippines _____ located in south-east Asia. (be)

4) A number of people _____ English very well. (speak)

3) be located in
   ~에 위치해 있다

04 우리말과 일치하도록 빈칸에 알맞은 말을 쓰시오.

1) 이 방에 있는 아이들의 수는 다섯이다.

→ _____ _____ _____ _____ in

this room _____ five.

2) 부자들이 항상 행복한 것은 아니다.

→ _____ _____ _____ _____

always happy.

3) 수학은 나에게 쉽다.

→ _____ _____ _____ for me.

2) the rich 부자들

Unit 37 시제의 일치

시제의 일치란 주절과 종속절로 이루어진 복문에서 주절의 시제와 종속절의 시제를 일치시키는 것을 말한다.

A | 시제 일치의 원칙

1 주절의 시제가 현재일 때 종속절에는 모든 시제가 올 수 있다.

2 주절의 시제가 과거일 때 종속절에는 과거나 과거완료가 올 수 있다.

주절(현재) + 종속절(모든 시제)		주절(과거) + 종속절(과거, 과거완료)	
I know	that he is rich. (현재) that he was rich. (과거) that he will come. (미래) that he has lost it. (현재완료)	I knew	that he was rich. (과거) that he had been rich. (과거완료) that he would come. (과거) that he had lost it. (과거완료)

B | 시제 일치의 예외

1 현재의 반복된 습관은 주절과 관계없이 현재시제로만 쓴다.

> ex • I knew that she takes a walk at 10 o'clock every morning.
> • She said that she always drinks coffee without sugar and cream.

2 일반적 진리, 속담, 격언은 주절과 관계없이 항상 현재시제로만 쓴다.

> ex • My mother said that walls have ears.
> • The teacher said that light travels faster than sound.

3 역사적 사실은 주절의 시제와 관계없이 반드시 과거시제로만 쓴다.

> ex • The teacher said that World War II ended in 1945.
> • The teacher said that World War II had ended in 1945. (×)

4 가정법의 시제는 변하지 않는다.

> ex • He says that he would go to Paris if he were rich.
>   → He said that he would go to Paris if he were rich.

Grammar Check-Up

Note

01 다음 중 알맞은 것을 고르시오.

1) He saved money so that he   may | might   buy a house.

2) She told me that she   goes | went   mountain climbing every Sunday.

3) I thought that she   has been | had been   to Europe before.

4) The teacher said that the earth   is | was   round.

02 다음 문장의 주절을 과거시제로 바꿀 때 종속절을 완성하시오.

1) I think that he has lost his MP3 player.

　→ I thought that _____.

2) They believe that he will arrive soon.

　→ They believed that _____.

3) I know that he was late for school.

　→ I knew that _____.

03 다음 문장의 틀린 부분에 밑줄을 긋고 바르게 고쳐 쓰시오.

1) The teacher said that World War II had broken out in 1939.

(→ _____)

2) My little sister learned that two plus five was seven.

(→ _____)

3) My mother taught me that the sun set in the west.

(→ _____)

1) break out
　발생하다, 발발하다
3) set 지다

04 다음 우리말을 영작하시오.

1) 그는 해가 동쪽에서 뜬다고 말했다.

　→ He said that _____.

2) 그는 열심히 공부하겠다고 약속했다.

　→ He promised that _____.

1) rise 뜨다, 떠오르다

38 평서문의 화법전환

A 직접화법과 간접화법

1 직접화법은 다른 사람의 말을 그대로 인용하여 전달하는 것을 의미한다.

> ex • He said, "I was sick yesterday."

2 간접화법은 다른 사람의 말을 전달자의 입장으로 바꾸어서 말하는 것을 의미한다.

> ex • He said that he had been sick the day before.

B 평서문의 화법전환

> ⓐ 전달동사 say는 say로 say to는 tell로 바꾼다.
> ⓑ 콤마와 인용부호(" ")를 없애고 that을 쓴다. 이때 that은 생략이 가능하다.
> ⓒ 인용부호(" ") 안에 있는 인칭대명사는 전달하는 사람에 맞춘다.
> → 주로 인용부호 안의 1인칭은 주어에, 2인칭은 목적어에 맞춘다.
> ⓓ 시제를 일치시킨다. (현재 → 과거 / 과거, 현재완료 → 과거완료)

> ex • She said, "I am pretty."
> → She said that she was pretty.
> • He said to her, "I met your sister."
> → He told her that he had met her sister.

C 화법전환 시 부사와 지시대명사

직접화법을 간접화법으로 바꿀 때 부사나 지시대명사는 말하는 사람의 입장에 따라 바뀐다.

> • this → that   • here → there   • now → then
> • ago → before   • today → that day   • tomorrow → the next day, the following day
> • yesterday → the day before, the previous day

> ex • He said to me, "I am helping my mom now."
> → He told me that he was helping his mom then.
> • She said to him, "I was sick yesterday."
> → She told him that she had been sick the day before.

Grammar Check-Up

정답 및 해설 p.22

Note

O1 다음 중 알맞은 것을 고르시오.

1) He   said | says   that he will leave this country.

2) She   said | told | asked   him that she didn't like her job.

3) They said that they   had been | have been   there.

O2 직접화법을 간접화법으로 바꾸어 쓰시오.

1) My father said, "I am on vacation now."

→ My father _____.

2) He said to them, "You can't swim across the river."

→ He told them that _____.

3) She said to him, "I will meet your brother tomorrow."

→ She _____.

4) She said to me, "I haven't seen you for a long time."

→ She _____.

O3 간접화법을 직접화법으로 바꿀 때 빈칸에 알맞은 말을 쓰시오.

1) She told me that my sister had given a book to her.

→ She said to me, "_____ sister gave a book to _____."

2) He said that he was reading the novel.

→ He said, "I _____ _____ the novel."

O4 우리말과 일치하도록 빈칸에 알맞은 말을 쓰시오.

1) 그는 "나는 그 모임에 참석할 거야."라고 말했다.

→ He said, "_____ _____ _____ the
meeting."

→ He _____ that _____ _____
_____ the meeting.

2) 그는 나에게 행복해 보인다고 말했다.

→ He _____ me that _____ _____
_____.

1) attend 참석하다

39 의문문과 명령문의 화법전환

A 의문문의 화법전환

ⓐ 전달동사는 ask를 쓴다.
ⓑ 의문사가 있을 때는 〈의문사 + 주어 + 동사〉가 되며, 의문사가 없을 때는 〈if/whether + 주어 + 동사〉가 된다.
ⓒ 인칭대명사, 부사, 지시대명사의 전환과 시제 일치는 평서문과 동일하다.

ex • He said to her, "Where do you live?"
→ He asked her where she lived.
• He said to her, "Do you know my name?"
→ He asked her if she knew his name.

━⊕ 의문사가 주어일 경우는 〈의문사(= 주어) + 동사〉의 순으로 온다.

ex • My mother said to me, "Who broke this vase?"
→ My mother asked me who had broken that vase.
　　　　　　　　　　　　　　(의문사 주어) (동사)

B 명령문의 화법전환

ⓐ 명령문의 전달동사는 다음과 같이 바뀐다.
• 지시, 명령 → tell
• 부탁 → ask
• 충고 → advise
ⓑ 인용부호(" ") 안의 동사를 to부정사로 만든다.

ex • He said to me, "Read the sentence."
→ He told me to read the sentence.
• She said to me, "Please help me."
→ She asked me to help her.
• The doctor said to him, "Don't smoke too much."
→ The doctor advised him not to smoke too much.

Grammar Check-Up

정답 및 해설 p.22

O1 다음 중 알맞은 것을 고르시오.

1) He   said ǀ told   me to take medicine three times a day.

2) She   told ǀ said ǀ asked   me when my sister would leave.

3) He asked me what time   was it ǀ it was .

4) My father asked her where   did she live ǀ she lived .

1) take medicine
   약을 먹다

O2 직접화법을 간접화법으로 바꿀 때 문장을 완성하시오.

1) The doctor said to me, "Go to bed early."

   → The doctor advised me _____ .

2) The teacher said to me, "Don't be nervous."

   → The teacher told me _____ .

3) She said to me, "How did the accident happen?"

   → She asked me _____ .

4) I said to him, "May I use your cell phone?"

   → _____

2) nervous
   긴장한, 초조해 하는

3) accident 사고

O3 간접화법을 직접화법으로 바꿀 때 빈칸에 알맞은 말을 쓰시오.

1) He told me not to play the computer game.

   → He said to me, "_____ _____ the computer game."

2) My mother asked me where I had put the meat.

   → My mother said to me, "_____ _____ _____
     put the meat?"

O4 우리말과 일치하도록 문장을 완성하시오.

1) 그녀는 나에게 수영할 수 있는지 물었다.

   → She asked me _____ .

2) 그는 나에게 조용히 해 달라고 부탁했다.

   → He asked _____ .

3) 나는 그녀에게 무엇이 필요한지 물었다.

   → I asked her _____ .

내신 족집게 문제

[01-03] 빈칸에 알맞은 단어를 순서대로 바르게 짝지은 것을 고르시오.

01
- Growing flowers _____ my hobby.
- Economics _____ popular at this university.

① is – is   ② is – are   ③ are – are
④ are – is   ⑤ has – is

02
- Some of the furniture _____ secondhand.
- Some of the chairs _____ broken.

① is – is   ② is – are   ③ are – are
④ are – is   ⑤ has – is

03
- A number of old people _____ helped by him.
- The number of old people _____ increasing.

① is – is   ② is – are   ③ are – are
④ are – is   ⑤ has – is

[04-06] 빈칸에 들어갈 알맞은 것을 고르시오.

04
I learned that the moon _____ around the earth.

① went   ② goes   ③ had gone
④ will go   ⑤ has gone

05
Did you know that the American War of Independence _____ in 1775?

① had begun   ② began   ③ has begun
④ begins   ⑤ begun

06
She asked me _____.

① how much is it   ② how much it is
③ how much was it   ④ how much it was
⑤ how it was much

[07-10] 직접화법을 간접화법으로 바꿀 때 빈칸에 알맞은 말을 쓰시오.

07
He said to me, "I am waiting for you."

→ He _____ me that _____
_____.

08
My father said to me, "Shine my shoes."

→ My father told me _____.

09
She said to me, "What can I do for you?"

→ She _____ me _____
_____.

10
He said to her, "Do you remember my name?"

→ He asked her _____
_____.

11 다음 중 올바른 문장을 고르시오.

① She said that she will keep her promise.
② My mother asked me to open the window.
③ The rich is getting richer.
④ He said that Columbus had discovered America in 1492.
⑤ The United States have a population of around 250 million.

[12-13] 보기의 문장을 간접화법으로 바르게 바꾼 것을 고르시오.

12 보기 He said to me, "Don't eat junk food."

① He told me don't to eat junk food.
② He told me that he didn't eat junk food.
③ He told me to didn't eat junk food.
④ He told me to not eat junk food.
⑤ He told me not to eat junk food.

13 보기 My mother said to me, "Who broke the cup?"

① My mother told me who broke the cup.
② My mother asked me who the cup had broken.
③ My mother asked me who had broken the cup.
④ My mother asked me who broke the cup.
⑤ My mother told me who had broken the cup.

14 다음 중 어법상 <u>틀린</u> 문장을 고르시오.

① Each of the students have his own locker.
② Most children like to go to the zoo.
③ She said that she takes a shower every day.
④ She told me that she had met my brother the day before.
⑤ My teacher taught us that water boils at 100°C.

15 빈칸에 들어갈 알맞은 것을 고르시오.

> She asked him _____.

① that how often he played tennis
② how often did he play tennis
③ how often did you play tennis
④ how often he played tennis
⑤ how often he plays tennis

[16-17] 간접화법을 직접화법으로 바꿀 때 빈칸에 알맞은 말을 쓰시오.

16 He asked me whether I was angry.

→ He said to me, "_____ _____ angry?"

17 My mother asked her when she had eaten lunch.

→ My mother said to her, "_____ _____ _____ eat lunch?"

[18-20] 우리말과 일치하도록 빈칸에 알맞은 말을 쓰시오.

18 모든 학생들이 지금 노래를 부르고 있다.

→ Every _____ _____ singing now.

19 그녀는 나에게 몇 살인지 물었다.

→ She asked me _____ _____ _____ _____.

20 나는 그녀에게 휴식을 취하라고 충고했다.

→ I advised _____ _____ _____ _____ _____.

정답 및 해설 p.23

01 다음 글의 밑줄 친 부분 중 어법상 틀린 것을 고르시오.

> When I was a high school student, the number of the students in my class ① were 60. Most of them didn't bring a lunch box ② because of their poverty. Also, a number of ③ students didn't go to college and had to get a job after graduation. On the other hand, these days, there ④ are about 30 students in one class. Some of them go on a diet to lose weight. In addition, most students go to college or go abroad to study. As time has passed, a lot of things ⑤ have changed.

■ poverty 가난　■ graduation 졸업

01 거리에서 친구를 만났다. 보기처럼 그 친구가 내게 말한 것들을 각각 간접화법으로 바꾸어 쓰시오.

> 보기　"How are you?"
>　　→ He asked me how I was.

1) "Where are you going?"

→ He asked me _____.

2) "Did you get a job?"

→ He asked me _____.

3) "Say hello to your parents."

→ He told me _____.

02 다음 빈칸에 들어갈 말로 가장 적절한 것을 고르시오.

> My roommate came into the room and asked me why I wasn't in class. I said that I had a cold. She asked me Ⓐ_____.
> I replied that there was nothing to eat. She boiled rice oatmeal for me. She advised me Ⓑ_____ to a doctor. After I ate the oatmeal, I said Ⓒ_____ to the doctor after a while. She said that she hoped I would get well soon and she went out. I said, "Thank you for the oatmeal."

■ oatmeal 죽

	Ⓐ	Ⓑ	Ⓒ
①	what did I need	go	that I will go
②	what did I need	to go	that I would go
③	what I needed	go	that I would go
④	what I needed	to go	that I will go
⑤	what I needed	to go	that I would go

02 다음 우리말을 읽고 바르게 영작하시오.

나는 어제 소개팅을 했다. 그는 나에게 취미가 뭐냐고 물었다. 그는 피아노 치는 것을 좋아한다고 말했다. 그는 나에게 피아노를 칠 수 있는지 물었다. 나는 칠 줄 모른다고 말했다.

_____

_____

_____

_____

_____

■ have a blind date 소개팅을 하다

Chapter 12

가정법

- ♠ **Unit 40** 가정법 과거, 과거완료, 현재
- ♠ **Unit 41** I wish, as if, without/but for

Chapter 미리보기

가정법 과거	If + 주어 + 동사의 과거형, 주어 + would/could + 동사원형
I wish 과거	I wish + 주어 + 동사의 과거형
as if 과거	as if + 주어 + 동사의 과거형
without/but for 과거	without/but for + 명사, 주어 + would/could + 동사원형
가정법 과거완료	If + 주어 + had p.p, 주어 + would/could have p.p
I wish 과거완료	I wish + 주어 + had p.p
as if 과거완료	as if + 주어 + had p.p
without/but for 과거완료	without/but for + 명사, 주어 + would/could have p.p

If at first you don't succeed, try, try again.
만약 처음에 당신이 성공하지 못하면, 시도하고 또 다시 시도하라.

▶ 칠전팔기

Unit 40 가정법 과거, 과거완료, 현재

A 가정법 과거

현재 사실과 반대되는 일이나 실현 가능성이 희박한 일을 가정하여 말할 때 사용한다.

> If + 주어 + 동사의 과거형/were, 주어 + would/could + 동사원형 (만약 ~한다면, …할 텐데)

ex
- If I were an American, I could speak English fluently.
  = As I am not an American, I can't speak English fluently.

B 가정법 과거완료

과거 사실과 반대되는 일을 가정하여 말할 때 사용한다.

> If + 주어 + had p.p, 주어 + would/could have p.p (만약 ~했다면, …했을 텐데)

ex
- If we had finished our homework, we could have gone to the cinema.
  = As we didn't finish our homework, we couldn't go to the cinema.
- If I had had money, I could have bought some ice cream.
  = As I didn't have money, I couldn't buy any ice cream.

C 가정법에서 if의 생략

가정법에서 if를 생략할 수 있는데, 이 때 주어와 동사의 위치가 바뀌어 동사가 문장의 맨 앞에 나온다.

ex
- If I were a prince, I would marry a princess.
  = Were I a prince, I would marry a princess.

D 가정법 현재

현재나 미래에 대한 불확실한 상황을 가정할 때 사용한다.

> If + 주어 + 동사의 현재형, 주어 + will/can + 동사원형 (만약 ~한다면, …할 것이다)

ex
- If it is sunny tomorrow, we will go to the park.

E 가정법 과거, 과거완료 그리고 현재의 비교

	실현 가능성	문장 형식
가정법 과거	×	If + 주어 + 동사의 과거형, 주어 + would/could + 동사원형
가정법 과거완료	×	If + 주어 + had p.p, 주어 + would/could + have p.p
가정법 현재	○	If + 주어 + 동사의 현재형, 주어 + will/can + 동사원형

Grammar Check-Up

정답 및 해설 p.23

01 다음 중 알맞은 것을 고르시오.

1) Kate didn't wear her coat. If she   wears | wore | had worn   her coat, she   caught | wouldn't catch | wouldn't have caught   a cold.

2) They are not here. If they   are | were | had been   here, they   enjoy | will enjoy | would enjoy   the party.

1) catch a cold
감기에 걸리다

02 빈칸에 주어진 동사의 알맞은 형태를 쓰시오.

1) If he _____ a girl, he would wear a skirt. (be)

2) If I had studied hard, I _____ a good grade. (get)

3) If it _____ rainy, they will stay at home. (be)

03 두 문장의 뜻이 같도록 문장을 완성하시오.

1) Were I you, I would study abroad.

  = If _____ .

2) As it didn't snow, we couldn't make a snowman.

  = If _____ .

04 밑줄 친 부분에 주의하여 다음 문장을 우리말로 해석하시오.

1) If it weren't raining, we would go to the park.

  → _____

2) If we had woken up late, we would have been late for school.

  → _____

05 우리말과 일치하도록 주어진 말을 바르게 배열하시오.

1) 내가 선생님이라면, 학생들에게 숙제를 내주지 않을 텐데.
   (homework, if, give, I, would, students, a, were, not, I, any, teacher, my)

  → _____

2) 우리가 그 경기에서 이긴다면, 상금을 받을 것이다.
   (get, the, we, will, game, we, if, win, some, prize money)

  → _____

2) prize money 상금

Unit 41 I wish, as if, without/but for

A I wish

I wish + 주어 + 동사의 과거형 (~라면 좋을 텐데)
I wish + 주어 + had p.p (~이었다면 좋을 텐데)

ex
- I wish I were a magician. (내가 마술사라면 좋을 텐데.)
  = I am sorry I am not a magician. (직설법)
- I wish I had been a millionaire. (내가 백만장자였다면 좋을 텐데.)
  = I am sorry I wasn't a millionaire. (직설법)

B as if

주어 + 동사 + as if + 주어 + 동사의 과거형 (마치 ~인 것처럼 …한다)
주어 + 동사 + as if + 주어 + had p.p (마치 ~였던 것처럼 …한다)

ex
- She talks as if she were a princess. (그녀는 마치 공주인 것처럼 말한다.)
  = In fact she is not a princess. (직설법)
- She talks as if she had met the prince. (그녀는 마치 왕자를 만났던 것처럼 말한다.)
  = In fact she didn't meet the prince. (직설법)

C without/but for

Without/But for + 명사, 주어 + would/could + 동사원형 (~가 없다면 …할 텐데)
Without/But for + 명사, 주어 + would/could have p.p (~가 없었다면 …했을 텐데)

ex
- Without/But for email, I couldn't keep in touch with him.
  = If it were not for email, I couldn't keep in touch with him.
  = Were it not for email, I couldn't keep in touch with him.
- Without/But for his help, I wouldn't have passed the test.
  = If it had not been for his help, I wouldn't have passed the test.
  = Had it not been for his help, I wouldn't have passed the test.

I wish, as if, without/but for절에서는 if 가정법에서처럼 현재 사실과 반대되는 일을 말할 때 과거시제를, 과거 사실과 반대되는 일을 말할 때 과거완료시제를 사용한다.

Note

01 다음 중 알맞은 것을 고르시오.

1) He isn't a police officer. He acts as if he   is | were | had been   a police officer.

2) Kate didn't meet the Queen. She talks as if she   meets | met | had met   the Queen.

3) I don't have a bicycle. I wish I   have | had | had had   a bicycle.

02 두 문장의 뜻이 같도록 빈칸에 알맞은 말을 쓰시오.

1) Without fast food, she would be healthier.

= If _____, she would be healthier.

2) But for our teacher, we would have failed the exam.

= If _____, we would have failed the exam.

3) In fact he is not a lawyer.

= He acts as if _____.

3) lawyer 변호사

03 밑줄 친 부분에 주의하여 다음 문장을 우리말로 해석하시오.

1) Susan talks <u>as if she had been to</u> Africa.

→ _____

2) <u>Without you</u>, I <u>couldn't have finished</u> my homework.

→ _____

3) <u>I wish I had already finished</u> my homework.

→ _____

04 다음 우리말을 영작하시오.

1) 그들은 마치 서로 모르는 것처럼 말한다.

→ _____

2) 그때 내게 카메라가 있었다면 좋을 텐데.

→ _____

1) each other 서로
2) then 그때

[01-02] 우리말과 일치하도록 빈칸에 알맞은 말을 쓰시오.

01 내가 머리가 아프지 않다면, 잠을 잘 잘 텐데.

→ If I _____ _____ a headache, I
would sleep well.

02 그가 영어를 열심히 공부했다면, 영어를 잘했을 텐데.

→ If he _____ _____ English hard,
he would have been good at English.

03 두 문장의 뜻이 같도록 빈칸에 알맞은 말을 고르시오.

In fact Kevin is unhappy.

= Kevin acts as if he _____ happy.

① be   ② were   ③ has been
④ had been   ⑤ is being

04 대화의 빈칸에 들어갈 알맞은 것을 고르시오.

A: Do you have a car?

B: No, I don't. I wish I _____ one.

① have   ② don't have   ③ have not
④ had   ⑤ having

05 문맥상 빈칸에 들어갈 알맞은 문장을 고르시오.

Jane is in trouble. She is your friend. _____.

① If I were you, I would not have helped her
② If I were not you, I would help her
③ If I were you, I would help her
④ If I had not been you, I would have helped her
⑤ If I had been you, I would have helped her

[06-08] 두 문장의 뜻이 같도록 문장을 완성하시오.

06 I wish I could play the violin.

= I am sorry _____.

07 They act as if nothing had happened to them.

= In fact _____.

08 If it had not been for you, he wouldn't have
finished the project.

= _____ you, he wouldn't
have finished the project.

[09-10] 가정법을 이용하여 다음 문장을 완성하시오.

09 John isn't a millionaire but he talks as if

_____.

10 Ann didn't see a real penguin but she talks
as if _____.

[11-12] 빈칸에 들어갈 알맞은 것을 고르시오.

11 If he _____ home early, he wouldn't have
missed the school bus.

① leave   ② leaves   ③ left
④ has left   ⑤ had left

12 What would you do if you _____ your
school bag?

① lose   ② loses   ③ lost
④ to lose   ⑤ losing

13 다음 문장을 if를 생략하여 다시 쓰시오.

If I had known your address, I would have sent you a letter.

→ _____

_____

14 두 문장의 뜻이 같도록 빈칸에 알맞은 말을 쓰시오.

If I _____ the cup, I _____ _____ another one.

= As I broke the cup, I bought another one.

15 빈칸에 들어갈 수 <u>없는</u> 것을 고르시오.

_____ computers, our lives would be different.

① Without   ② But for
③ If it were not for   ④ Were it not for
⑤ If it had not been for

16 보기의 문장과 의미가 같은 것을 고르시오.

보기 As Tom didn't like it, he gave it to me.

① If Tom had not liked it, he would not have given it to me.
② If Tom had liked it, he would have given it to me.
③ If Tom had liked it, he would not have given it to me.
④ If Tom liked it, he would give it to me.
⑤ If Tom didn't liked it, he would not give it to me.

[17-18] 주어진 단어를 알맞은 형태로 바꾸어 빈칸에 쓰시오.

17 If I had lived near my school, I _____ _____ late for school. (not, be)

18 If it _____ sunny tomorrow, we will go hiking. (be)

19 다음 중 올바른 문장을 고르시오.

① If I were her, I would have been sad.
② If it were sunny, we will go hiking.
③ If they had come to the concert, they would like it.
④ If we had some money, we could have had lunch.
⑤ If he hadn't played games, he could have finished his homework.

20 두 문장의 뜻이 같지 <u>않은</u> 것을 고르시오.

① I wish I had known his phone number.
  = I am sorry I didn't know his phone number.
② If she heard the rumor, she would be surprised.
  = As she doesn't hear the rumor, she won't be surprised.
③ If it had not been for water, they wouldn't have survived.
  = Had it not been for water, they wouldn't have survived.
④ She acts as if she were a princess.
  = In fact she isn't a princess.
⑤ If I spoke French, I could sing a French song.
  = As I don't speak French, I couldn't sing a French song.

O1 다음 글의 밑줄 친 부분 중 어법상 **틀린** 것을 고르시오.

> Pluto was the brother of Zeus. He was the god of the underworld. He also controlled some demons and they helped him ① to rule over dead people. His main concern was to increase the number of his subjects. He didn't allow his subjects ② to leave his underworld. He ③ will become very angry if anyone tried to leave, or ④ if someone tried to steal his food from him. ⑤ Very few escaped from the underworld.

■ underworld 저승　■ demon 악마　■ subject 신하

O2 다음 괄호 안에서 어법에 맞는 표현으로 가장 적절한 것을 고르시오.

> The bird flu usually only infects birds or pigs. Some kinds of bird flu cause only mild symptoms in birds. For example, if I Ⓐ(am / were) a bird, I would produce less eggs. Others are more dangerous to birds. They spread quickly, and kill the birds. A few years ago a kind of bird flu infected people in Asia. It cannot be spread from person to person. If they Ⓑ(didn't touch / hadn't touched) infected birds, they wouldn't have become infected. If you Ⓒ(will want / want) to protect yourself from bird flu, you should wash your hands with soap and water many times a day.

■ bird flu 조류 독감　■ infect 전염시키다
■ symptom 증상

	Ⓐ	Ⓑ	Ⓒ
①	am	– didn't touch	– will want
②	am	– didn't touch	– want
③	were	– didn't touch	– will want
④	were	– hadn't touched	– want
⑤	were	– hadn't touched	– will want

O1 다음 문장을 I wish로 시작하는 문장으로 다시 쓰시오.

1) It was raining. I didn't have an umbrella.

→ I wish _____ .

2) I am hungry. I don't have anything to eat.

→ I wish _____ .

3) I love music but I am not a good singer.

→ I wish _____ .

O2 다음 우리말을 읽고 바르게 영작하시오.

우리 반 친구 케빈은 키가 크고 잘생겼다. 그는 왕자처럼 행동한다. 그는 항상 나비넥타이를 맨다. 만약 내가 그라면 나비넥타이는 매지 않을 텐데. 만약 그가 우리에게 호의적이었다면 우리는 그를 회장으로 선출했을 텐데. 우리는 그를 회장으로 뽑지 않았다.

My classmate, Kevin, is tall and handsome.

_____

_____

_____

_____

We didn't elect him president.

■ bow tie 나비넥타이　■ friendly 호의적인
■ president 회장

Chapter

13

특수구문
- ⚙ **Unit 42** 강조구문과 부정구문
- ⚙ **Unit 43** 도치와 생략

Chapter 미리보기

강조 구문	It is/was ~ that …	It was the book that I lost yesterday.
	do/does/did + 동사원형	Kate does speak five languages.
	의문사 + on earth	What on earth are you doing?
부정 구문	부분 부정 : 부정어 + all, every, always, both	Not all of us liked the movie. The rich are not always happy.
	전체 부정 : neither, no one, none, never	None of them cried.
도치	장소 부사(구) + 동사 + 주어(명사) 장소 부사(구) + 주어(대명사) + 동사	Here comes the train. Here it comes.
	부정 부사(never, hardly) + 조동사 + 주어	Never will I forget it.
	긍정문 : So + 동사 + 주어 부정문 : Neither + 동사 + 주어	So do I. Neither do I.

All that glitters is not gold. 반짝이는 것이 모두 금은 아니다.
▶ 겉만 보고 판단하지 마라.

42 강조구문과 부정구문

A 강조구문

1 It is/was ~ that … : '~한 것은 바로 …이다'

① 강조하는 부분을 It is/was와 that 사이에 둔다. 그러나 동사는 강조할 수 없다.

ex • Kate went to the restaurant to have lunch with Jessica.

→ It was Kate that went to the restaurant to have lunch with Jessica.

→ It was to the restaurant that Kate went to have lunch with Jessica.

→ It was went that Kate to the restaurant to have lunch with Jessica. (×)

② 강조하는 부분에 따라 that 대신에 who(m), which, when, where 등을 사용할 수 있다.

ex • It was Kate that/who went to the restaurant to have lunch with Jessica.

2 강조의 do : '정말로, 진짜로'
동사를 강조하며 〈do/does/did + 동사원형〉의 형태로 쓴다.

ex • I do like to watch football.

• Kate does play basketball on Saturday.

• Kate did bake a delicious chocolate cake.

3 의문사 + on earth : '도대체'

ex • What on earth are you doing?

• Why on earth did you go there?

B 부정구문

1 부분 부정 : '항상/모두/반드시 ~인 것은 아니다'라고 해석하며, 〈부정어 + all, every, always, both〉의
형태로 사용한다.

ex • The rich are not always happy.

• Not all of them cried.

2 전체 부정 : '결코(아무도) ~하지 않다'라고 해석하며, neither, no one, none, never를 사용한다.

ex • None of them cried.

• Neither of us is shy.

= Either of us is not shy.

• They are never happy.

Grammar Check-Up

Note

O1 밑줄 친 부분을 강조하고자 할 때 빈칸에 알맞은 말을 쓰시오.

1) Paul <u>helps</u> them with their homework.

→ Paul _____ help them with their homework.

2) John <u>met</u> Jane for lunch.

→ John _____ meet Jane for lunch.

3) I <u>buy</u> books at a secondhand bookstore.

→ I _____ buy books at a secondhand bookstore.

1) help A with B
   A가 B하는 것을 돕다

3) secondhand
   중고의

O2 두 문장의 뜻이 같도록 빈칸에 알맞은 말을 쓰시오.

1) Some students went to the stadium, but others didn't.

= _____ _____ of the students went to the stadium.

2) Neither of us knew him.

= _____ of us _____ know him.

O3 밑줄 친 부분을 강조하여 다음 문장을 다시 쓰시오.

1) <u>Kate</u> went to the supermarket to buy eggs.

→ It _____ to the supermarket to buy eggs.

2) Kevin likes to make <u>model cars</u>.

→ It _____ to make.

3) Susan met Tom <u>at a restaurant</u> yesterday.

→ It _____ yesterday.

O4 다음 우리말을 영작하시오.

1) 아기가 항상 우는 것은 아니다.

→ _____

2) 그들 중 어느 누구도 도서관에 가지 않았다.

→ _____

3) 너는 도대체 왜 그렇게 했어?

→ _____

43 도치와 생략

보통 문장의 어순은 〈주어 + 동사 + 보어(또는 목적어) + 수식어〉이나 문장에서 특정한 어구가 주어 앞에 와서 문장의 어순이 바뀌는 것을 도치라고 한다.

A 장소, 방향 부사(구)의 도치

1 주어가 명사일 때는 〈부사구 + 동사 + 주어〉의 형태이다.

> **ex** • Your teacher comes here. → Here comes your teacher.

2 주어가 대명사일 때는 〈부사구 + 주어 + 동사〉의 형태이다.

> **ex** • He comes here. → Here he comes.

B 부정부사의 도치

Tips
• 부정부사
never, hardly, little,
seldom, rarely 등

부정부사가 문장의 맨 앞으로 나오면 〈부정부사 + 조동사 + 주어 + 동사원형〉의 어순이 된다.

> **ex** • I will never do that again. → Never will I do that again.

C so, neither 도치

1 긍정문일 때는 〈So + 동사 + 주어〉의 어순으로 쓰고, '~도 그래'의 의미이다.

> **ex** • A: I am so happy.   B: So am I.
> • A: I like skiing.   B: So do I.

2 부정문일 때는 〈Neither + 동사 + 주어〉의 어순으로 쓰고, '~도 그래'의 의미이다.

> **ex** • A: I am not busy.   B: Neither am I.
> • A: I didn't meet her.   B: Neither did I.

D 생략

1 부사절에서 〈주어(대명사) + be동사〉는 생략이 가능하다.

> **ex** • Though (he is) poor, he is happy.

2 목적격 관계대명사나 〈주격 관계대명사 + be동사〉는 생략이 가능하다.

> **ex** • This is the man (whom) my sister invited to the party.
> • The girl (who is) running there is my daughter.

3 목적절을 이끄는 접속사 that은 생략이 가능하다.

> **ex** • I think (that) she will come soon.

4 반복 어구는 생략이 가능하다.

> **ex** • I love him more than she (loves him).

Note

Q1 다음 중 알맞은 것을 고르시오.

1) **A** I have seen a koala. **B** So｜Neither have I.

2) **A** I am not good at math. **B** So｜Neither am I.

3) **A** She bought the book. **B** So does｜did he.

Q2 주어진 단어로 시작하여 문장을 다시 쓰시오.

1) I have never been to such a beautiful place.

→ Never _____ to such a beautiful place.

2) A gingko nut fell down.

→ Down _____.

3) He comes here.

→ Here _____.

4) He hardly agrees with me.

→ Hardly _____.

2) gingko nut 은행

Q3 다음 문장에서 생략된 부분을 넣어 문장을 다시 쓰시오.

1) She was very wise when young.

→ _____

2) Look at the old castle built 100 years ago.

→ _____

3) These are the glasses we bought in this shop.

→ _____

2) castle 성

Q4 우리말과 일치하도록 문장을 완성하시오.

1) 나는 그녀의 이름을 결코 잊지 못할 것이다.

→ Never _____.

2) 나는 아프리카에 가 본 적이 없다. 그녀도 또한 그렇다.

→ I have never been to Africa. _____

01 밑줄 친 부분을 강조할 때 빈칸에 알맞은 말을 쓰시오.

Kevin <u>went</u> to the zoo with Jane yesterday.

→ Kevin _____ _____ to the zoo
with Jane yesterday.

02 괄호 안의 말을 강조하여 다음 질문에 대한 답을 완성하시오.

A: What did you buy at the shop yesterday?

B: It _____ _____ _____

_____ _____ _____ at the
shop yesterday. (a bag)

03 보기의 밑줄 친 do동사와 쓰임이 같은 것을 고르시오.

보기 Kate <u>does</u> speak five languages.

① I <u>don't</u> believe what she said.
② They <u>did</u> win a championship last year.
③ Why <u>did</u> you do that?
④ We don't know the answer, <u>do</u> we?
⑤ He <u>did</u> his homework.

04 보기와 의미가 같은 문장을 고르시오.

보기 Not all of them were police officers.

① Any of them were not police officers.
② None of them were police officers.
③ They were police officers.
④ They were not police officers.
⑤ Some of them were police officers.

05 동사를 강조하여 질문에 대답할 때 빈칸에 알맞은 말을 쓰시오.

A: Why didn't you have lunch?

B: I _____ _____ lunch. I ate a tuna
sandwich.

[06-07] 두 문장의 뜻이 같도록 빈칸에 알맞은 말을 쓰시오.

06 Kate had breakfast yesterday but she didn't
have breakfast today.

= Kate does not _____ have breakfast.

07 Neither of us liked to play football with them.

= _____ of us _____ to play football
with them.

08 다음 보기의 밑줄 친 that과 쓰임이 같은 것을 고르시오.

보기 It was the English textbook <u>that</u> Kate lost
yesterday.

① <u>That</u> car is my uncle's.
② I think <u>that</u> he is genius.
③ I read the book <u>that</u> you gave me.
④ The problem is <u>that</u> someone stole the bag.
⑤ It is a new MP3 player <u>that</u> I want to buy.

09 밑줄 친 do동사의 쓰임이 나머지와 <u>다른</u> 것을 고르시오.

① We <u>do</u> like to play table tennis with them.
② They <u>did</u> finish their homework yesterday.
③ Please <u>do</u> come in.
④ Paul <u>did</u> his best.
⑤ Kate <u>does</u> have a question to ask.

10 보기를 강조한 문장이 <u>잘못된</u> 것을 고르시오.

> 보기 Kate and Kevin met Harry and Susan in the gymnasium yesterday.

① It was Kate and Kevin that met Harry and Susan in the gymnasium yesterday.

② It was met that Kate and Kevin Harry and Susan in the gymnasium yesterday.

③ It was Harry and Susan that Kate and Kevin met in the gymnasium yesterday.

④ It was in the gymnasium that Kate and Kevin met Harry and Susan yesterday.

⑤ It was yesterday that Kate and Kevin met Harry and Susan in the gymnasium.

[11-13] 주어진 단어로 시작하여 문장을 다시 쓰시오.

11 The bird flew away.

→ Away _____.

12 I have never thought her to be beautiful.

→ Never _____ her to be beautiful.

13 She hardly goes to the movies.

→ Hardly _____ to the movies.

[14-15] 우리말과 일치하도록 빈칸에 알맞은 말을 쓰시오.

14 A: I couldn't get up early in the morning.

B: _____ _____ I. (나도 그래.)

15 A: He thought the exam was easy.

B: _____ _____ she. (그녀도 그래.)

16 밑줄 친 부분 중 생략할 수 <u>없는</u> 것을 고르시오.

① He fell asleep while <u>he was</u> watching TV.

② I tried to forget her, but I failed to <u>forget her</u>.

③ He told me <u>that</u> he would be here at five.

④ This is the man <u>who</u> Jane loves.

⑤ The woman <u>who</u> won the lottery is very happy.

17 다음 중 어법상 틀린 문장을 고르시오.

① There lived a poor farmer in a village.

② Here comes it.

③ Little did I dream of seeing her here.

④ On the bench is a book.

⑤ Here comes the bus.

18 다음 문장에서 생략된 부분을 넣어 문장을 다시 쓰시오.

> The woman drinking coffee next to me is a famous actress.

→ _____

_____

19 두 문장에서 공통으로 생략된 것을 고르시오.

- They expect the president will lose the election.
- The woman he fell in love with was very beautiful.

① who   ② which   ③ whom
④ that   ⑤ whose

20 다음 중 올바른 것을 고르시오.

① A: I need a vacation.   B: So I do.

② A: She isn't a student.   B: Neither isn't he.

③ He did made this pizza.

④ It is you that is wrong.

⑤ Down came the rain.

정답 및 해설 **p.26**

O1 다음 글의 밑줄 친 부분 중 어법상 틀린 것을 고르시오.

It is global warming ① that threatens human lives and wildlife. ② Some international climate organizations warn that the world's poorer nations ③ does face rising rates of death and disease. This is because greenhouse gas emissions ④ increase the risk of droughts, floods, storms and other severe climate effects. Weather specialists have said that a global temperature rise of 1.5 to 2.5℃ could ⑤ kill 30 percent of animal and plant species.

- threaten 위협하다   - organization 협회
- greenhouse gas emission 온실가스 배출   - drought 가뭄

O2 다음 빈칸에 들어갈 말로 가장 적절한 것을 고르시오.

When Ⓐ_____ I used to go fishing with my grandfather at night. At that time, fishing with him was only my pleasure. The night sky of the country was very clear, so we could see a lot of stars in the very dark night sky. They were shining Ⓑ_____ for us not to get lost on our way to the sea. While he was fishing, I liked counting stars or hearing fish swimming. My grandfather passed away. I have never fished at night since then. Never Ⓒ_____ forget fishing with him at night.

	Ⓐ		Ⓑ		Ⓒ
①	young	–	brightly enough	–	will I
②	young	–	enough brightly	–	I will
③	I young	–	enough brightly	–	I will
④	I young	–	brightly enough	–	will I
⑤	I was young	–	enough brightly	–	I will

O1 보기의 문장을 참고하여 각각의 질문에 강조구문을 사용하여 대답하시오.

보기 Kate gave Paul an English book yesterday.

1) Ⓐ What did Kate give Paul yesterday?

Ⓑ It _____

_____.

2) Ⓐ When did Kate give Paul an English book?

Ⓑ It _____

_____.

3) Ⓐ Who gave Paul an English book yesterday?

Ⓑ It _____

_____.

O2 다음 우리말을 읽고 바르게 영작하시오.

케빈 : 나는 여기서 만났던 친절한 사람들을 결코 잊지 못할 거야.

톰 : 나도 그래. 내가 미래에 살고 싶은 곳은 바로 시골이야.

케빈 : 나도 그래.

Kevin : _____

_____

Tom : _____

_____

Kevin : _____

불규칙
동사 변화표

불규칙 동사 변화표

현재	과거	과거분사
blow 불다	blew	blown
broadcast 방송하다	broadcast	broadcast
build 세우다	built	built
buy 사다	bought	bought
catch 잡다	caught	caught
choose 고르다	chose	chosen
cost 비용이 들다	cost	cost
creep 기다	crept	crept
deal 다루다	dealt	dealt
dig 파다	dug	dug
draw 그리다	drew	drawn
eat 먹다	ate	eaten
fight 싸우다	fought	fought
fit ~에 적합하다	fit	fit
forget 잊다	forgot	forgotten
forgive 용서하다	forgave	forgiven
freeze 얼리다	froze	frozen
give 주다	gave	given
hang 걸다	hung	hung
hide 숨다, 숨기다	hid	hidden

현재	과거	과거분사
hit 치다	hit	hit
hold 잡다, 개최하다	held	held
hurt 다치다	hurt	hurt
keep 간직하다	kept	kept
lay ~을 눕히다	laid	laid
lead 이끌다, 인도하다	led	led
lie 눕다, 놓여 있다	lay	lain
light 불을 켜다	lit(lighted)	lit(lighted)
lose 잃어버리다	lost	lost
mean 의미하다	meant	meant
meet 만나다	met	met
pay 지불하다	paid	paid
put 놓다	put	put
quit 그만두다	quit	quit
ride 타다	rode	ridden
rise 오르다	rose	risen
set ~을 놓다	set	set
seek 찾다	sought	sought
shake 흔들다	shook	shaken
shine 비추다	shone(shined)	shone(shined)

현재	과거	과거분사
shoot 쏘다, 발사하다	shot	shot
show 보여주다	showed	shown(showed)
shut 닫다	shut	shut
sleep 잠자다	slept	slept
slide 미끄러지다	slid	slid
speak 말하다	spoke	spoken
spread 펴다, 살포하다	spread	spread
steal 훔치다	stole	stolen
stick 찌르다, 들러붙다	stuck	stuck
strike 일격을 가하다	struck	struck
swear 맹세하다	swore	sworn
take 데리고 가다	took	taken
tear 찢다	tore	torn
throw 던지다	threw	thrown
understand 이해하다	understood	understood
wake 잠을 깨다	woke	woken
wear 입다	wore	worn
weep 울다	wept	wept
withdraw (뒤로) 물러나다	withdrew	withdrawn
write 쓰다	wrote	written

불규칙이니까
무조건
외워야 해!

다음 동사의 과거형과 과거분사형을 써보세요.

현재	과거	과거분사
blow 불다		
broadcast 방송하다		
build 세우다		
buy 사다		
catch 잡다		
choose 고르다		
cost 비용이 들다		
creep 기다		
deal 다루다		
dig 파다		
draw 그리다		
eat 먹다		
fight 싸우다		
fit ～에 적합하다		
forget 잊다		
forgive 용서하다		
freeze 얼리다		
give 주다		
hang 걸다		
hide 숨다, 숨기다		

현재	과거	과거분사
hit 치다		
hold 잡다, 개최하다		
hurt 다치다		
keep 간직하다		
lay ～을 눕히다		
lead 이끌다, 인도하다		
lie 눕다, 놓여 있다		
light 불을 켜다		
lose 잃어버리다		
mean 의미하다		
meet 만나다		
pay 지불하다		
put 놓다		
quit 그만두다		
ride 타다		
rise 오르다		
set ～을 놓다		
seek 찾다		
shake 흔들다		
shine 비추다		

현재	과거	과거분사
shoot 쏘다, 발사하다		
show 보여주다		
shut 닫다		
sleep 잠자다		
slide 미끄러지다		
speak 말하다		
spread 펴다, 살포하다		
steal 훔치다		
stick 찌르다, 들러붙다		
strike 일격을 가하다		
swear 맹세하다		
take 데리고 가다		
tear 찢다		
throw 던지다		
understand 이해하다		
wake 잠을 깨다		
wear 입다		
weep 울다		
withdraw (뒤로) 물러나다		
write 쓰다		

Memo

꽉! 잡은 중학 영문법

3 Book

GRAMMAR
CATCH

저자 김명이 · 이재림

초판 1쇄 발행 2007년 8월 6일
개정판 1쇄 발행 2015년 8월 1일
개정판 4쇄 발행 2023년 9월 8일

편집장 조미자
책임편집 류은정 · 권민정 · 김미경 · 정진희 · 최수경
표지디자인 김교빈
디자인 김교빈 · 임미영
마케팅 도성욱 · 문신영 · 김성준
관리 이성희
인쇄 북토리

펴낸이 정규도

펴낸곳 Happy House

주소 경기도 파주시 문발로 211 다락원 빌딩
전화 02-736-2031 (내선 250)
팩스 02-732-2037
출판등록 1977년 9월 16일 제406-2008-000007호

ISBN 978-89-6653-189-9 53740

[Grammar Catch] 시리즈는 [오! 마이 그래머] 시리즈의 개정 증보판입니다.

정답 및 해설 무료 다운로드 www.ihappyhouse.co.kr
*Happy House는 다락원의 임프린트입니다.

꽉! 잡은 중학 영문법

GRAMMAR CATCH

★ Workbook ★

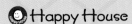

꼭! 잡은 중학 영문법

GRAMMAR CATCH

★ Workbook ★

Contents

Happy House

Chapter 01

Unit 01 ▶ 1, 2, 3형식 문장

01 밑줄 친 부분을 목적어, 보어, 수식어로 구분하여 괄호 안에 쓰시오.

1) He was <u>at the zoo</u> last weekend.   (_____)

2) They became <u>popular professors</u>.   (_____)

3) We saw <u>a movie star</u> on the street.   (_____)

4) His hobby is <u>to read comic books</u>.   (_____)

5) He agreed <u>to go to the gallery</u>.   (_____)

6) My father enjoys <u>playing tennis</u>.   (_____)

7) His job is <u>training golfers</u>.   (_____)

8) They believed <u>that the sun revolved around the earth</u>.   (_____)

02 보기와 같이 다음 문장의 밑줄 친 부분을 문장 요소로 구분하여 표시하시오.

> **보기**
> <u>She</u> <u>sings</u> <u>very well</u>.
> 주어 동사 수식어

1) There <u>are</u> <u>many kinds of animals</u> <u>in Kenya</u>.

2) <u>My sister and I</u> <u>borrowed</u> <u>some novels</u> from the library.

3) <u>The wild fox</u> <u>became</u> <u>quite tame</u>.

4) <u>Her brother's dream</u> <u>is</u> <u>to be a pilot</u>.

5) <u>The boys</u> <u>like</u> <u>playing basketball</u> after school.

03 다음 중 알맞은 것을 고르시오.

1) The cake tastes   sweet | sweetly .

2) Your sister looks   friendly | kindly .

3) A lot of members   attended | attended at   the meeting.

4) Many tourists   arrived | arrived at   Incheon International Airport.

5) My parents   reached | reached in   Seoul last night.

6) They decided   to buy | buying   coffee beans from Africa.

04 다음 문장의 틀린 부분에 밑줄을 긋고 바르게 고쳐 쓰시오. 틀린 부분이 없으면 ok라고 쓰시오.

1) The priest listened his prayer carefully.   (→ _____)

2) The students are discussing about their spring picnic.   (→ _____)

3) The members of the club have talked the plan.   (→ _____)

4) My elder sister is going to marry with a German man.   (→ _____)

5) My mom and I entered into the high building to meet him.   (→ _____)

6) The crackers I bought yesterday taste salty.   (→ _____)

7) Her voice sounds anxiously.   (→ _____)

8) My brother resembles my grandfather.   (→ _____)

05 우리말과 일치하도록 주어진 말을 바르게 배열하시오.

1) 그녀의 어머니는 그녀가 그 남자와 결혼하기를 바라신다.

(that, she, will, mother, her, marry ,the man, hopes)

→ _____

2) 그녀가 만든 피자는 매우 맛있는 냄새가 난다.

(smells, made, that, very, the pizza, delicious, she)

→ _____

3) 이 동네에 있는 대부분의 아이들은 같은 학교에 다녔다.

(the children, school, in, attended, the same, most of, this village)

→ _____

4) 옛날에 그 숲 속에는 가난한 한 농부가 한 명 살았다.

(lived, farmer, once upon a time, there, in, a poor, the forest)

→ _____

06 주어진 말을 이용하여 다음 우리말을 영작하시오.

1) 그의 조부모님은 건강해 보이신다. (look)

→ _____

2) 해외여행을 하는 것은 많은 시간과 돈이 필요하다. (require)

→ _____

3) 나는 내 학급친구들과 그 문제에 관해서 토론하고 싶다. (would like to, discuss)

→ _____

4) 우리 커피숍에 들어갈까? (shall, enter)

→ _____

01 두 문장의 뜻이 같도록 빈칸에 알맞은 말을 쓰시오.

1) Tim lent her some money a month ago.

= Tim lent some money _____ _____ a month ago.

2) My mother bought me an expensive cell phone.

= My mother bought an expensive cell phone _____ _____.

3) You may ask me a few questions

= You may ask a few questions _____ _____.

4) I wrote my friend a Christmas card.

= I wrote a Christmas card _____ _____ _____.

5) The teacher gave a piece of advice to him.

= The teacher gave _____ a piece of advice.

02 다음 중 알맞은 것을 고르시오.

1) He   made | sent   kites for children.

2) The movie made the actress   famous | famously .

3) His parents allowed him   go | to go   to the amusement park.

4) You should keep your hands and feet   warm | warmly .

5) He heard somebody   shouting | to shout   outside.

6) He has his right arm   bandage | bandaged .

03 다음 문장을 우리말로 해석하고 문장의 형식을 쓰시오.

1) He found his grandmother a seat.

→ _____ (_____ 형식)

2) He found the movie interesting.

→ _____ (_____ 형식)

3) His parents made him read this book.

→ _____ (_____ 형식)

4) His parents made him a toy car.

→ _____ (_____ 형식)

04 다음 문장의 틀린 부분에 밑줄을 긋고 바르게 고쳐 쓰시오.

1) She told a secret for her sister.　　　　　　(→ ＿＿＿＿＿＿＿＿)

2) My mother cooked dinner to us.　　　　　　(→ ＿＿＿＿＿＿＿＿)

3) He helped his father inventing the machine.　(→ ＿＿＿＿＿＿＿＿)

4) We should keep animals and plants safely.　(→ ＿＿＿＿＿＿＿＿)

5) You must have students remembering the rules.　(→ ＿＿＿＿＿＿＿＿)

6) She had her purse steal somewhere.　　　　(→ ＿＿＿＿＿＿＿＿)

7) They heard birds to sing in the forest.　　　(→ ＿＿＿＿＿＿＿＿)

05 우리말과 일치하도록 주어진 말을 바르게 배열하시오.

1) 태양은 지구에 빛과 에너지를 준다.

(and, gives, energy, to, light, the sun, the earth)

→ ＿＿＿＿＿＿＿＿＿＿＿＿＿＿＿＿＿＿＿＿＿＿＿＿＿＿＿＿＿

2) 나는 매일 나의 조카에게 커피콩을 갈게 한다.

(had, coffee beans, every day, I, my, nephew, grind)

→ ＿＿＿＿＿＿＿＿＿＿＿＿＿＿＿＿＿＿＿＿＿＿＿＿＿＿＿＿＿

3) 그 의사는 나에게 그 약을 하루에 세 번 먹으라고 충고했다.

(advised, a day, the medicine, the doctor, three, me, to, take, times)

→ ＿＿＿＿＿＿＿＿＿＿＿＿＿＿＿＿＿＿＿＿＿＿＿＿＿＿＿＿＿

4) 그녀는 지난달에 신발 두 켤레를 부모님께 사드렸다.

(she, parents, of, shoes, last, two, pairs, bought, her, month)

→ ＿＿＿＿＿＿＿＿＿＿＿＿＿＿＿＿＿＿＿＿＿＿＿＿＿＿＿＿＿

06 주어진 말을 이용하여 다음 우리말을 영작하시오.

1) 우리는 그녀가 우리에게 약간의 충고를 해 주기를 요청했다. (ask)

→ ＿＿＿＿＿＿＿＿＿＿＿＿＿＿＿＿＿＿＿＿＿＿＿＿＿＿＿＿＿

2) 나는 그들이 수업 중에 떠드는 것을 들었다. (make a noise)

→ ＿＿＿＿＿＿＿＿＿＿＿＿＿＿＿＿＿＿＿＿＿＿＿＿＿＿＿＿＿

3) 우리는 그가 방으로 들어가는 것을 보았다. (enter)

→ ＿＿＿＿＿＿＿＿＿＿＿＿＿＿＿＿＿＿＿＿＿＿＿＿＿＿＿＿＿

4) 우리는 그 책이 재미있고 유용하다는 것을 알았다. (find, useful)

→ ＿＿＿＿＿＿＿＿＿＿＿＿＿＿＿＿＿＿＿＿＿＿＿＿＿＿＿＿＿

01 다음 중 알맞은 것을 고르시오.

1) The French Revolution   had ended | ended   in 1799.

2) Many hands   make | made   light work.

3) Water   freezes | froze   at zero degrees centigrade.

4) After we   will eat | eat   lunch, we will watch the movie.

5) He said that Edison   had invented | invented   electricity.

6) My mom told me that honesty   is | was   the best policy.

7) My sister   will get | gets   married next month.

8) If it   will snow | snows   tomorrow, we will go skiing.

02 주어진 단어를 이용하여 문장을 완성하시오.

1) She _____ from high school next year. (graduate)

2) Korean students _____ to school five days a week. (go)

3) We _____ some cookies and bread yesterday. (bake)

4) France _____ the Statue of Liberty to the United States in 1884. (give)

5) The sun _____ about 109 times larger than the earth. (be)

6) The Winter Olympic Games _____ held in this city soon. (be)

7) I will say nothing to her until she _____ me the truth. (tell)

03 빈칸에 주어진 동사의 알맞은 형태를 쓰고 해석하시오.

1) (arrive)   Do you know when the singer _____ at the airport next week?

→ _____

When the singer _____ at the airport, one of his fans will give him flowers.

→ _____

2) (attend)   I don't know if he _____ the meeting next weekend.

→ _____

I will forgive him if he _____ the meeting next weekend.

→ _____

04 다음 문장의 **틀린** 부분에 밑줄을 긋고 바르게 고쳐 쓰시오.

1) Yesterday he is sick but now he is not sick.　　　　　　(→ ＿＿＿＿＿＿＿)

2) He said that a friend in need was a friend indeed.　　　(→ ＿＿＿＿＿＿＿)

3) If it will be rainy tomorrow, we will read comic books at home.　(→ ＿＿＿＿＿＿＿)

4) My father leaves for LA two weeks ago.　　　　　　　(·＿＿＿＿＿＿＿)

5) As soon as he will do his homework, he will play games.　(→ ＿＿＿＿＿＿＿)

6) We don't close our coffee shop at 11:30 last night.　　　(→ ＿＿＿＿＿＿＿)

7) I will stay beside her until she will sleep.　　　　　　(→ ＿＿＿＿＿＿＿)

8) My sister going to buy a secondhand car next Saturday.　(→ ＿＿＿＿＿＿＿)

05 우리말과 일치하도록 주어진 말을 바르게 배열하시오.

1) 그녀는 집으로 돌아오자마자 아기를 침대에 눕힐 것이다.

(home, will, she, as soon as, comes, the bed, she, lay, her baby, on)

→ ＿＿＿＿＿＿＿＿＿＿＿＿＿＿＿＿＿＿＿＿＿＿＿＿＿＿

2) 그 과학 선생님은 빛이 소리보다 빠르다고 말씀하셨다.

(that, faster, light, than, the science teacher, travels, said, sound)

→ ＿＿＿＿＿＿＿＿＿＿＿＿＿＿＿＿＿＿＿＿＿＿＿＿＿＿

3) 우리는 언젠가 가난한 사람들에게 음식과 물을 제공할 것이다.

(food, and, we, poor people, will, provide, with, water, someday)

→ ＿＿＿＿＿＿＿＿＿＿＿＿＿＿＿＿＿＿＿＿＿＿＿＿＿＿

4) 한국은 매년 많은 종류의 차들을 다른 나라에 수출한다.

(exports, kinds, Korea, many, to, every year, other, of, cars, countries)

→ ＿＿＿＿＿＿＿＿＿＿＿＿＿＿＿＿＿＿＿＿＿＿＿＿＿＿

06 주어진 말을 이용하여 다음 우리말을 영작하시오.

1) 그녀는 어제 그 목걸이를 서랍 속에 숨겼다. (hide, necklace, drawer)

→ ＿＿＿＿＿＿＿＿＿＿＿＿＿＿＿＿＿＿＿＿＿＿＿＿＿＿

2) 나의 언니는 프랑스로 막 떠나려고 하고 있다. (be about to)

→ ＿＿＿＿＿＿＿＿＿＿＿＿＿＿＿＿＿＿＿＿＿＿＿＿＿＿

3) 그녀는 일주일에 두 번 영어 수업을 받는다. (take an English class)

→ ＿＿＿＿＿＿＿＿＿＿＿＿＿＿＿＿＿＿＿＿＿＿＿＿＿＿

4) 다음 주말에 시간이 있으면 우리는 야구를 할 것이다. (have time)

→ ＿＿＿＿＿＿＿＿＿＿＿＿＿＿＿＿＿＿＿＿＿＿＿＿＿＿

01 주어진 단어를 이용하여 진행형 문장으로 쓰시오.

1) My sister _____ the cello now. (play)

2) My parents _____ a walk when I met them in the park. (take)

3) Mr. Smith _____ breakfast tomorrow morning. (cook)

4) They _____ about the problem at this time yesterday. (argue)

5) My father _____ his car at that time. (wash)

6) It is 10 o'clock. The train _____ soon. (leave)

7) We should not make any noise. Some students _____ here. (study)

02 다음 중 알맞은 것을 고르시오.

1) He   has ∣ is having   two houses and a tall building.

2) My brother   has ∣ is having   bread and juice for breakfast now.

3) Her children   play ∣ are playing   with a toy car twice a week.

4) The boys   play ∣ are playing   baseball in the park at the moment.

5) She   is smelling ∣ smells   the coffee that I made.

6) The coffee   is smelling ∣ smells   good.

7) That blue bike   belongs ∣ is belonging   to my nephew.

03 우리말과 일치하도록 빈칸에 알맞은 말을 쓰시오.

1) 나의 아버지는 그때 앞마당에 사과나무를 심고 계셨다.
   → My father _____ _____ an apple tree in the yard then.

2) 내일 5시에 그 클럽의 회원들은 골프를 치고 있을 것이다.
   → The members of the club _____ _____ _____ golf
     at five tomorrow.

3) 그들은 스키장을 건설하기 위해서 인공 눈을 만들고 있다.
   → They _____ _____ artificial snow to build a ski slope.

4) 내가 집에 도착했을 때 나의 어머니는 저녁을 준비하고 계셨다.
   → My mother _____ _____ dinner when I got home.

5) 소라야, 들어봐! 누군가가 피아노를 연주하고 있어.
   → Sora, listen! Someone _____ _____ the piano.

04 밑줄 친 부분에 주의하여 다음 문장을 우리말로 해석하시오.

1) We <u>are going</u> on a picnic tomorrow.

→ _____

2) We <u>are going</u> on a picnic now.

→ _____

3) My father <u>was fixing</u> the door when we arrived.

→ _____

4) My father <u>will be working</u> when we arrive at his office.

→ _____

05 우리말과 일치하도록 주어진 말을 바르게 배열하시오.

1) 내가 그녀를 봤을 때 그녀는 한 남자와 이야기를 하고 있었다.

(talking, she, was, with, I, saw, a man, when, her)

→ _____

2) 그녀는 지금 친구에게 이메일을 쓰는 중이다.

(writing, to, at the moment, is, her friend, she, an email)

→ _____

3) 우리는 내일 이맘때 빵과 쿠키를 굽고 있을 것이다.

(be, bread, will, baking, and, this time, we, cookies, at, tomorrow)

→ _____

06 주어진 말을 이용하여 다음 우리말을 영작하시오.

1) 나의 할머니는 지금 나의 여동생을 돌보는 중이시다. (take care of)

→ _____

2) 유명한 가수들 몇 명이 무대에서 노래하고 춤을 추고 있다. (on the stage)

→ _____

3) 그의 어머니가 문을 노크했을 때 그는 음악을 듣고 있었다. (knock at the door)

→ _____

4) 오늘 오후 3시에 그는 도서관에서 공부하고 있을 것이다. (this afternoon)

→ _____

O1 다음 중 알맞은 것을 고르시오.

1) Soccer   has been | was   very popular in Korea in 2002.

2) Soccer   has been | was   very popular in Korea since 2002.

3) My father   has been | has gone   to Europe twice.

4) He   has raised | raised   two cats since last month.

5) He   has raised | raised   two cats last month.

6) They   have attended | attended   a wedding a week ago.

7) The famous actor   hasn't arrived | doesn't have arrived   at the airport yet.

8) When   have you written | did you write   the grammar book?

9) The house has been empty   for | since   two years.

10) It   has been raining | has been rained   since yesterday.

O2 두 문장을 한 문장으로 바꿀 때 빈칸에 알맞은 말을 쓰시오.

1) Sora started to play the piano three years ago. She still plays the piano.

→ Sora _____ _____ the piano _____ three years.

2) He lost his wallet. He still doesn't have it.

→ He _____ _____ his wallet.

3) My grandparents moved to Jejudo when I was a child. They still live there.

→ My grandparents _____ _____ in Jejudo _____
I was a child.

4) My brother went to England a month ago. He is there now.

→ My brother _____ _____ to England.

5) We were busy yesterday. We are still busy.

→ We _____ _____ busy _____ yesterday.

6) My teacher started to teach English in 1999. He still teaches English.

→ My teacher _____ _____ English _____ 1999.

7) She began to wait for a train thirty minutes ago. She is still waiting for it.

→ She _____ _____ _____ for a train
_____ thirty minutes.

03 밑줄 친 부분에 주의하여 다음 문장을 우리말로 해석하시오.

1) My mom has been to India before.

→ _____

2) My mom has gone to India.

→ _____

3) My nephew has been in Korea since 1997.

→ _____

4) My nephew was in Korea in 1997.

→ _____

04 다음 문장의 틀린 부분에 밑줄을 긋고 바르게 고쳐 쓰시오.

1) He has taken part in a funeral a week ago.　　　　　　(→ _____)

2) Ⓐ Have you ever been to Jejudo before?　　Ⓑ No, I don't.　　(→ _____)

3) We import a lot of bags from France since last year.　　(→ _____)

4) My friend has stayed in this hotel yesterday.　　　　(→ _____)

5) Ⓐ Where have you been?　　Ⓑ I have gone to the drug store.　　(→ _____)

6) It has been snowed heavily since last Sunday.　　　　(→ _____)

7) My brother has already leaves for Busan.　　　　　(→ _____)

8) When has your mom come back to Korea?　　　　　(→ _____)

05 주어진 말을 이용하여 다음 우리말을 영작하시오.

1) 그녀는 10년 전에 여기서 살았다. (live)

→ _____

2) 그녀는 10년 동안 여기서 살고 있다. (live)

→ _____

3) 나는 그녀가 한국을 떠난 이후로 그녀를 만난 적이 없다. (leave)

→ _____

4) 그 여배우는 그때 이후로 유명하다. (then)

→ _____

5) 나는 호주에 한 번 가 본 적이 있다. (Australia, once)

→ _____

6) 그녀는 시각장애인들에게 두 시간 동안 책을 읽어 주고 있다. (read, blind people)

→ _____

O1 주어진 동사를 이용하여 완료시제 문장으로 쓰시오.

1) Lucy _____ busy for a week when I visited her. (be)

2) The plane _____ before we arrived. (already leave)

3) My family _____ in Ilsan for two years next month. (be)

4) He lost his cell phone that he _____ the day before. (buy)

5) He _____ England three times if he goes there again. (visit)

6) She _____ her project by 5 p.m. tomorrow. (finish)

7) I _____ the *Mona Lisa* before I visited the Louvre Museum. (never see)

8) When he retires next year, he _____ here for 35 years. (work)

O2 밑줄 친 부분에 유의하여 다음 문장을 우리말로 해석하시오.

1) We have lived in this village for ten years until now.

→ _____

2) We had lived in the village for ten years before we moved to Seoul.

→ _____

3) We will have lived in the village for ten years by the end of this year.

→ _____

4) It has been raining for a week.

→ _____

5) It had been raining for a week when we arrived in Korea.

→ _____

6) It will have been raining for a whole week by tomorrow.

→ _____

O3 빈칸에 알맞은 be동사의 시제를 쓰시오.

1) He _____ sick last Sunday.

2) He _____ sick in bed since last Sunday.

3) He _____ sick in bed for two days when I entered his room.

4) He _____ sick in bed for a week if he doesn't feel well tomorrow.

O4 다음 중 알맞은 것을 고르시오.

1) The movie   has | had   already started when I got to the theater.

2) He   has | had   wanted a brand-new cell phone since last month.

3) She   had | will have   studied for 5 hours if she studies for another hour.

4) Sora met John yesterday. She   has | had   never talked to him until then.

5) My uncle   moved | had moved   to Incheon five years ago.

6) My father told me that my uncle   has | had   moved to Incheon five years before.

7) My headache   has | had   already disappeared before I took a painkiller.

8) She   will have | has   helped me for a year by the end of next month.

O5 우리말과 일치하도록 주어진 말을 바르게 배열하시오.

1) 제임스는 한달 동안 독일에 있었다고 나에게 말했다.

(that, a month, told, James, had, Germany, for, he, me, been, in)

→ _____

2) 나이아가라 폭포를 가기 전에는 나는 그렇게 큰 폭포를 본 적이 없었다.

(had, such a, waterfall, seen, I, before, big, went, to, never, I, Niagara Falls)

→ _____

3) 내가 떠날 때 쯤이면 나는 미국에 2달 동안 머무르는 셈이다.

(leave, I, will, been, have, in, two, by the time, America, for, I, months)

→ _____

4) 내가 전화를 끊었을 때 그 기술자는 2시간 동안 냉장고를 고치고 있었다.

(been, the refrigerator, the engineer, had, for, fixing, two hours, hung up, when, I , the phone)

→ _____

O6 주어진 말을 이용하여 다음 우리말을 영작하시오.

1) 그는 우산을 버스에 두고 온 것을 알았다. (find, leave)

→ _____

2) 그 영화를 보기 전에 나는 이미 그것에 대해서 여러 번 들었다. (already)

→ _____

3) 한국 전쟁이 일어나기 전에 나의 할아버지는 돌아가셨다. (pass away, break out)

→ _____

01 다음 문장의 <u>틀린</u> 부분에 밑줄을 긋고 바르게 고쳐 쓰시오.

1) They don't have to making a dress for her.　　　(→ _____)

2) She will can play the flute.　　　(→ _____)

3) You ought to not laugh at him.　　　(→ _____)

4) She doesn't need take the exam.　　　(→ _____)

5) He will has to follow the rules.　　　(→ _____)

02 우리말과 일치하도록 빈칸에 알맞은 조동사를 쓰시오.

1) 그녀가 비싼 다이아몬드 반지를 가지고 있을 리가 없다.

　→ She _____ have an expensive diamond ring.

2) 그들은 3D 프린터를 사용할 수 있을 것이다.

　→ They _____ _____ _____ _____ use
　 a 3D printer.

3) 그녀는 도시락을 가지고 올 필요가 없다.

　→ She _____ _____ _____ bring lunch.

4) 그는 그의 자녀들을 보호해야 한다.

　→ He o_____ _____ protect his children.

5) 너는 전학을 가야 하니?

　→ Do you _____ _____ transfer to another school?

6) 그들이 그 화랑에서 그 그림을 훔칠지도 모른다.

　→ They m_____ steal the painting from the gallery.

03 두 문장의 뜻이 같도록 빈칸에 알맞은 말을 쓰시오.

1) Can I open the window?

　= _____ I open the window?

2) She must concentrate on studying.

　= She _____ _____ concentrate on studying.

3) We should not follow the wrong direction.

　= We _____ _____ _____ follow the wrong direction.

4) They don't have to worry about the test results.

　= They don't _____ _____ worry about the test results.

O4 다음 문장을 우리말로 해석하시오.

1) She will have to borrow some books.

→ _____

2) You must not touch the paintings in the gallery.

→ _____

3) We don't have to paint the ceiling.

→ _____

4) They can't be police officers.

→ _____

5) You ought not to bring a pet here.

→ _____

O5 우리말과 일치하도록 주어진 말을 바르게 배열하시오.

1) 그는 여기서 스케이트보드를 타면 안 된다.

   (should, skateboard, not, he, ride, here, a)

→ _____

2) 그 공장은 휴대전화를 생산할 수 있을 것이다.

   (able, cell phones, be, factory, produce, will, to, the)

→ _____

3) 그는 수술을 받지 않을지도 모른다.

   (operation, not, have, he, may, an)

→ _____

4) 그들은 마술을 행하면 절대로 안 된다.

   (magic tricks, not, perform, must, they)

→ _____

O6 주어진 말을 이용하여 다음 우리말을 영작하시오.

1) 그녀는 메모할 필요가 없다. (take notes)

→ _____

2) 그는 우리 담임선생님임에 틀림없다. (homeroom teacher)

→ _____

3) 그들은 댄스 수업을 빠져야 할 것이다. (miss)

→ _____

01 다음 문장의 <u>틀린</u> 부분에 밑줄을 긋고 바르게 고쳐 쓰시오.

1) She has better save some money. (→ _____)

2) I would not rather remain here. (→ _____)

3) The machine is used to cutting wood. (→ _____)

4) He used to skiing but he doesn't ski now. (→ _____)

5) Should you like to turn the volume down? (→ _____)

02 우리말과 일치하도록 빈칸에 알맞은 말을 쓰시오.

1) 너는 혼자 거기에 가지 않는 것이 좋다.

→ You _____ _____ _____ go there alone.

2) 그들은 스쿠버다이빙을 하러 가곤 했다.

→ They _____ _____ _____ scuba diving.

3) 우리는 TV를 보느니 차라리 자겠다.

→ We _____ _____ sleep _____ _____ TV.

4) 샐리는 걸어서 학교에 가는 것에 익숙해졌다.

→ Sally_____ _____ _____ _____ to
school.

5) 녹차를 드시겠어요?

→ Would you_____ _____ _____ green tea?

03 빈칸에 알맞은 조동사를 보기에서 골라 쓰시오.

| 보기 | used to | had better | would rather |

1) I am good at swimming but I don't like running. I _____ swim than run.

2) Mina often went fishing with her dad, but she doesn't do it anymore.
She _____ go fishing.

3) John has to hand in the essay by tomorrow, but he hasn't started it yet.
He _____ write the essay right now.

04 밑줄 친 부분에 유의하여 다음 문장을 우리말로 해석하시오.

1) My brother used to bite his nails.

→ _____

2) They used to be basketball players.

→ _____

3) She is used to singing in front of people.

→ _____

4) Plastic is used to make PET bottles.

→ _____

05 우리말과 일치하도록 주어진 말을 바르게 배열하시오.

1) 그녀는 대통령과 인터뷰하기를 원한다.

(to, the president, would, she, interview, like)

→ _____

2) 너는 에스컬레이터에서 뛰지 않는 것이 좋다.

(escalator, not, you, had, run, on, better, the)

→ _____

3) 나는 요리하는 것보다는 차라리 설거지를 하겠다.

(cook, I, than, do, would, the dishes, rather)

→ _____

4) 모퉁이에는 예전에 서점이 있었다.

(around the corner, be, there, a bookstore, used to)

→ _____

06 주어진 말을 이용하여 다음 우리말을 영작하시오.

1) 우리는 영어로 말하는 것에 익숙하다. (speak)

→ _____

2) 나는 차라리 그 제안을 거절하겠다. (refuse the proposal)

→ _____

3) 너는 그에게 미안하다고 말하는 것이 좋다. (say sorry)

→ _____

01 다음 중 알맞은 것을 고르시오.

1) She has a toothache. She   should | must   have brushed her teeth three times a day.

2) This shirt was only for dry-cleaning. I   should | shouldn't   have washed it.

3) Kevin seems to know Mia. He   must | can't   have met her before.

4) My brother doesn't have a driver's license. He   can't | should   have driven the truck.

5) Susan has a pain in her ankle. She   may | can't   have sprained it.

02 우리말과 일치하도록 주어진 말을 이용하여 문장을 완성하시오.

1) 그들은 그를 야단치지 말았어야 했다. (scold)

→ They _____ him.

2) 그녀는 직장을 그만두었을지도 모른다. (quit)

→ She _____ her job.

3) 폴이 그 소문을 퍼트렸음에 틀림없다. (spread)

→ Paul _____ the rumor.

4) 그들이 그를 시장으로 선출했을 리가 없다. (choose)

→ They _____ him as a mayor.

03 주어진 동사와 보기의 말을 이용하여 다음 문장을 완성하시오.

보기   should have p.p   must have p.p   can't have p.p   might have p.p

1) She didn't wear a coat so she caught a cold.

She _____ a coat. (wear)

2) He said he didn't study for the test, but he got a perfect score.

He _____ hard last night. (study)

3) I had a delicious dinner at Tim's house, but Tim is not a good cook.

He _____ dinner. (made)

4) Sam was supposed to come to the meeting, but he didn't.

He _____ the meeting. (forget)

O4 다음 문장을 우리말로 해석하시오.

1) We shouldn't have listened to him.

→ _____

2) They must have followed my advice.

→ _____

3) Jane can't have remembered me.

→ _____

4) He may have lost his key.

→ _____

O5 우리말과 일치하도록 주어진 말을 바르게 배열하시오.

1) 그들은 수상한 사람을 경찰에 신고했어야 했는데.
(should, the police, they, have, the stranger, reported, to)

→ _____

2) 그는 요리하는 법을 배웠음에 틀림없다.
(how, must, he, have, cook, learned, to)

→ _____

3) 누군가 범죄현장을 목격했을지도 모른다.
(have, crime scene, may, someone, witnessed, the)

→ _____

4) 그녀가 컴퓨터를 분해했을 리가 없다.
(cannot, the computer, have, she, taken apart)

→ _____

O6 주어진 말을 이용하여 다음 우리말을 영작하시오.

1) 나는 할머니 병문안을 갔어야 했는데. (visit, in the hospital)

→ _____

2) 내 사촌이 그 빵을 먹었음에 틀림없다. (cousin)

→ _____

3) 그녀는 교통체증으로 꼼짝하지 못했을지도 모른다. (stick in traffic)

→ _____

4) 나의 언니가 배구를 했을 리가 없다. (volleyball)

→ _____

Chapter 04 — Unit 10 ▶ 수동태의 시제

01 다음 중 알맞은 것을 고르시오.

1) The famous designer   designed | was designed   our school uniform.

2) The public library   designed | was designed   for children by a famous architect.

3) A lot of animals are   killing | being killed   by hunters.

4) The thief has just   arrested | been arrested   on the spot.

5) The police have   chased | been chased   the robber for two hours.

6) Your socks will   find | be found   somewhere.

7) They   founded | was founded   the university in 1985.

8) The company   founded | was founded   in 2001.

9) New products have been   developing | developed   at this company.

02 다음 문장을 수동태로 바꾸어 쓰시오.

1) They use their cell phones everywhere.

→ _____

2) My father found the key under the bed.

→ _____

3) We will protect animals and plants.

→ _____

4) Brian is writing an English grammar book.

→ _____

5) My nephew has collected many kinds of coins.

→ _____

03 밑줄 친 부분에 유의하여 다음 문장을 우리말로 해석하시오.

1) She is putting a coin into the machine.

→ _____

2) A coin is being put into this machine by her.

→ _____

3) The leader of the club has canceled the meeting.

→ _____

4) The meeting has been canceled by the leader of the club.

→ _____

04 주어진 동사를 알맞은 형태로 바꾸어 문장을 완성하시오.

1) (publish)   She _____ her book three years ago.

Her book _____ by her three years ago.

2) (wash)   These dishes will _____ by my sister soon.

My sister will _____ these dishes soon.

3) (fix)   My father _____ the car now.

The car _____ by my father now.

05 우리말과 일치하도록 주어진 말을 바르게 배열하시오.

1) 그 마을은 이틀 전에 적에 의해 공격을 받았다.

(days, was, the enemy, two, attacked, by, the village, ago)

→ _____

2) 그 큰 집은 두 마리의 개에 의해 지켜지고 있다.

(two, the big, being, by, guarded, dogs, house, is)

→ _____

3) 그 책들은 나의 학급친구들에 의해 도서관으로 옮겨질 것이다.

(my classmates, the books, moved, to, by, will, be, the library)

→ _____

4) 지난 몇 년 동안 많은 종류의 예술 작품들이 이 화랑에서 전시되어 왔다.

(kinds of, many, been, art works, have, exhibited, in, the past, this gallery, for, few years)

→ _____

06 주어진 말을 이용하여 다음 우리말을 영작하시오.

1) 약간의 돈이 그녀에 의해 저축되었다. (save)

→ _____

2) 그 신문은 한 노인에 의해 매일 배달된다. (deliver)

→ _____

3) 이 벤치는 나의 아버지에 의해 페인트칠 되고 있다. (paint)

→ _____

4) 그녀는 많은 학생들에 의해 기억될 것이다. (remember)

→ _____

O1 다음 중 알맞은 것을 고르시오.

1) He   lent | was lent   his sister 20,000 won.

2) The flowers   call | are called   cherry blossoms by people.

3) My grandfather   made | was made   us many kinds of kites.

4) The food   made | was made   for us by my mom.

5) The expensive bags   bought | were bought   for | to   his wife by Mr. Brown.

6) A lot of questions   asked | were asked   of | to   the teacher by the students.

7) Brian   asked | was asked   Sumi her age.

8) Most mothers   ask | are asked   many questions by their children.

9) She was told   opening | to open   the window by her dad.

O2 다음 문장을 수동태로 바꾸어 쓰시오.

1) The Internet gives people much information.

→ _____

→ _____

2) Bora will tell her mother the truth.

→ _____

→ _____

3) Terry bought his brother a glass of apple juice.

→ _____

4) Jenny kept the house tidy.

→ _____

5) I saw a thief enter the house.

→ _____

6) The game made people excited.

→ _____

7) The doctor advised her to take this pill after meals.

→ _____

8) Mrs. Johnson made her son practice the cello.

→ _____

03 주어진 동사를 알맞은 형태로 바꾸어 문장을 완성하시오.

1) (show)   Some old pictures _____ to her boyfriend by Sora yesterday.

Sora _____ her boyfriend some old pictures yesterday.

2) (teach)   My uncle will _____ students Korean history.

Students will _____ Korean history by my uncle.

Korean history will _____ to students by my uncle.

3) (watch)   A boy _____ carrying a big suitcase by me ten minutes ago.

I _____ a boy carrying a big suitcase ten minutes ago.

4) (name)   The couple _____ their daughter Sera when she was born.

Their daughter _____ Sera by the couple when she was born.

04 밑줄 친 부분에 유의하여 다음 문장을 우리말로 해석하시오.

1) He handed Sora a few coins.

→ _____

2) Sora was handed a few coins by him.

→ _____

3) A few coins were handed to Sora by him.

→ _____

4) We saw the baby playing with toys.

→ _____

5) The baby was seen playing with toys by us.

→ _____

05 주어진 주어로 시작하여 다음 우리말을 영작하시오.

1) 그 거리는 사람들에 의해 미리내(Mirinae)라고 불린다.

→ The street _____.

2) 몇몇 새들이 숲에서 노래를 하는 것이 들렸다.

→ Some birds _____.

3) 이 편지는 나에 의해 나의 부모님에게 쓰였다.

→ This letter _____.

4) 그는 그의 아버지에 의해 그 컴퓨터를 사용할 것을 허락받았다.

→ He _____.

01 다음 중 알맞은 것을 고르시오.

1) My cell phone   stole | was stolen   in Italy.

2) The computer   was turned off by | was turned off   him before he went out.

3) The cars   are produced | produce   in Germany.

4) Red pepper   introduced | was introduced   to Korea a long time ago

5) My friend will   introduce | be introduced   her brother to me.

6) Tim would   treat | be treated   like a prince when he was young.

7) Sheldon must   treat | be treated   Karen like his girlfriend.

8) The students may   punish | be punished   because they are late.

02 우리말과 일치하도록 빈칸에 알맞은 말을 쓰시오.

1) 그 사람은 고용되어서는 안 된다. (hire)
   → The man should not _____ _____ .

2) 캥거루는 호주에서 볼 수가 있다.
   → Kangaroos _____ _____ _____ in Australia.

3) 어머니는 나의 성적에 만족하셨다.
   → My mother was _____ _____ my grade report.

4) '해리포터' 시리즈는 전 세계 사람들에게 알려졌다.
   → The *Harry Potter* series is _____ _____ people all over the world.

5) 에드워드는 내일의 큰 발표에 대해서 걱정한다.
   → Edward is _____ _____ his big presentation tomorrow.

03 빈칸에 알맞은 전치사를 쓰시오.

1) The bucket is filled _____ water.

2) Some boys are interested _____ playing soccer.

3) This desk was made _____ my uncle

4) This desk is made _____ wood.

5) Butter is made _____ milk.

6) My dad was pleased _____ our presents

7) She was disappointed _____ the result.

O4 다음 문장을 수동태로 바꾸어 쓰시오.

1) We must keep our promise.

→ _____

2) Some students laughed at a new student.

→ _____

3) My friend will marry an English man soon.

→ _____

4) Tommy should look after the poor puppy.

→ _____

5) A truck ran over a cat.

→ _____

O5 우리말과 일치하도록 주어진 말을 바르게 배열하시오.

1) 학생들의 휴대전화는 교실에서 꺼져 있어야 한다.

(cell phones, must, students', be, off, in, turned, the classroom)

→ _____

2) 이 고아는 누군가에 의해 보살핌을 받아야 한다.

(be, orphan, has to, taken, of, this, by, care, someone)

→ _____

3) 시골에서는 밤에 많은 별들을 볼 수 있다.

(be, the countryside, at, stars, can, a lot of, seen, in, night)

→ _____

4) 여러 해 동안 그 선생님은 학생들에 의해 존경을 받아 왔다.

(has, by, been, many years, to, the teacher, looked, up, for, students)

→ _____

O6 주어진 말을 이용하여 다음 우리말을 영작하시오.

1) 모든 종이는 재활용되어야 한다. (recycle, should)

→ _____

2) 많은 군인들이 베트남 전쟁에서 전사했다. (kill, the Vietnam War)

→ _____

3) 모든 사람들이 그 사고에 놀랐다. (all, accident)

→ _____

01 다음 문장의 <u>틀린</u> 부분에 밑줄을 긋고 바르게 고쳐 쓰시오.

1) It is important study steadily.　　　　　(→ _____)

2) He planned run for school president.　　(→ _____)

3) She wanted to not meet him again.　　　(→ _____)

4) They know when visit New York.　　　　(→ _____)

5) To talk with friends are very interesting.　(→ _____)

6) This is important to read many kinds of books.　(→ _____)

02 우리말과 일치하도록 to부정사를 이용하여 문장을 완성하시오.

1) 그의 꿈은 역사드라마를 쓰는 것이다.
→ His dream is _____ a historical drama.

2) 동굴을 탐험하는 것은 흥미롭다.
→ It _____ a cave.

3) 그 카페매니저는 직원에게 언제 카페를 열어야 하는지 말했다.
→ The cafe manager told the staff _____ the cafe.

4) 그는 컴퓨터 게임을 너무 많이 하지 않기로 결심했다.
→ He _____ computer games too much.

03 두 문장의 뜻이 같도록 빈칸에 알맞은 말을 쓰시오.

1) To hit a home run in a baseball game is great.
= _____ _____ _____ _____ _____ a home run in a baseball game.

2) My mom told me what to do.
= My mom told me _____ _____ _____ _____.

3) They discussed when to open a shop.
= They discussed _____ _____ _____ _____ a shop.

4) She will explain to him how to handle stress.
= She will explain to him _____ _____ _____ _____ stress.

04 문장의 밑줄 친 부분이 어떤 역할을 하는지 구분하고 우리말로 해석하시오.

1) It is difficult to make a decision.

→ _____ (주어, 보어, 목적어)

2) His dream is to experience space travel.

→ _____ (주어, 보어, 목적어)

3) The man decided to stop fighting with others.

→ _____ (주어, 보어, 목적어)

4) They know how to save the earth from pollution.

→ _____ (주어, 보어, 목적어)

05 우리말과 일치하도록 주어진 말을 바르게 배열하시오.

1) 많은 노력을 하는 것은 중요하다.

(make, it, a lot of, is, to, important, effort)

→ _____

2) 그의 목표는 로봇을 만드는 것이다.

(is, robot, to, a, his, make, goal)

→ _____

3) 그들은 한 시간 동안 줄 서서 기다릴 것이라고 예상한다.

(an hour, to, they, for, expect, in line, wait)

→ _____

4) 그녀는 여름방학 동안 어디로 여행할지 안다.

(vacation, to, during, she, where, summer, knows, travel)

→ _____

06 주어진 말을 이용하여 다음 우리말을 영작하시오.

1) 뮤직비디오를 만드는 것은 흥미롭다. (music video)

→ _____

2) 그의 꿈은 투명망토를 발명하는 것이다. (invisible cloak)

→ _____

3) 그들은 지구온난화를 공부할 계획이다. (global warming)

→ _____

4) 그녀는 아침을 거르지 않겠다고 결심했다. (skip)

→ _____

01 다음 문장의 <u>틀린</u> 부분에 밑줄을 긋고 바르게 고쳐 쓰시오.

1) The patients have a counselor to talk.   (→ _____)

2) She is looking for the key in order open the locker.   (→ _____)

3) They don't have a chair to sit.   (→ _____)

4) He must be honest to telling the truth.   (→ _____)

5) Do you have a pen to write?   (→ _____)

6) The girl grew up become a lawyer.   (→ _____)

02 우리말과 일치하도록 to부정사를 이용하여 문장을 완성하시오.

1) 나는 같이 여행할 친구가 있다.

　→ I have _____ .

2) 우리는 공룡을 보기 위하여 과학박물관에 갔다. (dinosaurs)

　→ We went to the Science Museum _____ .

3) 그녀는 돌볼 아이들이 많다.

　→ He has a lot of _____ .

4) 그녀가 그렇게 말하는 것을 보니 현명한 것이 틀림없다.

　→ She must be wise _____ .

5) 그는 무언가 걱정할 것이 있다.

　→ He has _____ .

03 두 문장의 뜻이 같도록 빈칸에 알맞은 말을 쓰시오.

1) We went to Paris so that we could see the Eiffel Tower.

　= We went to Paris _____ _____ the Eiffel Tower.

2) They wanted to play on a water slide so they went to a water park.

　= They went to a water park _____ _____ _____

　　_____ on a water slide.

3) She was embarrassed because she fell on the stage.

　= She was embarrassed _____ _____ on the stage.

4) He studies hard because he wants to get a scholarship.

　= _____ _____ a scholarship, he studies hard.

04 문장의 밑줄 친 부분이 어떤 역할을 하는지 구분하고 우리말로 해석하시오.

1) She has a ticket to fly to London.

→ _____ (형용사, 부사)

2) We were happy to meet them again.

→ _____ (형용사, 부사)

3) The mountain is not easy to climb.

→ _____ (형용사, 부사)

4) Her family was to go on a trip.

→ _____ (형용사, 부사)

05 우리말과 일치하도록 주어진 말을 바르게 배열하시오.

1) 그는 99세까지 살았다.

(ninety-nine, he, be, lived, years, to, old)

→ _____

2) 그 영화는 이해하기 아주 어렵다.

(understand, the, difficult, to, movie, very, is)

→ _____

3) 우리는 점심을 먹기 위해 한 식당에서 만났다.

(a, lunch, we, restaurant, to, met, at, have)

→ _____

4) 그는 그녀와 사랑에 빠질 운명이었다.

(her, he, fall, was, in, love, to, with)

→ _____

06 주어진 말을 이용하여 다음 우리말을 영작하시오.

1) 그녀는 그녀의 친구와 헤어지게 되어서 슬펐다. (part from)

→ _____

2) 그 커피는 마시기에는 뜨겁다. (coffee)

→ _____

3) 그는 자라서 과학자가 되었다. (grow up)

→ _____

4) 그들은 살 집이 없다. (live)

→ _____

01 다음 문장의 <u>틀린</u> 부분에 밑줄을 긋고 바르게 고쳐 쓰시오. 맞는 문장은 ok라고 쓰시오.

1) The doctor told him stop smoking.　　　(→ _____)

2) He got them do the laundry.　　　(→ _____)

3) She heard someone to laugh.　　　(→ _____)

4) The teacher let us going home.　　　(→ _____)

5) My mom allowed me to bring my friends.　　　(→ _____)

6) I helped her washing her dog.　　　(→ _____)

7) They felt someone move.　　　(→ _____)

02 빈칸에 알맞은 말을 보기에서 골라 알맞은 형태로 쓰시오.

보기				
catch	dig	forgive	hide	look for
shake	ride	set	light	

1) 우리는 땅이 약간 흔들리는 것을 느꼈다.

　→ We felt the ground _____ a little.

2) 그는 정원사에게 마당을 파라고 시켰다.

　→ He had the gardener _____ in the yard.

3) 미나는 그녀의 어머니에게 용서해 달라고 간청했다.

　→ Mina asked her mother _____ her.

4) 그녀는 그에게 촛불을 켜게 했다.

　→ She let him _____ the candle.

5) 그는 딸에게 자전거를 타고 학교에 가라고 시켰다.

　→ He made his daughter _____ her bike.

6) 그들은 그가 직업을 찾는 것을 도왔다.

　→ They helped him _____ a job.

7) 나의 어머니는 내가 나비 잡는 것을 허락하셨다.

　→ My mother allowed me _____ the butterfly.

8) 나는 도둑이 벽 뒤에 숨는 것을 보았다.

　→ I saw the thief _____ behind the wall.

9) 나의 아버지는 나에게 자명종을 6시에 맞추라고 하셨다.

　→ My father got me _____ the alarm for 6 o'clock.

○3 다음 중 알맞은 것을 고르시오.

1) They could smell something   burning | to burn .

2) We   asked | saw   him to take photos of us.

3) The dolphin trainer   made | told   the dolphins jump.

4) Susan got us   to help | help   her.

5) Karl   helped | wanted   me do my homework.

○4 우리말과 일치하도록 주어진 말을 바르게 배열하시오.

1) 우리는 그가 유명한 배우가 될 거라고 예상하지 않았다.

(famous, expect, we, become, didn't, him, to, a, actor)

→ _____

2) 그녀는 그녀의 아이들이 시소를 타는 것을 보았다.

(seesaw, she, her, children, a, saw, riding)

→ _____

3) 나는 그 인기 있는 록스타가 무대에서 노래 부르는 것을 들었다.

(stage, the, I, rock star, on, the, listened to, popular, singing)

→ _____

4) 그들은 그들의 적을 항복하게 만들었다.

(enemy, they, surrender, their, made)

→ _____

○5 주어진 말을 이용하여 다음 우리말을 영작하시오.

1) 나는 그들이 농구하는 것을 봤다. (see)

→ _____

2) 나의 어머니는 나를 친구의 생일파티에 가게 해 주셨다. (let)

→ _____

3) 그들은 그 노인이 길을 건너는 것을 도왔다. (cross)

→ _____

4) 그녀는 누군가 그녀를 부르는 것을 들었다. (call)

→ _____

5) 그 선생님은 우리에게 교실을 청소하라고 시키셨다. (get, clean)

→ _____

O1 다음 문장의 <u>틀린</u> 부분에 밑줄을 긋고 바르게 고쳐 쓰시오.

1) He is enough brave to fight against the robber.   (→ _____)

2) They seemed to finding a solution.   (→ _____)

3) The book is too hard for me to read it.   (→ _____)

4) He seems that he got married.   (→ _____)

O2 우리말과 일치하도록 빈칸에 알맞은 말을 쓰시오.

1) 그 상자가 너무 작아서 그들은 책들을 모두 집어넣을 수 없었다.

→ The box was _____ small _____ they _____ put the books in it.

2) 이 책은 아주 쉬워서 누구나 읽을 수 있다.

→ This book is _____ easy _____ everyone _____ read it.

3) 이 노래는 우리가 감동받기에 충분히 아름다웠다.

→ This song was _____ _____ _____ _____ to be moved.

4) 그 강은 너무 깊어서 그녀가 건너갈 수 없다.

→ The river is _____ deep _____ _____ to cross.

O3 두 문장의 뜻이 같도록 문장을 완성하시오.

1) We were too sad to eat anything.

= We were so _____.

2) She is clever enough to get a perfect score.

= She is so _____.

3) The room is so dark that we can't see each other.

= The room is _____.

4) The book was so easy that they can read it.

= The book was _____.

5) He seemed to spread the rumor.

= It _____ spread the rumor.

O4 다음 문상을 우리말로 해석하시오.

1) She was too scared to say anything.

→ _____

2) He was lucky enough to find the lost bag.

→ _____

3) The children seem to like sunbathing.

→ _____

4) It was so hot that we could play on the beach all day.

→ _____

5) The map was so wrong that they couldn't find the way to the camp.

→ _____

O5 우리말과 일치하도록 주어진 말을 바르게 배열하시오.

1) 그들은 실수를 한 것 같았다.

(to, a, seemed, make, they, mistake)

→ _____

2) 기차는 너무 사람이 많아서 나는 내 친구를 찾을 수 없었다.

(my, friend, the, train, couldn't, crowded, was, so, I, that, find)

→ _____

3) 그 유리잔은 매우 깨지기 쉬워서 우리가 쉽게 깰 수 있다.

(break, glass, can, is, the, that, fragile, so, we, it, easily)

→ _____

4) 그 그림은 미술대회에서 이기기에 충분히 아름다웠다.

(art contest, painting, enough, the, was, win, beautiful, to, the)

→ _____

O6 주어진 말을 이용하여 다음 우리말을 영작하시오.

1) 그녀는 그녀의 돈을 잃어버린 것 같다. (it, lose)

→ _____

2) 그는 경찰이 되기에 충분히 용감하다. (enough, police officer)

→ _____

3) 그들은 너무 화가 나서 그를 용서할 수 없었다. (too, forgive)

→ _____

O1 다음 문장의 <u>틀린</u> 부분에 밑줄을 긋고 바르게 고쳐 쓰시오.

1) It is easy of us to speak Korean.   (→ _____)

2) It was wise them to do that.   (→ _____)

3) It took two hours me to come here.   (→ _____)

4) She seems to had been nervous.   (→ _____)

5) He seems to have been busy now.   (→ _____)

6) She seems to meet him yesterday.   (→ _____)

O2 우리말과 일치하도록 빈칸에 알맞은 말을 쓰시오.

1) 그가 중국어를 가르치는 것은 불가능하다.

   → It is impossible _____ _____ _____

         _____ Chinese.

2) 그녀가 그들에게 길을 알려주다니 잘했다.

   → It was nice _____ _____ _____ _____

     them the way.

3) 내가 숙제를 할 시간이다.

   → It is time _____ _____ _____ _____

     my homework.

4) 그들이 실망한 것 같았다.

   → They seemed _____ _____ disappointed.

O3 두 문장의 뜻이 같도록 문장을 완성하시오.

1) It seems that the coach trusts the players.

   = The coach _____ .

2) It seems that he has learned Chinese.

   = He _____ .

3) It seemed that they liked going skiing in the Alps.

   = They _____ .

4) It seemed that she had taken photos with the Olympic medalists.

   = She _____ .

04 다음 문장을 우리말로 해석하시오.

1) They seemed to have chosen the right leader.

→ _____

2) It is not easy for him to make an advertisement.

→ _____

3) It was wise of you to listen to your parents.

→ _____

4) It takes an hour for her to drive to work.

→ _____

05 우리말과 일치하도록 주어진 말을 바르게 배열하시오.

1) 그 팀의 주장은 다음 경기를 걱정하는 것 같았다.

(game, to, team captain, worried, the, seemed, the, about, next, be)

→ _____

2) 그 가수는 노래 가사를 잊어버렸던 것 같다.

(the, lyrics, the, to, have, the, of, singer, forgotten, song, seems)

→ _____

3) 우리는 그 집을 칠하는 데 5시간이 걸렸다.

(for, the, house, took, us, it, to, paint, five, hours)

→ _____

4) 그들이 그를 병원에 데려다 주다니 친절했다.

(to, them, it, take, was, him, of, the, to, hospital, kind)

→ _____

06 주어진 말을 이용하여 다음 우리말을 영작하시오.

1) 그 작가는 나를 기억하는 것 같았다. (writer)

→ _____

2) 그가 시험에서 부정행위를 하는 것은 어리석었다. (cheat on)

→ _____

3) 그녀가 마라톤을 뛰는 것은 불가능하다. (run a marathon)

→ _____

4) 내가 집에 가야 할 시간이다. (go home)

→ _____

O1 다음 중 알맞은 것을 고르시오.

1) They are bored with   do | doing   nothing.

2) The man finished   digging | to dig   in the ground to plant a tree.

3)   Dream | Dreaming   of my future makes me excited.

4) His duty is   inform | informing   them of any changes.

5) Because of   not wasting | wasting not   money, she could save some money.

6) She had a hard time   clean | cleaning   the house.

O2 다음 문장의 <u>틀린</u> 부분에 밑줄을 긋고 바르게 고쳐 쓰시오.

1) Kate is interested in invent a lot of things.   (→ _____)

2) She avoided be scolded by her mom.   (→ _____)

3) Don't making a noise in the library is a rule.   (→ _____)

4) Her brother feels like sleep all day.   (→ _____)

5) Bothering others are bad manners.   (→ _____)

O3 우리말과 일치하도록 빈칸에 알맞은 말을 보기에서 골라 알맞은 형태로 쓰시오.

| 보기 | discuss   organize   suffer   photograph   wrap   make |

1) 이 모임의 목적은 그의 선거운동을 조직하는 것이다.
   → The purpose of this meeting is _____ his election campaign.

2) 그 노부부는 어떤 병으로도 고통을 받지 않아서 만족했다.
   → The old couple was satisfied with _____ _____ from any disease.

3) 수지는 아름다운 풍경을 사진 찍는 것을 즐긴다.
   → Suzie enjoys _____ beautiful scenery.

4) 노력을 많이 하는 것이 너의 미래를 위해 좋다.
   → _____ a lot of effort is good for your future.

5) 우리는 크리스마스 선물을 포장하는 것을 끝냈다.
   → We finished _____ our Christmas gifts.

6) 그는 그녀와 그 문제에 대해 논의하는 것을 피곤해했다.
   → He is tired of _____ the matter with her.

04 다음 문장을 우리말로 해석하시오.

1) I can't help smiling when I see her.

→ _____

2) Not repeating the same error is necessary for them.

→ _____

3) The police stopped him from stealing the jewelry.

→ _____

05 우리말과 일치하도록 주어진 말을 바르게 배열하시오.

1) 다른 사람을 놀리지 않는 것은 그들에게 중요하다.

(important, not, fun, for, of, others, making, is, them)

→ _____

2) 그 소녀는 자신을 공주로 상상하는 것을 즐긴다.

(imagining, the, as, enjoys, princess, herself, a, girl)

→ _____

3) 그는 하버드대학에 입학하지 못해서 실망했다.

(disappointed, entering, with, he, Harvard University, not, was)

→ _____

4) 그녀는 그녀의 아들이 그녀의 차를 운전하는 것을 못하게 했다.

(her, driving, she, from, car, kept, son, her)

→ _____

06 주어진 말과 동명사를 이용하여 다음 우리말을 영작하시오.

1) 그들은 희망을 포기하지 않은 것을 자랑스러워 한다. (proud of, give up)

→ _____

2) 이 클럽의 목적은 작문 기술을 향상시키는 것이다. (purpose, writing skills)

→ _____

3) 규칙을 어기지 않는 것이 중요하다. (break)

→ _____

4) 케빈(Kevin)은 결승전을 보는 것을 학수고대하고 있다. (final game)

→ _____

5) 내 비밀을 말하지 않아서 고마워. (tell, secret)

→ _____

01 다음 문장의 **틀린** 부분에 밑줄을 긋고 바르게 고쳐 쓰시오.

1) I don't mind explain it again. (→ _____)

2) We hope improve our English in Canada. (→ _____)

3) Paul gave up run for president. (→ _____)

4) They planned protect the environment. (→ _____)

5) He avoided express his anger. (→ _____)

6) The boy wants behave himself. (→ _____)

02 두 문장의 뜻이 같도록 빈칸에 알맞은 말을 쓰시오.

1) Kate remembers that she booked a table for two.

= Kate remembers _____ a table for two.

2) He expects that he will persuade her to come to the meeting.

= He expects _____ her to come to the meeting.

3) The teacher forgot that she printed the handout a week ago.

= The teacher forgot _____ the handout a week ago.

4) I forgot that I had to review the lesson before the test.

= I forgot _____ the lesson before the test.

03 빈칸에 주어진 단어의 알맞은 형태를 쓰시오.

1) The reporter will remember _____ the mayor tomorrow. (interview)

2) He tried _____ his daughter until the final test ended. (not, bother)

3) Susan doesn't have the English text book now as she forgot _____ it. (bring)

4) We regret _____ you that we are not able to go to your party. (tell)

5) They are on a diet so they have stopped _____ fatty food. (eat)

6) The firefighters remembered _____ the children from the fire last month. (save)

7) She was bored so she tried _____ her friend. (call)

8) I forgot _____ Jason to my sister so I did it again. (introduce)

O4 다음 문장을 우리말로 해석하시오.

1) They remembered complaining about the bus service.

→ _____

2) They remembered to complain about the bus service.

→ _____

3) I regret saying that he did it.

→ _____

4) I regret to say that I am not able to help you.

→ _____

O5 우리말과 일치하도록 주어진 말을 바르게 배열하시오.

1) 수지는 그녀의 롤모델을 만났던 것을 잊지 못할 것이다.
(will, forget, meeting, Suzie, role model, her, never)

→ _____

2) 우리는 그 콘서트에 늦지 않겠다고 약속했다.
(late, we, to, concert, promised, be, not, the, for)

→ _____

3) 당신의 지원서는 받아들여지지 않았다고 말하게 되어 유감입니다.
(your, I, you, to, regret, application, tell, accepted, that, isn't)

→ _____

4) 경찰은 용의자를 쫓아다니는 것을 포기했다.
(the, chasing, the, gave, suspect, police, up)

→ _____

O6 주어진 말을 이용하여 다음 우리말을 영작하시오.

1) 우리는 약간의 정보를 수집하는 것을 잊었다. (collect)

→ _____

2) 해리(Harry)는 북극을 탐험하는 것을 끝마쳤다. (the Arctic)

→ _____

3) 그들은 위기에서 살아남았던 것을 기억했다. (survive the crisis)

→ _____

4) 그녀는 그를 친절하게 대하지 않았던 것을 후회한다. (treat, kindly)

→ _____

01 다음 문장의 <u>틀린</u> 부분에 밑줄을 긋고 바르게 고쳐 쓰시오.

1) He doesn't mind she talking loudly.　　　　(→ _____)

2) Amy is fond of he playing the piano.　　　　(→ _____)

3) He was disappointed with have failed his driving test.　(→ _____)

4) They are proud of understand the difficult lecture.　(→ _____)

02 두 문장의 뜻이 같도록 문장을 완성하시오.

1) Mina was amazed that she had gotten a perfect score.

= Mina was amazed at _____.

2) The boy is frightened to do the bungee jump.

= The boy is frightened at _____.

3) We are shocked that they destroyed all the evidence.

= We are shocked at _____.

4) He doesn't mind if I use his laptop.

= He doesn't mind _____.

5) He was disappointed that he wasn't elected as school president.

= He was disappointed with _____.

6) The man was embarrassed that he had repeated the same mistakes.

= The man was embarrassed at _____.

03 빈칸에 알맞은 동명사의 형태를 쓰시오.

1) She told me a lie, but now she is ashamed of _____ _____ it.

2) He hit a homerun yesterday. We are amazed at _____ _____ _____ homerun.

3) I will get third prize. I am satisfied with _____ third prize.

4) We want to complain about the product. The company doesn't mind _____ _____ about it.

5) They had completed the project. We were surprised at _____ _____ _____ the project so quickly.

04 다음 문장을 우리말로 해석하시오.

1) He was surprised at her speaking English fluently.

→ _____

2) Suzie was moved by him helping the poor.

→ _____

3) They were depressed by her scolding them.

→ _____

4) We are interested in their having solved a mysterious murder.

→ _____

05 우리말과 일치하도록 주어진 말을 바르게 배열하시오.

1) 우리는 그들이 암호를 풀었던 것에 매료되었다.

(fascinated, we, having, the code, were, their, with, broken)

→ _____

2) 그들은 그가 적에게 무기를 공급한다는 것에 충격을 받았다.

(shocked, they, arms, were, enemy, supplying, at, to, the, him)

→ _____

3) 그녀는 그가 그의 의견을 바꿔서 혼란스럽다.

(having, she, is, about, opinion, confused, his, changed, his)

→ _____

4) 나는 그가 변명을 해서 놀랐다.

(making, I, at, his, was, excuses, surprised)

→ _____

06 주어진 말을 이용하여 다음 우리말을 영작하시오.

1) 우리는 그가 세계신기록을 세웠던 것에 놀라고 있다. (set)

→ _____

2) 나는 그녀가 나의 제안을 받아들여서 신이 난다. (accept, proposal)

→ _____

3) 제임스(James)는 그들이 최고의 서비스를 제공해서 만족했다. (offer)

→ _____

4) 그들은 그가 천 년 전에 나라를 구했다는 것을 자랑스러워 했다. (save)

→ _____

01   다음 중 알맞은 것을 고르시오.

1) Ann has already   locking | locked   the gate.

2) They are looking for a   losing | lost   puppy.

3) A   barking | barked   dog never bites.

4) Is your brother the boy   wearing | worn   a yellow shirt?

5) I got an invitation card   sending | sent   by one of my friends.

6) Many people were   exciting | excited   because the game was very   exciting | excited .

7) We were   shocking | shocked   because of the   shocking | shocked   news.

8) Karen saw a boy   standing | stood   at the bus stop.

9) Sora and I heard the song   playing | played   somewhere.

10) Many travelers had their cell phones   steal | stolen   in France and Italy.

02   주어진 단어를 빈칸에 알맞은 형태로 바꿔 쓰시오.

1) (bore)   ① His speech was _____.

               ② All of us felt _____ with his presentation.

               ③ I don't like a _____ man. I like a man of humor.

               ④ Look at the _____ people. They are yawning.

               ⑤ She tried to read _____ books.

               ⑥ I found the game _____.

               ⑦ Listening to classical music makes me _____.

2) (disappoint)   ① He was _____ with her lies.

               ② Her answer to the question was _____.

               ③ The research showed _____ results.

               ④ The people _____ with the movie looked angry.

               ⑤ Don't make me _____.

3) (scold)   ① Sumi saw the teacher _____ a student.

               ② Sumi saw him _____ in front of the students.

4) (carry)   ① We got him _____ the suitcase.

               ② We got the suitcase _____.

03 우리말과 일치하도록 빈칸에 주어진 단어의 알맞은 형태를 쓰시오.

1) 혼자 남겨진 그 아이는 울고 있다. (leave)

→ The child _____ alone is crying.

2) 무대에서 노래를 부르고 있는 소녀들은 매우 행복해 보인다. (sing)

· The girls _____ on the stage look happy.

3) 팬들의 의해 둘러싸인 그 배우는 당황한 것처럼 보였다 (surround, confuse)

→ The actor _____ by fans seemed _____.

4) 우리는 거리에서 한 남자가 체포되는 것을 보았다. (arrest)

→ We saw a man _____ on the street.

5) 방을 떠나는 마지막 사람이 불을 꺼야 한다. (leave)

→ The last man _____ the room must turn off the light.

6) 나의 어머니는 장미가 마당에 심겨지도록 했다. (plant)

→ My mother had roses _____ in the yard.

04 다음 문장의 틀린 부분에 밑줄을 긋고 바르게 고쳐 쓰시오.

1) The book written by him looks interested.　　　　(→ _____)

2) Walking on the falling leaves is pleasant.　　　　(→ _____)

3) She was surprising at his sudden gift.　　　　(→ _____)

4) Sheldon had his eyesight test last week.　　　　(→ _____)

5) Whose car key was putting on the table?　　　　(→ _____)

6) Minho bought two books publishing this year.　　　　(→ _____)

7) Many workers didn't feel satisfying with their pay.　　　　(→ _____)

8) The work they finished was satisfied.　　　　(→ _____)

05 주어진 말을 이용하여 다음 우리말을 영작하시오.

1) 인사동에는 많은 흥미로운 가게들이 있다. (interest, Insa-dong)

→ _____

2) 설리(Shelly)는 그들이 버스를 타는 것을 보았다. (take a bus)

→ _____

3) 케이트(Kate)는 그녀의 컴퓨터가 수리되도록 했다. (get, repair)

→ _____

4) 나는 나의 별명이 불리는 것을 들었다. (nickname)

→ _____

01 다음 문장을 분사구문으로 바꿀 때 빈칸에 알맞은 말을 쓰시오.

1) As she plays the piano, she sings a song.

→ _____ the piano, she sings a song.

2) When he was in New York, he often went to see musicals.

→ _____ in New York, he often went to see musicals.

3) If you watch the movie, you can understand what he said.

→ _____, you can understand what he said.

4) Though Tommy caught a cold, he didn't take any medicine.

→ _____, Tommy didn't take any medicine.

5) While Ann was cooking food, she listened to rock music.

→ _____, Ann listened to rock music.

6) Because she had no close friends, she felt lonely

→ _____, she felt lonely.

7) As my sister didn't have enough money, she couldn't buy the bag.

→ _____, my sister couldn't buy the bag.

8) We watched the movie as we ate popcorn.

→ We watched the movie _____ popcorn.

02 두 문장의 뜻이 같도록 빈칸에 알맞은 말을 쓰시오.

1) Walking along the river, I saw two dogs playing together.

= When _____ along the river, I saw two dogs playing together.

2) Getting up late, he didn't eat breakfast.

= _____ up late, he didn't eat breakfast.

3) Arriving at the station in a hurry, we missed the train.

= _____ at the station in a hurry, we missed the train.

4) Eating fast food at night, you will gain weight.

= _____ fast food at night, you will gain weight.

5) Not knowing what to do, she stood quietly.

= _____ what to do, she stood quietly.

○3 우리말과 일치하도록 밑줄 친 부분을 바르게 고쳐 쓰시오.

1) 나의 어머니는 전화통화를 하면서 그 방을 청소하셨다.

→ <u>Talk on the phone</u>, my mother cleaned the room. (→ _____)

2) 나는 버스정류장에 서 있었을 때 나의 친구를 만났다.

→ <u>Stood at the bus stop</u>, I met my friend. (→ _____)

3) 우리는 충분한 시간이 없었기 때문에 택시를 타야 했다.

→ <u>Don't have enough time</u>, we had to take a taxi. (→ _____)

4) 그녀는 TV를 보는 동안에 장갑을 짰다.

→ <u>She watching TV</u>, she knitted gloves. (→ _____)

○4 우리말과 일치하도록 주어진 말을 바르게 배열하시오.

1) 유리는 그녀의 여동생의 이름을 부르면서 집으로 달려 들어갔다.

(her sister's, ran, calling, into, name, Yuri, the house)

→ _____

2) 그는 할 것이 없었기 때문에 낮잠을 잤다.

(having, do, he, nothing, a nap, to, took)

→ _____

3) 나의 어머니는 책을 읽은 후에 저녁을 준비하셨다.

(reading, prepared, a book, my mother, dinner)

→ _____

4) 운전하는 법을 몰랐기 때문에 나는 자동차를 사고 싶지 않다.

(not, want, how, to, knowing, drive, I, don't, a car to, buy)

→ _____

○5 주어진 말과 분사구문을 이용하여 다음 우리말을 영작하시오.

1) 그는 혼자 살지만 외롭지 않았다. (alone, feel lonely)

→ _____

2) 나는 숲 속을 걷고 있을 때 잠자리 한 마리를 잡았다. (forest, dragonfly)

→ _____

3) 나는 거기에 간다면 많은 종류의 꽃을 볼 것이다. (see)

→ _____

01 다음 문장을 분사구문으로 바꿀 때 빈칸에 알맞은 말을 쓰시오.

1) Because Terry studied hard, he passed the exam.

→ _____ hard, Terry passed the exam.

2) As he finished doing his homework yesterday, he is free now.

→ _____ doing his homework yesterday, he is free now.

3) After she had cleaned the house, she planted a few trees.

→ _____, she planted a few trees.

4) As I have never met Sora, I don't know about her at all.

→ _____ Sora, I don't know about her at all.

5) When she was invited to Edward's birthday party, she was very pleased.

→ _____ to Edward's birthday party, she was very pleased.

→ _____ to Edward's birthday party, she was very pleased.

6) Because he was born in Germany, he can speak German.

→ _____ in Germany, he can speak German.

→ _____ in Germany, he can speak German.

7) When she is compared with her mother, she is not so beautiful.

→ _____ with her mother, she is not so beautiful.

02 우리말과 일치하도록 밑줄 친 부분을 바르게 고쳐 쓰시오.

1) 그녀는 작년에 중학교를 졸업했기 때문에 지금 고등학생이다.

→ Graduating from middle school last year, she is a high school student now.

(→ _____)

2) 나는 계란에 싫증이 났기 때문에 더 이상 그것을 먹고 싶지 않다.

→ Tiring of eggs, I don't want to eat them anymore. (→ _____)

3) 그녀는 선생님한테 벌을 받은 후에 매우 우울했다.

→ Having punished by the teacher, she felt depressed. (→ _____)

4) 브라이언은 그녀에게 꽃 한 송이를 주면서 그녀를 좋아한다고 말했다.

→ Given her a flower, Brian said he liked her. (→ _____)

03 다음 중 알맞은 것을 고르고 우리말로 해석하시오.

1) Asking | Asked   Terry how to use the machine, Sora handed him a cup of coffee.

→ _____

2) Asking | Asked   how old she was, the girl didn't answer the question.

→ _____

3) Painting | Painted   the portrait, the painter was 90 years old.

→ _____

4) Painting | Painted   by the famous painter, the pictures sold well.

→ _____

5) Seeing | Seen   from a plane, the houses looked like matchboxes.

→ _____

6) Seeing | Seen   my grandmother, I ran toward her.

→ _____

7) Spending | Spent   hours playing computer games, the boy did his homework.

→ _____

8) Being spent | Having spent   all our money yesterday, we can't stay at a hotel.

→ _____

04 우리말과 일치하도록 주어진 말을 바르게 배열하시오.

1) 그 책은 프랑스어로 쓰였기 때문에 읽기 어렵다.

(in, written, hard, to, the book, French, is, read)

→ _____

2) 그 책은 오랫동안 읽혀지지 않았기 때문에 먼지로 덮여있었다.

(a long time, having, covered, been, read, for, with, the book, not, was, dust)

→ _____

3) 우리는 어젯밤에 그 정보를 얻었으므로 그에게 연락할 것이다.

(gained, keep in touch, we, having, last night, him, the information, will, with)

→ _____

01 다음 문장을 분사구문으로 바꿀 때 빈칸에 알맞은 말을 쓰시오.

1) When I went to bed, I always turned off the lights.

→ _____ _____ to bed, I always turned off the lights.

2) As it got too hot, we turned on the air conditioner.

→ _____ _____ too hot, we turned on the air conditioner.

3) After the game was over, Juliet came home in a hurry.

→ _____ _____ _____ over, Juliet came home in a hurry.

4) Although there are many houses in Seoul, I have no house.

→ _____ _____ many houses in Seoul, I have no house.

5) If we speak frankly, the food you made is not good.

→ _____ _____, the food you made is not good.

6) If we judge from her appearance, she must be an actress.

→ _____ _____ her appearance, she must be an actress.

02 다음 중 알맞은 것을 고르시오.

1) Speaking strictly | Strictly speaking , this tree is different from that one.
2) Raining | It raining at the moment, the picnic was canceled.
3) Considering | Considered her good grades, she can go to university.
4) While taking | taken a rest, we drank some water.
5) Mrs. Brown lay on the bed with her baby crying | cried beside her.
6) The woman stood in front of me with her arms crossing | crossed .
7) Don't leave a baby alone in the room with the door locking | locked .

03 밑줄 친 부분에 유의하여 다음 문장을 우리말로 해석하시오.

1) She sat on the train with her legs crossed.

→ _____

2) The princess was walking around the garden with her servants following her.

→ _____

3) Considering her age, she must be smart.

→ _____

04 우리말과 일치하도록 빈간에 알맞은 말을 쓰시오.

1) 일반적으로 말하면 여성이 남성보다 오래 산다.

→ _____ _____, women live longer than men.

2) 앤은 불을 켠 채로 잠이 들었다.

→ Ann fell asleep with the light _____ on.

3) 그는 그의 아들이 게임을 하게 하면서 TV를 보는 중이다.

→ He is watching TV with his son _____ games.

4) 그는 창문이 닫힌 채로 볼륨을 크게 올렸다.

→ He turned the volume up _____ the window _____.

05 우리말과 일치하도록 주어진 말을 바르게 배열하시오.

1) 에이미는 그녀의 숙제를 끝낸 후에 친구들과 시간을 보냈다.

(her, after, her friends, homework, with, Amy, finishing, hung out)

→ _____

2) 그 도둑은 손이 묶인 채로 그 경찰 뒤에서 걸어갔다.

(behind, walked, his hands, the police officer, the thief, with, tied)

→ _____

3) 태양이 진 후에 우리는 정동진에 도착했다.

(arrived, having, the sun, set, at, we, Jeongdongjin)

→ _____

4) 모든 학생들이 쳐다보는 가운데 그 선생님이 교실 안으로 들어왔다.

(the teacher, the students, with, all, looking, at, entered, the classroom, her)

→ _____

06 주어진 말을 이용하여 다음 우리말을 영작하시오.

1) 솔직히 말하면 케이트(Kate)가 거짓말을 했다. (tell a lie)

→ _____

2) 나의 남동생은 책을 덮고서 시를 암기하고 있다. (memorize, a poem, with)

→ _____

3) 날씨가 덥고 건조하기 때문에 우리는 자주 물을 마셨다. (it, dry)

→ _____

01 다음 문장의 <u>틀린</u> 부분에 밑줄을 긋고 바르게 고쳐 쓰시오.

1) She is so ambitious as he is.   (→ _____)

2) Jane is more brighter than James.   (→ _____)

3) He is less luckiest than his friend.   (→ _____)

4) His hair is not as shorter as hers.   (→ _____)

5) She is the most intelligent student of her school. (→ _____)

6) He is the more creative of all the researchers.   (→ _____)

7) Cathy earns much than Karl does.   (→ _____)

02 두 문장이 같은 뜻이 되도록 빈칸에 알맞은 말을 쓰시오.

1) Kate is more active than Jane.

= Jane is _____ active than Kate.

2) A bike is not as expensive as a car.

= A bike is _____ than a car.

3) Kevin is more generous than Paul.

= Paul is _____ _____ generous _____ Kevin.

4) Mt. Seorak is not as high as Mt. Halla.

= Mt. Halla is _____ _____ Mt. Seorak.

03 우리말과 일치하도록 주어진 단어를 이용하여 빈칸을 채우시오.

1) 면은 실크만큼 부드럽지 않다. (smooth)

→ Cotton is _____ _____ _____ _____ silk.

2) 그는 그녀보다 영어를 더 유창하게 말한다. (fluently)

→ He speaks English _____ _____ than her.

3) 이 문제는 저 문제보다 덜 심각하다. (serious)

→ This problem is _____ _____ than that one.

4) 이 건물은 이 도시에서 가장 좋은 교회이다. (good)

→ This building is _____ _____ church in the city.

04 주어진 단어의 원급, 비교급, 최상급을 이용하여 문장을 완성하시오.

1) His essay is as _____ as hers. (good)

2) They are _____ singers in this country. (good)

3) Her English is _____ than I thought. (good)

4) His acting is _____ than hers. (bad)

5) There is _____ traffic than we thought. (much)

05 우리말과 일치하도록 주어진 말을 바르게 배열하시오.

1) 그 소설은 그 영화만큼 지루하지 않다.

(as, not, the, so, novel, is, movie, boring, the)

→ _____

2) 1월은 가장 추운 달이다.

(coldest, all, January, of, months, is, the)

→ _____

3) 그 아기는 인형보다 더 사랑스럽다.

(than, the, more, is, baby, doll, the, adorable)

→ _____

4) 그녀의 기술이 내가 예상했던 것보다 더 빠르게 향상하고 있다.

(improving, her, expected, faster, skill, I, is, than)

→ _____

06 주어진 말을 이용하여 다음 우리말을 영작하시오.

1) 그는 그의 남동생만큼 부정적이지 않다. (negative)

→ _____

2) 이것은 세상에서 가장 멋진 사원이다. (wonderful, temple)

→ _____

3) 그들은 그들의 사촌보다 더 민감하다. (sensitive)

→ _____

4) 그는 그녀의 모든 선생님들 중에서 가장 엄격하다. (strict)

→ _____

5) 내 친구는 내가 가지고 있는 것보다 더 많은 책을 가지고 있다. (have)

→ _____

O1 우리말과 일치하도록 주어진 단어를 이용하여 빈칸을 채우시오.

1) 그 마을은 점점 더 평화로워지고 있다. (peaceful)

→ The town is becoming _____ _____ _____

_____.

2) 그 의사는 환자보다 훨씬 더 당황했다. (embarrassed)

→ The doctor was _____ _____ _____ than his patient.

3) 그 선생님은 우리에게 가능한 한 많이 가르쳐 주시려고 했다. (much)

→ The teacher tried to teach us _____ _____ _____

possible.

4) 이 엔진은 저 엔진보다 세 배 더 강력하다. (powerful)

→ This engine is _____ _____ _____

_____ as that one.

O2 보기와 같이 다음 문장을 바꾸어 쓰시오.

> 보기
>
> As you have more, you want more.
> → The more you have, the more you want.

1) As we run faster, we get there earlier.

→ _____

2) As the sky is clearer, you can see more stars.

→ _____

O3 두 문장의 뜻이 같도록 빈칸에 알맞은 말을 쓰시오.

1) We will take the train as early as possible.

= We will take the train as early as _____ _____.

2) Susan went to bed as late as possible.

= Susan went to bed as late as _____ _____.

3) The bracelet is four times as expensive as the earrings.

= The bracelet is four times _____ _____ _____ the
earrings.

O4 다음 문장을 우리말로 해석하시오.

1) The faster you get there, the longer you can take a rest.

→ _____

2) My classroom is even more crowded than his.

→ _____

3) This bridge is four times as long as that one.

→ _____

4) All my classmates will jump as high as possible.

→ _____

O5 우리말과 일치하도록 주어진 말을 바르게 배열하시오.

1) 그는 더 많이 걸을수록 더 건강해질 것이다.

(the, be, he, healthier, walks, the, he, more, will)

→ _____

2) 나의 언니와 나는 가능한 한 멀리 여행하고 싶어 한다.

(far, my, want, sister, possible, travel, as, and, I, to, as)

→ _____

3) 로봇은 점점 더 지능적이 되고 있다.

(more, getting, more, robots, are, and, intelligent)

→ _____

4) 그 노인은 그 소년보다 10배 더 참을성이 있다.

(the, is, the, ten, as, old, times, boy, as, man, patient)

→ _____

O6 주어진 말을 이용하여 다음 우리말을 영작하시오.

1) 그 그림은 점점 더 가치 있어 지고 있다. (valuable)

→ _____

2) 그 시험이 어려울수록 그는 더 긴장할 것이다. (nervous)

→ _____

3) 폴(Paul)은 가능한 한 빨리 그 문제를 해결할 것이다. (quickly)

→ _____

O1 다음 문장의 <u>틀린</u> 부분에 밑줄을 긋고 바르게 고쳐 쓰시오.

1) Bach is one of the most famous composer in the world.　　(→ _____)

2) The man is the strange person that I have ever met.　　(→ _____)

3) No other boy in my class is tall as Paul.　　(→ _____)

4) She is happiest girl in the book club.　　(→ _____)

5) He is diligent than any other student in our school.　　(→ _____)

6) No other pilot in the airline is most skilled than James.　　(→ _____)

O2 두 문장의 뜻이 같도록 빈칸에 알맞은 말을 쓰시오.

1) She is the most creative artist in my country.

= She is _____ _____ _____ any other artist in my country.

2) No other barista in the cafe is as good as Harry.

= No other barista in the cafe is _____ _____ Harry.

3) He is the healthiest baby in my town.

= No _____ _____ in my town is _____ _____ _____ him.

4) This room is noisier than any other place in the building.

= No _____ _____ in this building is _____ _____ _____ this room.

O3 우리말과 일치하도록 주어진 단어를 이용하여 빈칸을 채우시오.

1) '해바라기'는 세계에서 가장 인상적인 명작들 중의 하나이다. (impressive, masterpiece)

→ *Sunflower* is one of _____ _____ _____ _____ in the world.

2) 여기는 내가 지금까지 가 본 도시 중에서 가장 멋진 도시이다. (fantastic)

→ This is _____ _____ _____ city that I have ever been to.

3) 이것은 다른 어떤 기계보다 더 유용하다. (useful)

→ This is _____ _____ than _____ _____ _____ machine.

O4 다음 문장을 우리말로 해석하시오.

1) No other boy in my class is as polite as Jack.

→ _____

2) No other food is more nutritious than this.

→ _____

O5 우리말과 일치하도록 주어진 말을 바르게 배열하시오.

1) 그는 이 공장에서 가장 기술 좋은 기계공들 중 한 명이다.

(skillful, is, the, he, one, mechanics, this, of, in, most, factory)

→ _____

2) 그녀는 내가 만나 본 사람 중 가장 야망 있는 사람이다.

(most, she, is, ever, that, met, person, the, have, ambitious, I)

→ _____

3) 그 미술관의 다른 어떤 그림도 이것만큼 비싸지는 않다.

(gallery, as, other, the, expensive, no, as, painting, in, is, this)

→ _____

4) 그는 팀에서 다른 어떤 선수보다 더 도전적이다.

(player, than, team, he, is, other, the, more, any, in, challenging)

→ _____

O6 주어진 말을 이용하여 다음 우리말을 영작하시오.

1) 이것은 내가 풀어본 문제 중에서 가장 복잡한 문제이다. (complicated)

→ _____

2) 반 고흐(Van Gogh)는 역사상 가장 위대한 화가들 중 한 명이다. (great)

→ _____

3) 그녀는 그 연구소에서 가장 호기심 많은 과학자이다. (curious, research center)

→ _____

4) 제임스(James)는 그 클럽에서 다른 누구보다도 더 관대하다. (generous)

→ _____

5) 그 잡지사의 다른 어떤 기자도 케이트(Kate)보다 더 바쁘지 않다. (no, reporter)

→ _____

01 우리말과 일치하도록 빈칸에 알맞은 접속사를 쓰시오.

1) 그녀는 대학에 입학했을 뿐만 아니라 장학금도 받았다.

→ She _____ _____ entered the university _____ _____ got a scholarship.

2) 그는 영화와 뮤지컬 둘 다 연출한다.

→ He produces _____ movies _____ musicals.

3) 우리는 그의 의견도 그녀의 의견도 받아들일 수 없다.

→ We can accept _____ his opinion _____ hers.

4) 나는 이탈리아가 아니라 스페인에 갈 것이다.

→ I will go to _____ Italy _____ Spain.

5) 영어클럽에 가입해라, 그러면 너의 영어 실력은 향상될 것이다.

→ Join the English club, _____ your English will improve.

6) 밤에 잠을 잘 자라, 그렇지 않으면 너는 낮에 피곤할 것이다.

→ Have a good night sleep, _____ you will be tired during the day.

02 빈칸에 주어진 동사의 알맞은 현재시제를 쓰시오.

1) Both Paul and Jane _____ to travel. (like)

2) Neither Sally nor I _____ to bring the dictionary to school. (want)

3) Not only Kate but also I _____ going to participate in the meeting. (be)

4) Not they but he _____ broken the rule. (have)

03 두 문장이 같은 의미가 되도록 빈칸에 알맞은 말을 쓰시오.

1) If you apply for the job, you will be able to get it.

= Apply for the job, _____ you will be able to get it.

2) If you don't learn English now, you will regret it later.

= Learn English now, _____ you will regret it later.

= _____ you learn English now, you will regret it later.

3) She wasted time as well as money.

= She wasted _____ _____ money _____ _____ time.

O4 다음 두 문장을 한 문장으로 만들 때 빈칸에 알맞은 상관접속사를 쓰시오.

1) She wants to go camping. I want to go camping, too.

→ _____ she _____ I want to go camping.

2) She can't speak English. She can't speak Spanish, either.

→ She can speak _____ English _____ Spanish.

3) They will elect him as class president. Or they will elect her as class president.

→ They will elect _____ him _____ her as class president.

O5 우리말과 일치하도록 주어진 말을 바르게 배열하시오.

1) 꿈을 가져라, 그러면 너는 더 많은 것을 성취할 수 있을 것이다.

(a, dream, you, achieve, and, things, more, have, be able to, will)

→ _____

2) 그들뿐만 아니라 우리도 그가 말하는 것을 잘 이해할 수 없다.

(what, well, as, he, can't, says, as, we, understand, they)

→ _____

3) 그도 나도 우리의 선생님으로부터 칭찬을 기대하지 않는다.

(from, praise, neither, expect, he, nor, our, teacher, I)

→ _____

4) 그녀가 아니라 내가 절벽에서 다이빙을 할 것이다.

(am, to, not, she, dive, but, from, the, going, cliff, I)

→ _____

O6 주어진 말을 이용하여 다음 우리말을 영작하시오.

1) 그녀와 연락해라, 그렇지 않으면 너는 그녀를 다시 못 만날 것이다. (keep in touch)

→ _____

2) 종이를 재활용해라, 그러면 너는 많은 나무를 살릴 수 있다. (save)

→ _____

3) 그녀뿐만 아니라 그녀의 아이들도 환경을 보호한다. (not only)

→ _____

4) 우리도 그녀도 게임을 하는 것을 좋아하지 않는다. (neither)

→ _____

01 다음 문장의 <u>틀린</u> 부분에 밑줄을 긋고 바르게 고쳐 쓰시오.

1) The fact is if the lake is frozen during winter. (→ _____)

2) I don't know that he drinks ice coffee. (→ _____)

3) Whether they have supernatural power isn't true. (→ _____)

4) What do you know he designed? (→ _____)

5) Do you believe who she depends on? (→ _____)

6) Do you know where did he stay yesterday? (→ _____)

7) I found what she loves traveling by train. (→ _____)

8) Do you know that he chose as a career? (→ _____)

02 주어진 말로 시작하여 다음 질문에 대한 대답을 완성하시오.

1) **A** Is she going to record her song?

   B I don't know _____ .

2) **A** Where did he bury his dog?

   B I don't know _____ .

3) **A** Will they offer guided tours?

   B I don't know _____ .

03 우리말과 일치하도록 빈칸에 알맞은 말을 쓰시오.

1) 나는 그 식당의 음식이 놀랄 정도로 맛있다고 생각한다.

   → I think _____ the food at the restaurant is amazingly delicious.

2) 유명한 아이돌 가수들이 개회식에서 노래한다는 것은 사실이다.

   → _____ famous idols will sing at the opening ceremony is true.

3) 나는 그 의사가 그 환자를 치료했는지 궁금하다.

   → I wonder _____ the doctor cured the patient.

4) 너는 그들이 무엇을 조직했는지 아니?

   → _____ _____ _____ _____ they organized?

5) 너는 그녀가 생일선물로 무엇을 받았다고 생각하니?

   → _____ _____ _____ _____ she received as a birthday present?

O4 다음 문장을 우리말로 해식하시오.

1) That Edison invented electricity is not true.

→ _____

2) She doesn't know if they will go on a school trip in May.

→ _____

3) What do you think she is proud of?

→ _____

O5 우리말과 일치하도록 주어진 말을 바르게 배열하시오.

1) 너는 그가 그녀를 언제 처음 만났다고 믿니?

(met, do, he, first, you, when, her, for, the, time, believe)

→ _____

2) 나는 그녀에게 그 올림픽경기가 어디에서 열렸었는지 물어봤다.

(took, her, I, where, place, asked, the Olympic Games)

→ _____

3) 나는 그가 우리가 말한 것을 엿들었는지 궁금하다.

(wonder, we, if, he, about, talked, I, what, overheard)

→ _____

4) 그는 그녀가 돈을 주식에 투자하는지 모른다.

(he, invests, whether, in, she, stocks, doesn't, her, money, know)

→ _____

O6 주어진 말을 이용하여 다음 우리말을 영작하시오.

1) 우리는 경찰이 그 도둑을 쫓아갔는지 궁금하다. (chase)

→ _____

2) 너는 그가 누구와 사랑에 빠졌다고 생각하니? (fall in love with)

→ _____

3) 그녀는 내가 그에게 무엇을 빌렸는지 안다. (borrow)

→ _____

4) 그 운전사가 그 소년을 구했다는 것은 사실이다. (save)

→ _____

01 우리말과 일치하도록 빈칸에 알맞은 접속사를 쓰시오.

1) 그가 숙제를 하는 동안 그의 남동생은 TV를 봤다.

→ His brother was watching TV _____ he was doing his homework.

2) 우리가 학교에 걸어가는 반면 그들은 학교에 자전거를 타고 간다.

→ They ride bikes to school _____ we walk to school.

3) 비록 그 아이디어는 창의적이지만 현실적이지는 않다.

→ _____ the idea is creative, it is not practical.

4) 그는 매우 수줍음이 많아서 사람들 앞에서 연설할 수 없다.

→ He is _____ shy _____ he _____ make a speech in public.

5) 정부는 사람들이 그 강을 건널 수 있도록 다리를 만들 것이다.

→ The government will build a bridge _____ _____ people can cross the river.

6) 날씨가 더 더워지고 있기 때문에 많은 사람들은 해변에 가기를 원한다.

→ _____ _____ it is getting hotter, a lot of people want to go to the beach.

02 두 문장의 뜻이 같도록 빈칸에 알맞은 말을 쓰시오.

1) He followed the map but he lost his way.

→ _____ he followed the map, he lost his way.

2) She returned the coat so she received a refund.

→ _____ she returned the coat, she received a refund.

3) If they don't protect themselves, nobody will protect them.

→ _____ they protect themselves, nobody will protect them.

4) Before she graduated from school, she did a lot of volunteer work.

→ _____ she did a lot of volunteer work, she graduated from school.

5) We came here by subway because the traffic was heavy.

→ We came here by subway _____ _____ heavy traffic.

O3 다음 문장을 우리말로 해석하시오.

1) She is practicing the piano hard so that she can win the music competition.

→ _____

2) The boy was so intelligent that he could solve the mystery.

→ _____

3) Now that he fastened his seat belt, he survived the car accident.

→ _____

4) Unless he reviews his decision, he can't get a good result.

→ _____

O4 우리말과 일치하도록 주어진 말을 바르게 배열하시오.

1) 이 그림은 아주 현대적이어서 그는 이해할 수 없다.

(that, can't, this, painting, understand, so, he, it, modern, is)

→ _____

2) 비록 그는 매우 참을성이 있었지만 그것을 참을 수 없었다.

(was, could, although, patient, tolerate, he, very, not, it, he)

→ _____

3) 그들은 미끄러지지 않기 위해서 얼음 위에서 조심스럽게 걸었다.

(slide, on, they, so, wouldn't, carefully, that, the, ice, walked, they)

→ _____

4) 그녀가 그를 설득한다면 그는 죄를 자백할 것이다.

(him, crime, if, persuades, will, his, confess, she, he)

→ _____

O5 주어진 말을 이용하여 다음 우리말을 영작하시오.

1) 비록 그는 그녀에게 무언가를 속삭였지만 그녀는 그것을 들을 수 없었다. (although, whisper)

→ _____

2) 만약 그가 그녀의 초대를 거절하지 않는다면 그는 파티에 올 것이다. (unless, refuse)

→ _____

3) 그녀는 너무 초조해서 아무것도 할 수 없었다. (nervous)

→ _____

4) 그는 자는 동안 하늘을 나는 꿈을 꾸었다. (dream about)

→ _____

O1 다음 중 알맞은 것을 고르시오.

1) A waiter is a person   who | which   works in a restaurant.

2) The woman   which | whom   he married works as a florist.

3) The lady   who | whose   bag is on the table is my friend.

4) A blender is a machine   who | which   mixes food.

5) He has an aunt   which | whose   house is a five-story building.

6) A doctor   which | that   treats skin problems is a dermatologist.

7) The flowers that   is | are   in the vase are roses and carnations.

O2 관계대명사를 이용하여 다음 두 문장을 한 문장으로 쓰시오.

1) Jenny supports the child. He has no parents.

→ _____

2) He has two cats. They are cute but fat.

→ _____

3) I know an author. Her book was published in 2014.

→ _____

4) The man is handsome. My sister wants to meet him.

→ _____

5) The town has a lot of traditional houses. We visited it last summer.

→ _____

6) The tree looks very beautiful. Its leaves turn red and yellow.

→ _____

O3 빈칸에 알맞은 관계대명사를 쓰시오.

1) Once there lived a king _____ had no child.

2) My friend Bora looks after dogs _____ got lost.

3) The professor _____ Brian met last week teaches history.

4) The food _____ Susan brought is pizza.

5) Tim spoke to the woman _____ hair is blond.

6) Please throw away the chairs _____ legs are broken.

O4 다음 문장의 밑줄 친 부분을 바르게 고쳐 쓰시오.

1) The reporter which wrote the article used to be a teacher.　　(→ _____)

2) The bus whose he takes every morning is always crowded.　　(→ _____)

3) I am not interested in the movie which storyline is boring.　　(→ _____)

4) The kids that is dancing on the stage look cute.　　(→ _____)

5) There is a boy who want to be an Edison.　　(→ _____)

6) The shop which owner is my friend sells a variety of tea.　　(→ _____)

O5 우리말과 일치하도록 주어진 말을 바르게 배열하시오.

1) 브라이언은 그의 여자친구가 보낸 소포를 받지 못했다.

(which, has, Brian, not, his girlfriend, the parcel, received, sent)

→ _____

2) 나는 많은 사람에게 이름이 알려진 시인을 알고 있다.

(a poet, know, name, is, whose, to, many, known, I, people)

→ _____

3) 그 선생님은 바닥에 쓰레기를 버린 학생을 야단치고 있다.

(is, the student, the teacher, scolding, who, garbage, on, threw, the floor)

→ _____

4) 그가 찾은 정보는 매우 유용했다.

(that, he, the information, very, found, was, useful)

→ _____

5) 그 외국인은 지붕이 한국 전통 기와로 만들어진 집에서 산다.

(lives, in, the foreigner, the house, roof, is, whose, made, Korean tiles, of, traditional)

→ _____

O6 주어진 말을 이용하여 다음 우리말을 영작하시오.

1) 나는 그 거지에게 내가 갖고 있는 동전을 주었다. (beggar)

→ _____

2) 소라(Sora)는 멕시코 출신의 친구 두 명이 있다. (Mexico)

→ _____

3) 나는 눈이 매우 큰 여자를 알고 있다. (whose)

→ _____

01 다음 중 알맞은 것을 고르시오.

1) Insu is the very boy   that | who   solved the hardest problem.

2) This spaghetti is the worst food   that | which   I have ever eaten.

3) Penny is the girl to   who | whom   I sent the letter.

4)   Which | What   she needs most is your help.

5) This cell phone is the thing   what | that   I want to buy.

6) Please show me   that | what   is in your pocket.

7) He has not found the cat for   which | that   he was looking.

02 다음 문장 중 생략할 수 있는 부분을 괄호 안에 넣으시오.

1) Tell me about the man that Jenny would like to marry.

2) There are a lot of endangered animals which we should protect.

3) The old man whom Mary helped lives next to my house.

4) The man who is wearing a black suit looks like my father.

5) The car which is parked outside is mine.

03 다음 문장의 <u>틀린</u> 부분에 밑줄을 긋고 바르게 고쳐 쓰시오.

1) I need a book what is easy to understand.　　　　　　　　　(→ _____)

2) She can't believe that Brian told me.　　　　　　　　　　　(→ _____)

3) They are discussing the problem about that we talked yesterday.   (→ _____)

4) Look at the boy and his dog which are running along the river.   (→ _____)

04 생략된 부분을 넣어서 문장을 다시 쓰시오.

1) The boy delivering milk every morning is an orphan.

　　→ _____

2) The pen Terry lent me yesterday looked very expensive.

　　→ _____

O5 문장의 뜻이 같도록 빈칸에 알맞은 말을 쓰시오.

1) This is the thing _____ she bought for my birthday.

= This is _____ she bought for my birthday.

2) Tim has a nephew _____ his aunt is proud of.

= Tim has a nephew his aunt is proud _____.

= Tim has a nephew _____ _____ his aunt is proud.

3) Someday I will visit the city _____ Mozart was born in.

= Someday I will visit the city Mozart was born _____.

= Someday I will visit the city _____ _____ Mozart was born.

O6 다음 문장을 우리말로 해석하시오.

1) What she has been looking for is a scarf.

→ _____

2) Don't postpone until tomorrow what can be done today.

→ _____

3) All the fish the fisherman caught last night were sold out.

→ _____

4) What is the name of the girl every boy wants to meet?

→ _____

O7 주어진 말을 이용하여 다음 우리말을 영작하시오.

1) 내가 원하는 것은 물 한 잔이다. (a glass of)

→ _____

2) 나의 어머니는 나에게 내가 가장 필요한 것을 사 주셨다. (need)

→ _____

3) 이것은 서울로 가는 마지막 기차이다. (leave)

→ _____

4) 브라이언(Brian)은 수지(Suzie)가 함께 어울렸던 바로 그 학생이다. (the very, hang out with)

→ _____

01 다음 중 알맞은 것을 고르시오.

1) Chicago is the city   when | where   my aunt lives.

2) Summer is the season   when | why   we can swim in the sea.

3) I do not know the reason   when | why   Jane gave up playing the piano.

4) Tell me   how | the way how   I can earn money.

5) Tony asked me the reason for   why | which   I didn't go there.

6) The coffee shop at   where | which   we drank coffee looks nice.

02 관계부사를 이용하여 다음 두 문장을 한 문장으로 쓰시오.

1) Bora didn't say the reason. She was late for the reason.

→ _____

2) She remembers the day. Her son got married on the day.

→ _____

3) The town is very small. We arrived in the town.

→ _____

4) I don't know the way. I download the program in the way.

→ _____

03 문장의 뜻이 같도록 빈칸에 알맞은 말을 쓰시오.

1) This is the park _____ my mom lost her bag in.

= This is the park _____ _____ my mom lost her bag.

= This is the park _____ my mom lost her bag.

2) Please tell me the time _____ _____ the train for Daegu leaves.

= Please tell me the time _____ the train for Daegu leaves at.

= Please tell me the time _____ the train for Daegu leaves.

3) I know the reason _____ my father stopped smoking.

= I know the reason _____ _____ my father stopped smoking.

4) Let me know the way in _____ you make the pancake.

= Let me know _____ _____ you make the pancake.

= Let me know _____ you make the pancake.

04 다음 문장의 **틀린** 부분에 밑줄을 긋고 바르게 고쳐 쓰시오.

1) Spring is the season why many kinds of flowers come out. (→ _____)

2) Here is a restaurant which we can eat Chinese food. (→ _____)

3) Tell students the way how they can solve the problem. (→ _____)

4) This is the apartment where my family used to live in. (· _____)

5) Do you remember the year which he came back home? (→ _____)

6) There is no reason for why you won't attend the meeting. (→ _____)

05 우리말과 일치하도록 주어진 말을 바르게 배열하시오.

1) 나의 여동생이 그 일을 그만둔 이유는 명확하지 않다.

(why, my sister, the reason, quit, not, the job, is, clear)

→ _____

2) 내 조카가 태어난 날에 몹시 눈이 많이 내렸다.

(born, it, heavily, on, snowed, the day, was, when, my nephew)

→ _____

3) 나는 내 컴퓨터의 바이러스를 제거하는 방법을 알고 싶다.

(to, the way, I, can, I, want, know, on, get rid of, the virus, my computer)

→ _____

4) 우리는 주차장이 있는 식당을 찾고 있어요.

(looking, for, we, are, a parking lot, which, there, is, the restaurant, in)

→ _____

06 관계부사와 주어진 말을 이용하여 다음 우리말을 영작하시오.

1) 화랑은 우리가 많은 종류의 그림을 볼 수 있는 곳이다. (gallery)

→ _____

2) 나는 우리가 처음으로 만난 날을 잊을 수가 없다. (for the first time)

→ _____

3) 이것이 우리가 그 기계를 사용할 수 있는 방법이다. (machine)

→ _____

4) 우리는 야단맞을 이유가 없다. (there, scold)

→ _____

01 다음 중 알맞은 것을 고르시오.

1) I often hang out with Jinsu,   that ǀ who   lives next to my house.

2) Mr. Lee went to Starbucks,   which ǀ who   is close to the subway station.

3) He employed Sora,   who ǀ whom   could speak English fluently.

4) Jiwon passed the test,   which ǀ that   made his parents happy.

5) My dog Cuty,   which ǀ whose   baby died, ate nothing.

6) Last year I went to Hungary,   where ǀ which   I visited my friend's house.

7) Penny said that she did not like Tony,   who ǀ which   was a lie.

8) My sister held a party yesterday,   where ǀ when   she wore a white dress.

9) There used to be a theater,   which ǀ where   was built before I was born.

10) He has three sisters,   whom ǀ that   Kelly invited to her birthday party.

02 밑줄 친 부분에 주의하여 다음 문장을 해석하시오.

1) He has an uncle, who teaches math at school.

→ _____

2) He has an uncle who teaches math at school.

→ _____

3) My sister has two dogs, which I bought.

→ _____

4) My sister has two dogs which I bought.

→ _____

5) Korea held the World Cup in 2002, when the Korean team went on to the semi-finals.

→ _____

6) 2002 is the year when Korea and Japan held the World Cup.

→ _____

7) Tomorrow my aunt will leave for England, where her daughter lives.

→ _____

8) My aunt wants to live in the country where her daughter lives.

→ _____

O3 두 문장의 뜻이 같도록 빈칸에 알맞은 말을 쓰시오.

1) He entered the house, but it was empty.

= He entered the house, _____ was empty.

2) Mary lives with her friend Bora, for her parents are in China.

= Mary lives with her friend Bora, _____ parents are in China.

3) My family traveled to India, and there we rode a camel in the desert.

= My family traveled to India, _____ we rode a camel in the desert.

4) J. K. Rowling wrote *Harry Potter*, _____ consists of 7 books.

= J. K. Rowling wrote *Harry Potter*, _____ _____ consists of 7 books.

5) On her way home, Jenny met Brian, _____ said that he would move to Busan.

= On her way home, Jenny met Brian, _____ _____ said that he would move to Busan.

6) My grandfather was born in 1950, _____ the Korean War broke out.

= My grandfather was born in 1950, _____ _____ the Korean War broke out.

O4 다음 문장의 <u>틀린</u> 부분에 밑줄을 긋고 바르게 고쳐 쓰시오.

1) Tony downloaded a song, that he listened to countless times.   (→ _____)

2) The boss fired Karen, which was absent frequently.   (→ _____)

3) My favorite restaurant is Smith & Jack, who is famous for pizza.   (→ _____)

4) My sister won first prize, it surprised us.   (→ _____)

5) Juno visited Italy, which he experienced unforgettable things.   (→ _____)

O5 우리말과 일치하도록 주어진 말을 바르게 배열하시오.

1) 그 아이는 그의 손톱을 자주 물어뜯는데, 그것은 그의 나쁜 버릇이다.

(the child, his, is, his, fingernails, which, bad, often, bites, habit)

→ _____

2) 나의 조카는 하버드 대학에 막 들어갔는데, 거기서 그는 경제학을 공부한다.

(has, my nephew, just, Harvard University, economics, entered, studies, where, he)

→ _____

3) 나는 두 명의 친한 친구가 있는데, 그들은 대학에 다닌다.

(close, university, have, two, friends, I, attend, who)

→ _____

O1 다음 중 알맞은 것을 고르시오.

1) Whoever | Whomever   passes the word test can go home earlier.

2) Please tell me   whoever | whatever   you need.

3) I will give the apples to   whoever | whomever   comes first.

4) However | Whatever   hard you may try, you will not finish the work in an hour.

5) My mother wants to live   wherever | however   there are a lot of flowers and trees.

6) You should take a rest   whatever | whenever   you are sick.

7) She will be satisfied with   whichever | whosever   she chooses.

8) I will welcome   whomever | whosever   my child takes home.

O2 밑줄 친 부분에 주의하여 다음 문장을 우리말로 해석하시오.

1) Whoever is late for school, he will be punished.

→ _____

2) Whoever reads this book can attend the debate.

→ _____

3) Mothers tend to give children whatever they want.

→ _____

4) Students should do their best whatever they do.

→ _____

O3 다음 문장의 <u>틀린</u> 부분에 밑줄을 긋고 바르게 고쳐 쓰시오.

1) Whomever you may tell her, she will never change her mind.   (→ _____)

2) You may lend your computer to whomever wants to use it.   (→ _____)

3) I will live next to her house whenever she lives.   (→ _____)

4) Whatever difficult the test is, you should take it.   (→ _____)

5) My dad scolds my brother wherever he lies.   (→ _____)

6) Whenever much money you have, you can't buy everything.   (→ _____)

O4 두 문장의 뜻이 같도록 빈칸에 알맞은 말을 쓰시오.

1) We will send these samples to anyone who filled in questionnaires.

= We will send these samples to _____ filled in questionnaires.

2) They helped themselves to anything that they wanted to eat.

= They helped themselves to _____ they wanted to eat.

3) You may call me at any time when you feel lonely.

= You may call me _____ you feel lonely.

4) No matter what may happen, all of us will stay here.

= _____ may happen, all of us will stay here.

5) However humble it may be, there is no place like home.

= _____ _____ _____ humble it may be, there is no place like home.

O5 우리말과 일치하도록 주어진 말을 바르게 배열하시오.

1) 이 규칙을 따르지 않는 사람은 누구든지 벌을 받을 것이다.

(whoever, follow, this, doesn't, be, punished, rule, will)

→ _____

2) 당신은 어디에 있을지라도 인터넷을 위해서 스마트폰을 사용할 수 있다.

(wherever, you, can, for, use, your smartphone, are, you, the Internet)

→ _____

3) 우리가 아무리 일찍 일어날지라도 5시까지 거기에 도착할 수 없다.

(we, can't, five, arrive, get up, early, we, there, by, however, o'clock)

→ _____

O6 주어진 말과 관계부사를 이용하여 다음 우리말을 영작하시오.

1) 진수(Jinsu)는 인하(Inha)를 기쁘게 하는 것은 무엇이든지 한다. (please)

→ _____

2) 축구를 좋아하는 사람은 누구든지 이 클럽에 가입할 수 있다. (join)

→ _____

3) 네가 원하는 것은 어느 것이든지 가져가도 좋다. (take)

→ _____

O1 다음 중 알맞은 것을 고르시오.

1) The Netherlands   is｜are   famous for tulips.

2) The poor   is｜are   often happier than the rich.

3) Economics   is｜are   important for students.

4) Three hours   is｜are   enough for you to watch the movie.

5) The number of old people   is｜are   increasing in Korea.

6) There   is｜are   a number of birds in this forest.

7) Each of the travelers   wears｜wear   a backpack.

8) The poems that the poet wrote   is｜are   being read by many people.

9) Some of the students   come｜comes   from other countries.

10) Every teacher   has｜have   to love students.

O2 우리말과 일치하도록 빈칸에 알맞은 말을 쓰시오.

1) 정치학은 우리 오빠의 전공이다.

→ _____ _____ my brother's major.

2) 그 책들 중 대부분은 읽기에 재미있다.

→ _____ of the books _____ interesting to read.

3) 그 교수들은 각자 그의 분야에서 전문가이다.

→ _____ of the professors _____ an expert in his field.

4) 학생들의 수는 25명이다.

→ _____ _____ of students _____ twenty five.

5) 그 거리에 있는 꽃들 중에서 4분의 3이 벚꽃이다.

→ Three quarters of the flowers in the street _____ cherry blossoms.

6) 많은 사람들이 주말마다 한강을 따라 자전거를 탄다.

→ _____ number of people _____ bikes along the Han river on weekends.

7) 3주는 유럽을 여행하기에 너무 짧다.

→ _____ _____ _____ too short to travel in Europe.

8) 그 가구들은 모두 먼지로 덮여있다.

→ _____ of the furniture _____ covered with dust.

O3 다음 문장의 밑줄 친 부분을 바르게 고쳐 쓰시오.

1) The United States <u>consist</u> of 50 states.　　　　　(→ _____)

2) Mathematics <u>are</u> the subject that she dislikes.　　　(→ _____)

3) Every boy <u>like</u> to watch soccer.　　　　　　　　(→ _____)

4) The young <u>has</u> to give up their seats.　　　　　　(→ _____)

5) Half of the paper <u>are</u> in this box.　　　　　　　(→ _____)

6) All of our classmates <u>was</u> present at the party.　　(→ _____)

7) Most of my money <u>were</u> left in the hotel.　　　　(→ _____)

O4 우리말과 일치하도록 주어진 말을 바르게 배열하시오.

1) 외국인들 중에서 3분의 2는 매년 이 궁전을 방문한다.

(of, visit, this, year, the foreigners, palace, every, two thirds)

→ _____

2) 그 회의에 참석한 사람들의 수는 7명이다.

(number, participating, the, people, of, in, is, the meeting, seven)

→ _____

3) 시각장애인들은 점자를 이용해서 책을 읽을 수 있다.

(blind, are, the, able, to, books, read, Braille, using)

→ _____

4) 10달러는 네가 이 가방을 사는 데 충분하지 않다.

(is, enough, ten dollars, not, buy, this, you, to, bag, for)

→ _____

5) 각 여성들은 자신의 몸무게에 민감하다.

(own, each, the women, is, of, sensitive, her, about, weight)

→ _____

O5 주어진 말을 이용하여 다음 우리말을 영작하시오.

1) 모든 군인들은 걸그룹을 좋아하는 경향이 있다. (every, tend)

→ _____

2) 물리학은 이해하기 어렵다. (physics)

→ _____

3) 우리들 대부분은 직업을 찾아야 한다. (have to, look for)

→ _____

01 다음 중 알맞은 것을 고르시오.

1) Tony said that Sora   is | was   in her car.

2) Mary thought that her mom   will | would   arrive soon.

3) My dad told me that I   had | have   to do my homework before dinner.

4) He was taught that Columbus   had discovered | discovered   America in 1492.

5) My grandmother always said that still waters   run | ran   deep.

6) They knew that Beijing   is | was   the capital of China.

7) Mr. Kim taught that water   consists | consisted   of oxygen and hydrogen.

8) She heard that her boyfriend   has left | had left   for Greece.

9) Tommy was so tired that he   can't | couldn't   attend the conference.

02 다음 문장의 주절을 과거시제로 바꿀 때 종속절을 완성하시오.

1) He promises me that he will not be late for school.

→ He promised me that _____.

2) My dad knows that my brother is lying.

→ My dad knew that _____.

3) We believe that Karen has already finished the work.

→ We believed that _____.

4) Students learn that the Industrial Revolution began in Britain in the 19th century.

→ Students learned that _____.

5) He thinks that if she were you, she would not go there.

→ He thought that _____.

03 다음 문장의 밑줄 친 부분을 바르게 고쳐 쓰시오.

1) My mom hoped that my dad will come back home soon.   (→ _____)

2) Brian told me that the French Revolution had taken place in 1789.   (→ _____)

3) My grandfather always said that no news was good news.   (→ _____)

4) She found that her mother has been sick for a week.   (→ _____)

5) Kate studied hard so that she may pass the exam.   (→ _____)

6) Jenny thought it is impossible.   (→ _____)

04 우리말과 일치하도록 주어진 말을 바르게 배열하시오.

1) 제니퍼는 항상 아침 7시에 일하러 간다고 말했다.
(goes, always, Jennifer, to, seven, in the morning, work, at, said, she)
→ _____

2) 나의 여동생은 나에게 절대로 학교에 결석하지 않을 것을 약속했다.
(my sister, she, me, that, promised, would, absent, school, not, be, at all, from)
→ _____

3) 너는 걸프전이 1991년에 일어났다는 것을 알고 있었니?
(that, did, know, out, in, the Gulf War, broke, 1991, you)
→ _____

4) 나는 너의 가족이 전에 아프리카에 가 본 적이 있다고 들었다.
(that, your family, heard, I, before, had, to, Africa, been)
→ _____

5) 그 선생님은 우리에게 오렌지 주스는 비타민 C가 많이 들어있다고 가르쳤다.
(us, that, taught, orange juice, vitamin C, a lot of, the teacher, contains)
→ _____

6) 한 친절한 여자가 우리에게 전철에서 버스로 갈아타야 한다고 말했다.
(kind, that, said, woman, we, to, from, a, transfer, had, subway, to, bus)
→ _____

05 주어진 말을 이용하여 다음 우리말을 영작하시오.

1) 브라이언(Brian)은 아침마다 산책을 한다고 말했다. (take a walk)
→ _____

2) 레이첼(Rachel)은 나에게 나의 어머니가 기다리고 있다고 말했다. (tell)
→ _____

3) 그 외국인은 일본인들이 1592년에 한국을 침입했다는 것을 몰랐다. (invade)
→ _____

4) 나의 가족은 나의 여동생이 일등을 할 거라고 생각했다. (win first prize)
→ _____

5) 나의 할아버지는 항상 피는 물보다 진하다고 말씀하셨다. (thicker)
→ _____

6) 케이트(Kate)는 3년 동안 한국에 머무르고 있다고 말했다. (be)
→ _____

O1 다음 중 알맞은 것을 고르시오.

1) My mom always   told | tells   me that I can do anything.

2) He said   that | if   Budapest is the capital of Hungary.

3) His aunt   said | told   that she would visit me.

4) Ms Brown   told | asked   the students that she was their homeroom teacher.

5) The boy said that he was waiting for Sumi   now | then .

O2 직접화법을 간접화법으로 바꾸어 쓰시오.

1) Tony often says, "I am lonely."

→ _____

2) She said to her parents, "I want to live with you."

→ _____

3) Mr. Lee said to his students, "You have to do your best."

→ _____

4) My grandfather said to me, "This is for you."

→ _____

5) He said to me, "I am looking for my dog now."

→ _____

6) The woman said to him, "I entered the building yesterday."

→ _____

7) Suzie said to her mother, "I will clean my room tomorrow."

→ _____

O3 간접화법을 직접화법으로 바꿀 때 빈칸에 알맞은 말을 쓰시오.

1) The girl said that she would join the club.

→ The girl said, "_____ _____ join the club."

2) My dad told me that I was good at playing soccer.

→ My dad said to me, "_____ _____ good at playing soccer."

3) Sora told me that she had reached Seoul the previous day.

→ Sora said to me, "_____ _____ Seoul _____."

04 직접화법을 간접화법으로 바꾼 문장에서 틀린 부분에 밑줄을 긋고 바르게 고쳐 쓰시오.

1) He said, "I will leave for London tomorrow."

→ He said that he would leave for London tomorrow. (→ _____)

2) He said to me, "There is a car in front of my house."

→ He told me that there was a car in front of my house. (→ _____)

3) The boss said to me, "You may use my pen."

→ The boss told me that I may use his pen. (→ _____)

4) Mary said to him, "I sent a gift to my parents yesterday."

→ Mary told him that she sent a gift to her parents the day before. (→ _____)

5) My brother said to her, "You look sad."

→ My brother told her that you looked sad. (→ _____)

05 우리말과 일치하도록 주어진 말을 바르게 배열하시오.

1) 그 유명한 가수는 곧 결혼할 것이라고 기자에게 말했다.

(the, told, that, famous, the reporter, get, singer, he, would, married, soon)

→ _____

2) 내 조카는 운전하는 법을 배우고 싶다고 말했다.

(that, my nephew, said, drive, he, learn, how, wanted, to, to)

→ _____

3) 나의 언니는 친구들과 여행을 갈 계획을 세웠다고 말했다.

(said, sister, friends, that, planned, she, take, my, her, to, a trip, with)

→ _____

06 주어진 말을 이용하여 다음 우리말을 영작하시오.

1) 켄(Ken)은 그녀를 위해 반지를 살 거라고 페니(Penny)에게 말했다. (ring)

→ _____

2) 나의 할머니는 내가 아버지를 닮았다고 나에게 말씀하셨다. (resemble)

→ _____

3) 보라(Bora)는 우리에게 "나는 전에 외국에 가 본 적이 없어."라고 말했다. (foreign)

→ _____

4) 케이트(Kate)는 자신이 그때 집에서 만화책을 읽고 있었다고 말했다. (comic book)

→ _____

O1 다음 중 알맞은 것을 고르시오.

1) He asked   that | if   the rumor was true.

2) His uncle   told | asked   me why my aunt didn't come.

3) My dad   said | told   us to exercise regularly.

4) Somi asked him   don't | not   to forget her name.

5) Tony asked my sister how   tall she was | she was tall .

6) The teacher advised her students   read | to read   a lot of books.

7) Mina asked the clerk how much   was it | it was .

8) Brian asked Bora when   she went | did she go   to school.

O2 직접화법을 간접화법으로 바꾸어 쓰시오.

1) A girl said to me, "Where is the cosmetics shop?"

→ _____

2) The woman said to him, "What time is it?"

→ _____

3) She said to me, "How long does it take for me to go there?"

→ _____

4) I said to John, "Where can I take a bus?"

→ _____

5) My mom said to me, "What are you doing now?"

→ _____

6) My dad said to me, "Who planted the tree?"

→ _____

7) A woman said to the librarian, "May I borrow this book?"

→ _____

8) I said to Sumi, "Have you ever been to Italy?"

→ _____

9) Ms Brown said to her son, "Did you do your homework?

→ _____

10) The teacher said to his students, "Do you have a pet?"

→ _____

O3 주어진 동사를 이용하여 직접화법을 간접화법으로 바꾸어 쓰시오.

1) He said to me, "Help yourself." (tell)

→ _____

2) She said to Brian, "Don't be absent." (tell)

→ _____

3) A girl said to her father, "Please buy me an umbrella." (ask)

→ _____

4) The doctor said to John, "Take the medicine three times a day." (advise)

→ _____

O4 간접화법을 직접화법으로 바꿀 때 빈칸에 알맞은 말을 쓰시오.

1) The reporter asked the singer when he would leave for China.

→ The reporter said to the singer, "_____ _____ _____ _____ for China?"

2) Terry asked me if I knew Sorim's phone number.

→ Terry said to me, "_____ _____ _____ Sorim's phone number?"

3) The teacher told her students to memorize the sentence.

→ The teacher said to her students, "_____ the sentence."

4) The doctor advised my father not to drink too much.

→ The doctor said to my father, "_____ _____ too much."

O5 우리말과 일치하도록 주어진 말을 바르게 배열하시오.

1) 내 친구는 내가 얼마나 자주 피아노 레슨을 받는지 물었다.

(me, often, I, asked, how, my friend, took, piano lessons)

→ _____

2) 브라이언은 내가 전에 제주도에 가 본 적이 있는지 물었다.

(asked, if, I, been, to, me, had, Jejudo, Brian, before)

→ _____

3) 케이트는 그녀의 남동생에게 개에게 먹이를 주라고 부탁을 했다.

(her brother, feed, Kate, to, asked, the dog)

→ _____

01 빈칸에 주어진 단어의 알맞은 형태를 쓰시오.

1) If he _____ one more goal, he would have been the MVP. (score)

2) If she believed in herself, the result _____ different. (will be)

3) If it _____ tomorrow, they will go skiing. (snow)

4) If she hadn't accepted his apology, he _____ disappointed. (will be)

5) If he _____ a student again, he would study harder. (become)

6) If the girl _____ a phone call from her mom, she will go home immediately. (receive)

02 두 문장의 뜻이 같도록 주어진 말로 시작하여 문장을 쓰시오.

1) As a traffic accident occurred, the road was jammed.

= If _____ .

2) As she doesn't like traveling, she will not be here with us.

= If _____ .

3) I lost contact with him so I couldn't talk to him again.

= If _____ .

4) He is not an architect so he can't design a nice building.

= If _____ .

03 우리말과 일치하도록 빈칸에 알맞은 말을 쓰시오.

1) 그녀가 신을 믿는다면 신에게 기도할 것이다. (pray)

→ If she _____ in God, she _____ _____ to God.

2) 우리가 무인도에 있다면 외로울 텐데.

→ If we _____ on a desert island, we _____ _____ lonely.

3) 내가 그 영화를 봤더라면 후회했을 텐데.

→ If I _____ _____ the movie, I _____ _____ _____ it.

4) 그들이 그 법을 따랐다면 벌을 받지 않았을 텐데. (obey, punish)

→ If they _____ _____ the law, they _____ _____ _____ _____ .

04 다음 문장을 우리말로 해석하시오.

1) If she had not wasted money, she would not have borrowed money.

→ _____

2) If they did not bother him, he could concentrate on his work.

→ _____

3) If he listens to online science lectures, he will understand science better.

→ _____

05 우리말과 일치하도록 주어진 말을 바르게 배열하시오.

1) 그가 많은 노력을 한다면 성공할 텐데.

(made, he, succeed, he, a lot of, would, if, effort)

→ _____

2) 그가 가난으로 힘겨워하지 않았더라면 대학에 갔을 텐데.

(gone, had, not, he, poverty, struggled, he, with, would, university, have, to)

→ _____

3) 그가 망설이지 않았더라면 그 기회를 잡았을 텐데.

(hesitated, if, had, the, chance, not, he, taken, would, he, have)

→ _____

4) 그가 핑계를 댄다면 야단맞을 것이다.

(makes, if, be, he, will, scolded, an, he, excuse)

→ _____

06 주어진 말을 이용하여 다음 우리말을 영작하시오.

1) 그가 그 배우를 만난다면 인터뷰할 텐데. (interview)

→ _____

2) 우리가 그 범죄를 목격했더라면 경찰에 신고했을 텐데. (witness, crime)

→ _____

3) 그녀가 그의 초대를 거절하지 않는다면 그는 행복할 것이다. (refuse)

→ _____

4) 그들이 독립을 위해 싸웠더라면 자유를 얻었을 텐데. (independence, freedom)

→ _____

01 다음 문장의 밑줄 친 부분을 바르게 고쳐 쓰시오.

1) He is lazy. I wish he <u>is</u> diligent. (→ _____)

2) She didn't win a medal but she behaves as if she <u>has won</u> one. (→ _____)

3) If it <u>were not</u> for water, she couldn't have survived. (→ _____)

4) If it were not for cancer, people could have <u>lived</u> longer. (→ _____)

5) <u>With</u> her, they couldn't have built the building. (→ _____)

6) I wish she <u>has followed</u> my advice. (→ _____)

02 빈칸에 주어진 단어의 알맞은 형태를 쓰시오.

1) Harry never joined the army but he talks as if he _____ in a war. (fight)

2) She is not an actress but she acts as if she _____ an actress. (be)

3) She hurt herself while jogging. I wish she _____ herself. (hurt)

4) He had an injury. But for the injury, he _____ football. (play)

03 두 문장의 뜻이 같도록 빈칸에 알맞은 말을 쓰시오.

1) Without his advice, she would have made an error.

= If _____ _____ _____ _____ for his
advice, she would have made an error.

= _____ _____ _____ _____ for his
advice, she would have made an error.

2) Without an instruction manual, I would not assemble the desk.

= If _____ _____ _____ for an instruction manual,
I would not assemble the desk.

= _____ _____ _____ for an instruction manual,
I would not assemble the desk.

3) In fact James didn't explore the Amazon.

= James talks _____ _____ _____ _____
_____ the Amazon.

4) I am sorry I don't remember the password of the locker.

= I wish _____ _____ the password of the locker.

O4 다음 문장을 우리말로 해석하시오.

1) I wish I had followed his advice.

→ _____

2) She acts as if she knew everything.

→ _____

3) If it were not for the flu, I would go on the school trip.

→ _____

4) If it had not been for love, they wouldn't have got married.

→ _____

O5 우리말과 일치하도록 주어진 말을 바르게 배열하시오.

1) 내가 그 영화의 주인공이라면 좋을 텐데.

(wish, the, a, leading, I, in, I, character, movie, were)

→ _____

2) 그들은 마치 올림픽메달을 땄던 것처럼 행동한다.

(medals, if, won, act, they, as, had, they, Olympic)

→ _____

3) 친구가 없다면 나는 외로울 텐데.

(feel, but, would, friends, I, for, lonely)

→ _____

O6 주어진 말을 이용하여 다음 우리말을 영작하시오.

1) 그녀의 격려가 없었다면 그는 그의 소설을 완성할 수 없었을 텐데. (without, encouragement)

→ _____

2) 많은 노력이 없다면 그들은 성공할 수 없을 텐데. (if, effort)

→ _____

3) 그녀가 내 제안에 동의했더라면 좋을 텐데. (agree, suggestion)

→ _____

4) 그는 마치 그들을 부러워하지 않는 것처럼 행동한다. (envy)

→ _____

01 밑줄 친 부분을 강조하여 다음 문장을 다시 쓰시오.

1) <u>Brian</u> likes Jenny.

→ It _____ .

2) My mom has been looking for <u>the lost ring</u>.

→ It _____ .

3) Penny did volunteer work <u>at an orphanage</u>.

→ It _____ .

4) My sister baked a cheesecake <u>last weekend</u>.

→ It _____ .

02 밑줄 친 부분을 강조하고자 할 때 빈칸에 알맞은 말을 쓰시오.

1) The author <u>wrote</u> the book.

→ The author _____ _____ the book.

2) The girl <u>plays</u> the piano every morning.

→ The girl _____ _____ the piano every morning.

3) The couple <u>welcome</u> people to their home.

→ The couple _____ _____ people to their home.

03 우리말과 일치하도록 빈칸에 알맞은 말을 쓰시오.

1) 도대체 누가 그 화병을 깼니?

→ Who _____ _____ broke the vase?

2) 거짓말을 하고 있는 사람은 바로 너야.

→ It is _____ _____ are telling a lie.

3) 어제 에이미가 산 것은 바로 양말이었다.

→ It was _____ _____ Amy bought yesterday.

4) 내가 브라이언을 만난 곳은 바로 은행에서였다.

→ It was _____ _____ _____ I met
Brian.

5) 그 남자는 정말로 그의 아내를 사랑한다.

→ The man _____ _____ his wife.

04 밑줄 친 부분에 주의하여 다음 문장을 우리말로 해석하시오.

1) Not all insects do harm to people.

→ _____

2) Teachers don't know everything.

→ _____

3) The boy doesn't always play computer games.

→ _____

05 두 문장의 뜻이 같도록 빈칸에 알맞은 말을 보기에서 골라 쓰시오.

보기   both   neither   all   none

1) Either of my parents doesn't work in the company.

= _____ of my parents works in the company.

2) Karen doesn't know any of them.

= Karen knows _____ of them.

3) Some birds can fly, but the others can't.

= Not _____ birds can fly.

06 주어진 말을 이용하여 다음 우리말을 영작하시오.

1) 그 책 둘 다 재미가 없다. (both)

→ _____

2) 만점을 맞은 사람은 바로 소미(Somi)였다. (perfect score)

→ _____

3) 나의 아버지가 이 소나무를 심은 때는 바로 10년 전이다. (pine tree)

→ _____

4) 우리는 지난 금요일에 대기오염에 대해 정말로 토론했다. (do, discuss, air pollution)

→ _____

5) 모든 소녀들이 다 치마 입는 것을 좋아하는 것은 아니다. (every, girl)

→ _____

6) 그 학생들 중에서 아무도 그 문제를 풀지 못했다. (none)

→ _____

01 다음 중 알맞은 것을 고르시오.

1) Here   is | are   some tips.

2) Here   he comes | comes he .

3) Next to the table   are | is   two cats.

4) On the hill   was | were   an old castle.

5) In front of the house   stand | stands   three big trees.

6) Never   I will | will I   be absent from school.

7) Hardly   Kate studied | did Kate study   math.

8) Karen is pretty and so   her sister is | is her sister .

9) She can't speak Spanish and   so | neither   can he.

10) The students had a good time yesterday and so   do | did   the teachers.

02 주어진 어구로 시작하여 다음 문장을 다시 쓰시오.

1) Your bus comes here.

→ Here _____ .

2) A small restaurant is behind the gas station.

→ Behind the gas station _____ .

3) My new hats were on your left.

→ On your left _____ .

4) I have never been to Jejudo.

→ Never _____ to Jejudo.

5) She little dreamed that she would meet him there.

→ Little _____ that she would meet him there.

03 다음 대화의 상황에 맞게 주어진 우리말 대답을 영어로 쓰시오.

1) Ⓐ I am hungry. Ⓑ _____ (나도 그래.)

2) Ⓐ I water my flowers every Saturday. Ⓑ _____ (수미도 그래.)

3) Ⓐ Bora can ski. Ⓑ _____ (나도 그래.)

4) Ⓐ He wasn't busy last night. Ⓑ _____ (그녀도 그래.)

5) Ⓐ She has never met the boy. Ⓑ _____ (그도 그래.)

6) Ⓐ Mary agreed with him. Ⓑ _____ (나도 그래.)

04 다음 문장의 밑줄 친 부분을 바르게 고쳐 쓰시오.

1) Under the bed is a few pairs of shoes.　　　　　(→ _____)

2) Between the houses were a parking lot.　　　　　(→ _____)

3) Never he tells a lie.　　　　　　　　　　　　　(→ _____)

4) Ⓐ My mom is a teacher.　Ⓑ So her daughter is.　(→ _____)

5) Ⓐ He will never do it.　Ⓑ So will his brother.　(→ _____)

6) Ⓐ My dad plays golf.　Ⓑ So is my mom.　　　(→ _____)

7) Ⓐ She doesn't like coffee.　Ⓑ Neither doesn't her sister.　(→ _____)

05 다음 문장에서 생략할 수 있는 부분을 괄호 안에 넣고 문장 전체를 우리말로 해석하시오.

1) People believe that seven is a lucky number.

→ _____

2) The man who is taking pictures of me is a famous photographer.

→ _____

3) When she was asked how old she was, the actress didn't answer the question.

→ _____

4) Here are some tips that I want to give students.

→ _____

5) The church which was partly destroyed by a fire last year was rebuilt last week.

→ _____

06 우리말과 일치하도록 주어진 말을 바르게 배열하시오.

1) 캐런은 그 사실을 거의 모른다.

(does, hardly, know, Karen)

→ _____

2) 나는 매일 비올라 연습을 한다, 그리고 내 여동생도 또한 그렇다.

(practice, viola, every, I, the, day, does, and, so, my sister)

→ _____

3) 소미는 그녀의 보고서를 제출하지 못했다, 그리고 보라도 또한 그렇다.

(didn't, report, did, Somi, submit, her, Bora, and, neither)

→ _____

꼭! 잡은 중학 영문법

3
Book

GRAMMAR
CATCH

✷ Workbook ✷